**PARK LEARNING CENTRE**

The Park Cheltenham
Gloucestershire GL50 2RH
Telephone: 01242 714333

# THE NAKED EMPLOYEE

# THE NAKED EMPLOYEE

How Technology Is Compromising Workplace Privacy

FREDERICK S. LANE III

## AMACOM

### American Management Association

New York • Atlanta • Brussels • Buenos Aires • Chicago • London • Mexico City
San Francisco • Shanghai • Tokyo • Toronto • Washington, D.C.

This publication is designed to provide accurate and authoritative information in regard to the subject matter covered. It is sold with the
understanding that the publisher is not engaged in rendering legal,
accounting, or other professional service. If legal advice or other expert assistance is required, the services of a competent professional
person should be sought.

Library of Congress Cataloging-in-Publication Data

Lane, Frederick S.
The naked employee : how technology is compromising workplace privacy
/ Frederick S. Lane.
p.   cm.
Includes bibliographical references and index.
ISBN 0-8144-7149-8
    1. Employee rights—United States.    2. Privacy, Right of—United
States.    3. Electronic monitoring in the workplace—United States.    4.
Supervision of employees—United States. I. Title.

HF5549.5.E428L36   2003
331'.01'1—dc21                                          2003000312

Printing number

10   9   8   7   6   5   4   3   2   1

*To my sons, Benton and Peter Lane, with great love,*
*and with thanks for their enthusiasm and*
*encouragement*

# Contents

CHAPTER 9

CHAPTER 10

# Introduction

## Surprising Levels of Surveillance

The idea for this book arose from research that I conducted for *Obscene Profits* (Routledge 2000), during which it became clear that online pornography was becoming a serious problem in the workplace. As I researched the issue of pornography at work, it quickly became apparent that employers were responding to the problem by installing increasingly sophisticated software to monitor what their employees were doing online. It was evident that the software used to monitor online activity was capable of recording far more than employee efforts to download sexually explicit images.

The other thing that quickly became obvious was that computer monitoring was merely the tip of the workplace surveillance iceberg. Every day, employees work under the unblinking gaze of video cameras (both hidden and overt), pee into little plastic cups in order to get or keep a job, swipe a card or wear a badge to create a trail of their movements, and/or drive a vehicle equipped with a Global Positioning System that closely monitors their out-of-office behavior.

Although the attacks of 9/11 have altered our expectations somewhat, the idea of so many Americans working under constant surveillance is still jarring. Personal privacy is a deeply ingrained theme in the mythos of this nation—after all, Daniel Boone picked up stakes and headed west when the smoke of his nearest neighbor appeared on the horizon.

The frontier disappeared more than a century ago, and not long afterwards, so did the practical availability of true personal privacy. Nonetheless, even in an era of highly detailed credit reports, invasive telemarketers, and pizza deliverers who track what we ordered last time, we cling fiercely to the myth of privacy—so fiercely, in fact, that we believe in personal privacy even in the workplace. Time and again, public opinion surveys show that employees do not think that their employers monitor their activities at work, or even have the right to do so.

That expectation may slowly be changing, at least with respect to computer-related activities, as well-publicized cases make it clear that employers *can* conduct computer surveillance, and more and more employers inform their employees that they do monitor e-mails and Web surfing. But computer-related monitoring is only one small piece of the surveillance that occurs, and few employers disclose all of the surveillance and investigation that actually takes place.

Frankly, our expectation of privacy in the workplace needs to change more quickly. Employer surveillance tools no longer necessarily discriminate between work-related and personal activities, and the steady expansion of workplace surveillance is threatening the privacy of our homes.

Equally important is the growing risk that the information gathered as part of workplace surveillance will be used to support a truly unprecedented level of government surveillance. In an era when legitimate concerns about homeland security are being used to rationalize new federal voyeurism, we need to consider more carefully than ever before the question of whether workplace surveillance is exceeding its legitimate rationalizations.

## The Total Information Awareness System

As I was writing the final pages of this book, a flurry of articles revealed that at the beginning of 2002, the Bush administration had put retired admiral John Poindexter, President Ronald Reagan's national security advisor, in charge of a newly created "Information Awareness Office." Armed with an initial budget of $200 million, Poindexter was asked to set up an enormously powerful computer system capable of collecting and analyzing data from thousands of federal, state, and commercial databases.

The ostensible purpose of the system, known as "Total Information Awareness" (TIA), is to identify and track the activities of people hostile to the United States by looking for suspicious patterns of behavior. With disturbing ease, however, the TIA system will allow Poindexter to compile, as columnist William Safire put it, "computer dossiers on 300 million Americans."[1] Concern over Poindexter's activities is creating strange bedfellows. In my own database of information on this issue, Safire's column wound up side-by-side with a similar piece by *The Village Voice's* Nat Hentoff, who declared that Poindexter's warrantless searches will make "individual privacy as obsolete as the sauropods of the Mesozoic era."[2]

It's not just their mutual fondness for the word "Orwellian" that binds those two writers. It's also their obvious understanding of the potential

unintended consequences of a system like TIA—the possibility, if not the
likelihood, that the collected information will be misused. As noted British
scholar Lord Acton observed almost exactly one century before Poindexter
was convicted of lying to Congress, "Power tends to corrupt, and absolute
power corrupts absolutely."[3]

Overlooked in the growing hubbub over Admiral Poindexter's resurfac-
ing, however, is the fact that to one degree or another, private businesses
have been creating and operating their own "information awareness offices"
for the last half century. As we'll see throughout this book, employers have
collected far more information about individuals in this country than the
federal government.

A certain amount of information about and supervision of employees
is a necessary component of a successful business. A company will fail if it
hires people who have lied about their experience and credentials; if it allows
employees to steal inventory or trade secrets; or if it allows employees to
spend excessive amounts of time talking on the phone, playing computer
games, or surfing the Web for personal reasons. The fact that on the first
Monday after Thanksgiving this year, Americans rang up $275 million in
online purchases during normal working hours may be good news for the
nation's economy, but less promising for the nation's productivity.

As justified as workplace surveillance may be in limited quantities, the
situation is rapidly getting out of hand. Advances in technology are making
it possible for companies to routinely gather unprecedented quantities of
information about the people who work for them. Unfortunately, as the
power and sophistication of surveillance tools steadily improve, an increasing amount of human intervention is required to sift relevant information
from the irrelevant. More often than not, it is simply easier and cheaper for
companies to collect information about their employees without regard to
whether it is actually relevant to an employee's qualifications or job performance.

The collection of excessive amounts of private information about employees is troubling enough when the collection, compilation, and analysis
is done by a single company. It is far more troubling in an era when the
federal government has the capability and increasingly the will to use that
information for public policy purposes. It's a trend directly related to times
of civic stress: The government first began collecting information about
employee salaries during the Great Depression, and today's search for total
information awareness is obviously driven by the threat of terrorism.

No one who watched the horrific events of 9/11 unfold on television
and computer screens around the world can legitimately question whether
the threat of terrorism is real or worthy of aggressive opposition. But as
numerous commentators have asked (and not just during the present con-

flict), if the cost of victory is the freedoms we value, then is it a victory worth having?

By itself, the issue of workplace privacy is worth examining for what it says about the economic and social structure of this nation. But in light of the growing collaboration and data exchange between government and business, workplace surveillance now has the potential to play an important role in undermining our most fundamental freedoms.

## Structure

*The Naked Employee* begins with a discussion of some of the reasons for workplace surveillance. In writing about this issue, it seemed important to me to recognize that the successful operation of any business does in fact depend on a certain amount of investigation about and surveillance of employees.

The remainder of the book, however, implicitly asks the questions of how much surveillance is too much. Beginning with the job application process, *The Naked Employee* looks at a wide variety of investigatory tools and surveillance techniques. Some, I argue, are clearly legitimate when they are designed to produce information that is relevant about an employee's job performance, and illegitimate when they are used to gather information beyond that. Other surveillance techniques, I believe, are inherently unreasonable (hidden cameras, for instance). My hope is that as readers work their way through this book, they will be able to decide for themselves where they would draw the line between reasonable and unreasonable surveillance. At the very least, readers may spend more time looking over their shoulder, which is not necessarily a bad thing. As the joke t-shirt puts it so well, "Just because you're paranoid doesn't mean they're not out to get you."

The book concludes with a summary of the efforts by Congress to impose some limits on workplace surveillance, most of which failed to pass. I believe that those various measures should have passed and in fact, did not go far enough. While the political tide is clearly running the other way, my hope is that this book (which is, after all, simply a snapshot of a rapidly moving target) will encourage employees, unions, and their elected representatives to seriously debate the issue and take action to impose some reasonable restrictions on workplace surveillance.

Frederick S. Lane III
Burlington, Vermont
December 11, 2002

# Acknowledgments

During the last two years, I have been fortunate to have the assistance of a large number of people in making this book a reality. I would like to take this opportunity to express my appreciation for all of the assistance I have received.

Initial thanks go to my agents, Christian Crumlish and Danielle Jatlow, at Waterside Productions in San Francisco, California. Both Christian and Danielle played a valuable role in helping me select the idea for this book from the hodgepodge that I handed to them two years ago. Danielle in particular played a critical role in helping me hone the idea, find a publisher, and shepherd the project to a successful conclusion. My thanks to both for their help, and to Dr. David Gardner for introducing me to them.

I was particularly fortunate to have had the opportunity to work with Ellen Kadin, the senior acquisitions editor at Amacom Books in New York. With unending patience, Ellen helped me refine the initial concept, adapt it to the changes that resulted from the events of 9/11, and see it through to a successful (if belated) conclusion. It has been a rewarding collaboration, and I am very thankful for her steady enthusiasm and encouragement.

In conversations via coffeehouse, phone, and e-mail, the direction of this project has been shaped by both friends and family. I'm fortunate to have had their interest, insights, suggestions, and support. Warm appreciation and thanks to: Warren and Anne Lane, Jessica Smith Lane, Brian Goetz, Bob Emmons, Adam Snyder and Sue Buckingham, Ted Pearcy and Tifani Greenwood, Amy Werbel, Christine Jensen, Christopher McVeigh, Karen Cody, and John Zeigle.

Two people deserve particular thanks for taking the time to read the entire manuscript for this book in the last feverish flurry of its creation. My thanks to Sarah Dunn for her stylistic suggestions and ongoing encouragement, and heartfelt appreciation to Dr. Madeline Waid for her valuable comments, including specifically the sections dealing with medical information.

As many writers have noted, editing is the aspect of book production that has taken the brunt of publisher cutbacks. I was fortunate that Amacom felt the project merited (and/or desperately needed) the attention of Janis Fisher Chan, who did a superb job of lopping off unnecessary boughs and posing tough but valuable questions about the text. This is a far better book than it would have been without her assistance, and I appreciate the obvious effort that she put into the editing process.

At AMACOM, my thanks to Christina McLaughlin and Mike Sivilli for their work in shepherding this book through the production process. I have also enjoyed my initial work with Irene Majuk, AMACOM's director of trade publicity & sales promotion, and look forward to our further efforts to promote the book. My thanks as well to AMACOM's President and Publisher, Hank Kennedy, for his support of this project, and for a very enjoyable meeting last spring.

I believe that environment plays an important role in the writing process and in that regard, I have been very fortunate to have found a marvelous environment. In Burlington, Vermont, Carrie and Mark MacKillop own and operate Muddy Waters, a wood-beamed coffeehouse on Main Street. The hours that I have spent drinking tea and writing at Muddy Waters have provided me with a valuable sense of community in the midst of a sometimes lonely process. I am very grateful to the two of them and to the entire Muddy Waters staff for their long-suffering patience. My thanks as well to my fellow coffeehouse travelers for their interest, encouragement, and often much-needed distraction.

Throughout the course of this project, the Web continued its phenomenal growth; the breadth of material now available online is staggering. One site in particular helped me wend my way through the potentially choking thicket of information: Google.com, which deserves tremendous kudos for the speed, smoothness, and simplicity of its operation. Although it was released relatively late in this project, it's clear that Google News has the potential to be a valuable aid to researchers in the future. In addition, there are a number of software programs that helped make this project far easier than it would have been otherwise. Despite the occasional frustrations, my sincere thanks to the programmers of Microsoft's *Windows XP* (operating system); Corel *Wordperfect 10.0* (word processing), Micro-Logic's *Infoselect 6.0* (an unbelievably useful information management program), Netscape *Communicator 7.0* (Web browser), Yahoo! *Mail,* and Adelphia Communication's *PowerLink* (broadband cable access).

# End Notes

1. William Safire, "You Are a Suspect," *The New York Times* (November 14, 2002).

2. Nat Hentoff, "We'll All Be Under Surveillance," *The Village Voice* (December 6, 2002). Sauropods were long-necked, plant-eating dinosaurs, the best-known example of which is the Jurassic period's Brachiosaurus. The gargantuan animals (fifty feet tall, up to eighty-five feet long) were one of the species featured in Steven Spielberg's enormously popular movie, *Jurassic Park.*

3. Lord Acton, in a letter to Bishop Mandell Creighton, 1887. Poindexter's conviction was entered in 1990, but was later overturned on the grounds that the basis of his conviction—his testimony to Congress—was given under a grant of immunity.

# CHAPTER ONE

# It's My Property and I'll Spy if I Want To...

It is fairly safe to say that virtually everyone in this country is physically naked at some point during the typical day. For most of us, it's usually in the morning, as we rush to change, bathe, or shower in order to get ready for the remainder of the day. Naturism is neither a practical nor an accepted choice for most of us, and so we dress according to our day's plans. A day spent puttering around the house may merit nothing more than a pair of sweat pants and a tattered t-shirt. For a trip to the mall, we might choose a polo shirt and a reasonably clean pair of jeans. And for many of us, a day in the office still requires a company uniform, a coat and tie, or at the very least, a nice button-down shirt and khaki slacks.

The clothing choices we make (or feel required to make) mirror the way our society treats personal privacy. When we stand naked before the mirror in the morning, our cloak of personal privacy is wrapped most tightly around us, and it takes extraordinary circumstances to strip it away. From the moment we cross our property line onto public property, however, the cloak of personal privacy begins to flap and flutter, and offers us only sporadic protection. And once we cross the line onto someone else's property, particularly as an employee, our cloak is at its thinnest and most revealing.

As we'll see in this chapter, there are a number of reasons—some of them quite compelling—for surveillance of employees. A major problem, however, is that technology makes it possible for employers to gather enormous amounts of data about employees, often far beyond what is necessary to satisfy safety or productivity concerns. And the trends that drive technology—faster, smaller, cheaper—make it possible for larger and larger numbers of employers to gather ever-greater amounts of personal data.

To date, the nation's legislatures and courts have made occasional efforts to reweave some threads of the privacy cloak for employees, but the result is little more than a patchwork of protection. A legitimate debate can be had over whether there should be any expectation of "workplace privacy," but the real issue is that without some limits on the surveillance of employees, our more closely guarded privacy in the home will vanish as well.

## Privacy in the Home

Most of us have quirks in our morning routine that we might not necessarily want to share with anyone else—the Oreos for breakfast that would horrify our granola-chewing buddies, the tea tree exfoliant and moisturizer that would greatly amuse our brick-laying coworkers, the leopard-spotted underwear that clashes with our sober pinstripe suits.

Such information is generally within what we consider to be our "zone of privacy," which Simson Garfinkle defined in his book *Database Nation* as the ability of people "to control what details about their lives stay inside their own houses and what leaks to the outside."[1]

Since the information about your morning ritual is under your control, you can choose to share it with others. It might be fun, for instance, to horrify your health-food buddies by regaling them with tales of how you start your day with a triple espresso and a six-pack of Oreos, and "oh, did you see the Danish in the break room?"

The very fact that we can choose to share such information if we want to do so demonstrates that the "right to privacy," at least compared to the other freedoms we enjoy (most notably life and liberty), is not a particularly strong right. We can't, after all, give or sell our life to someone else and, *Dilbert's* cynical outlook notwithstanding, we're not allowed to do so with our liberty either. But we can and do give away or sell pieces of our privacy every day.

As a "right," privacy suffers from two main flaws: First, it's very difficult to protect because the definition of "privacy" shifts so dramatically from generation to generation, and even from person to person. A century or so ago in this country, a glimpse of a woman's well-turned ankle was considered erotic, since clothing styles and social propriety put even that innocuous body part within the zone of privacy. Today, that woman's great-granddaughters are shopping for specially designed panties, so that they can wear low-rise jeans without letting their underwear show. By contrast, we have far less trouble defining "life" and "liberty." If you ask a random sampling of people if they're alive or free, most will be able to give you a correct answer.

The second main problem with the "right to privacy" is that it is not yet widely recognized as a fundamental human right, or at least has not yet become one. The explicit prohibition against invading someone's "privacy," for instance, is less than a century old, and we still really don't have a clear definition of what it means. By contrast, the laws against taking someone's life are well understood and have been on the books for centuries. Even the prohibition against slavery, which remarkably only predates the "right to privacy" in this country by about thirty-five years, is still easily defined.

A century after its creation, however, the "right to privacy" is still vague and amorphous, struggling to find its place in our list of its freedoms. The main challenge is that at bottom, "privacy" is a derivative right, one that is largely based on our attitudes toward the ownership of property. As we'll see throughout this book, the main practical consequence is that when a privacy interest comes in conflict with property rights, privacy is typically the loser. And in a nutshell, that's the basic reason that "workplace privacy" is largely an oxymoron: Your interest in personal privacy in the workplace is routinely overridden by your employer's property interests.

Before we explore the various tools and technologies that employers are using to protect their property rights, it's useful to take a look at how property became a more important principle than personal privacy. There are a number of potential starting places for this discussion, but as England's infamous King John discovered nearly 800 years ago, few things focus the attention as neatly as the point of a sword.

## The Magna Carta: Freedom from the Point of a Sword

On the edge of a sunlit green meadow in Runnymede, England (not far from Windsor Castle), there is a small monument. Ten straight beams of stone support a small dome, under which is a simple granite pillar that reads:

> To Commemorate
>
> Magna Carta
>
> Symbol of
>
> Freedom
>
> Under
>
> Law

The modest memorial—a gift to England in 1957 from the American Bar Association—marks the spot, approximately, where a group of rebellious barons forced King John, the younger brother of Richard the Lionheart, to place his seal on a document guaranteeing English freemen certain basic rights.

There is no question that John's confirmation of the Magna Carta in June 1215 was a momentous occasion—one of the first instances in which a sovereignty acknowledged that even it is not above the law. Despite the importance of the King's concession, however, the Magna Carta had far less to do with a recognition of fundamental human rights and more to do with the protection of feudal property.

In thirteenth-century England, power was measured in property and the resources that could be drawn from it. As the fourth son of Henry II and the legendary Eleanor of Aquitaine, John was unlikely to inherit property, which earned him the nickname "John Lackland." In an effort to maintain family harmony with his oft-difficult younger brother, however, Richard gave John vast tracts of land in England when Richard was crowned king in 1189.

The nickname "Lackland" proved prophetic: Ten years later, after being crowned king following Richard's death, John quickly proceeded to lose all of England's property holdings in Normandy during the first five years of his reign. He spent the next decade trying to win them back, but in 1214, a stinging military defeat at the hands of Philip II brought an end to John's efforts and led to the formation of what we know today as France.

On his return to England, King John tried to refill the Crown's depleted treasury by demanding scutage (a fee nobles paid to avoid military service—the medieval equivalent of stepping to the front of the line for National Guard assignments) from the barons who had failed to join him in his fight against King Philip. Most of the barons refused to pay, and civil war began to spread across England. In the spring of 1215, the rebellious nobles captured London and forced John to negotiate with them at Runnymede.

The document initially endorsed by John was not called the Magna Carta, but instead "The Articles of the Barons." Not surprisingly, the original draft was entirely concerned with the protection of the rights and interests of the nobility. Subsequent drafts of the document, however, inserted the word "freemen" into the text of the Magna Carta, and it was this language that was read to residents throughout England.

King John never had any real intention of abiding by the document; in fact, just three months after affixing his seal to the charter, he persuaded Pope Innocent III to annul the Magna Carta on the grounds that it was signed under duress. John had a point—after all, the barons were all but holding a sword to his throat.

Over time, most of the specific provisions of the Magna Carta have gradually become irrelevant, but the principles embedded in the document became part of the bedrock of English common law. The news of what took place at Runnymede—that the Crown had acknowledged *in writing* that the monarchy could not seize property or prosecute freemen without due process of law—spread rapidly, and affixed the concepts of due process and the sovereign's adherence to law in the popular imagination. Underlying both of those concepts was the sanctity of private property and its freedom from interference and invasion, even by a sovereign.

## The Declaration of Independence and the Bill of Rights

More than five hundred years later, belief in the Magna Carta's principles of due process and the sovereign's obedience to the law led another group of angry British subjects to gather together in Philadelphia. The complaint was essentially the same: that the Crown—then King George III—was arbitrarily disregarding the basic rights guaranteed to a free people.

Lacking the military strength needed to compel a distant monarch to sign a document like the Magna Carta, the colonists took a courageous leap and flatly declared their independence from Britain on July 4, 1776. "We hold these truths to be self-evident," the young Virginian Thomas Jefferson stirringly wrote, "that all men are created equal, that they are endowed by their Creator with certain unalienable Rights, that among these are Life, Liberty, and the pursuit of Happiness." Even in this clarion call for the recognition of basic human rights, the law of property was an important but hidden element: The term "unalienable" is defined as "incapable of being alienated, surrendered, or transferred," concepts that are traditionally applied to the ownership of land.[2]

Thanks to some timely help from the French army, the colonialists successfully resisted England's attempt to reassert its authority. Meeting again in Philadelphia in 1787, representatives of the thirteen colonies adopted the Constitution of the United States. On June 21, 1788, after a long and frequently feisty debate, the Constitution was ratified by a ninth state, New Hampshire, and the United States of America was formed.

With the battles against the British Crown still fresh in their minds, many of the political leaders of the new nation were concerned that the newly drafted Constitution did not do enough to guarantee the rights of individual citizens. When the inaugural Congress convened in 1789, the first thing that it did was to pass twelve proposed constitutional amendments, ten of which were ratified and form what we know today as the "Bill of Rights." Not surprisingly, given the often heavy-handed rule of King George and the British Parliament, half of the new amendments were specifically aimed at protecting the freedom of a person and his property from intrusions by the newly created federal government.

## Amendments Protecting Property

### Amendment III

No soldier shall, in time of peace be quartered in any house, without the consent of the owner, nor in time of war, but in a manner to be prescribed by law.

### Amendment IV

The right of the people to be secure in their persons, houses, papers, and effects, against unreasonable searches and seizures, shall not be violated, and no warrants shall issue, but upon probable cause, supported by oath or affirmation, and particularly describing the place to be searched, and the persons or things to be seized.

### Amendment V

No person shall be held to answer for a capital, or otherwise infamous crime, unless on a presentment or indictment of a grand jury, except in cases arising in the land or naval forces, or in the militia, when in actual service in time of war or public danger; nor shall any person be subject for the same offense to be twice put in jeopardy of life or limb; nor shall be compelled in any criminal case to be a witness against himself, nor be deprived of life, liberty, or property, without due process of law; nor shall private property be taken for public use, without just compensation.

### Amendment VI

In all criminal prosecutions, the accused shall enjoy the right to a speedy and public trial, by an impartial jury of the state and district wherein the crime shall have been committed, which district shall have been previously ascertained by law, and to be informed of the nature and cause of the accusation; to be confronted with the witnesses against him; to have compulsory process for obtaining witnesses in his favor, and to have the assistance of counsel for his defense.

### Amendment VIII

Excessive bail shall not be required, nor excessive fines imposed, nor cruel and unusual punishments inflicted.

More than 200 years later, it's still somewhat surprising to modern eyes that neither the Constitution nor the Bill of Rights even mention privacy, let alone specifically protect it. At the time that these documents were drafted, however, the concept of personal privacy barely existed. To the extent that privacy was an issue for the Founders at all, it meant primarily the right of citizens to be free from unjustified physical restraint and to be free from unlawful intrusion onto their property by agents of a central government.

## Crafting the Modern Concept of Privacy

As is so often the case, it was a technological innovation—the camera—that helped spur a rethinking of the legal principles that protect our rights. What we typically think of today as "privacy" (the right to be left alone) first entered the popular vocabulary in 1890, when two Boston law partners, Samuel D. Warren and Louis D. Brandeis, published an article in the *Harvard Law Review* entitled "The Right to Privacy."

"Instantaneous photographs and newspaper enterprise have invaded the sacred precincts of private and domestic life," the two attorneys wrote, "and numerous mechanical devices threaten to make good the prediction that 'what is whispered in the closet shall be proclaimed from the housetops.'"

Warren and Brandeis argued that the impact of these technological changes made it necessary for the common law to recognize an individual's right to prevent the collection and publication of personal information. Their warning, sounded nearly a century before *People* magazine, *Entertainment Tonight*, and nude celebrity websites, is uncannily prescient:

> The press is overstepping in every direction the obvious bounds of propriety and of decency. Gossip is no longer the resource of the idle and of the vicious, but has become a trade, which is pursued with industry as well as effrontery. To satisfy a prurient taste the details of sexual relations are spread broadcast in the columns of the daily papers. . . . The intensity and complexity of life, attendant upon advancing civilization, have rendered necessary some retreat from the world . . . so that solitude and privacy have become more essential to the individual; but modern enterprise and invention have, through invasions upon his privacy, subjected him to mental pain and distress. . . . When personal gossip attains the dignity of print, and crowds the space available for matters of real interest to the community, what wonder that the ignorant and thoughtless mistake its relative importance. Easy of comprehension, appealing to that weak side of human nature which is never

wholly cast down by the misfortunes and frailties of our neighbors, no one can be surprised that it usurps the place of interest in brains capable of other things. Triviality destroys at once robustness of thought and delicacy of feeling. No enthusiasm can flourish, no generous impulse can survive under its blighting influence.[3]

By the early 1930s, the "right to privacy" first proposed by Warren and Brandeis had earned a place in the First Restatement of Torts, one of the treatises that outlines the nation's generally accepted principles of law. According to the Restatement, "a person who reasonably and seriously interferes with another's interest in not having his affairs known to others or his likeness exhibited to the public is liable to the other."

Even as the U.S. legal system began to recognize a right to recover damages for invasion of privacy, technology was devising new and ingenious ways for our privacy to be invaded. Over the course of seventy or more years, both the U.S. Supreme Court and Congress have reacted to specific invasions of privacy (sometimes erroneously), yet neither has articulated or implemented a cohesive set of principles regarding personal privacy and its place in our list of freedoms.

## Privacy at Work

After 215 years, the Constitution is so firmly embedded in our national consciousness that it's difficult to imagine that we can still be on American soil and not enjoy the benefits of its protective principles. And yet, every single day, tens of millions of us spend hours in offices, cubicles, kitchens, laundry rooms, and work sites where the U.S. Constitution is completely inapplicable. It is, essentially, the equivalent of traveling each day to a foreign nation.

This somewhat disturbing state of affairs stems from the fact that when the Constitution was drafted, the concept of workplace privacy was even more remote than personal privacy. The purpose of the U.S. Constitution, after all, was to create a framework for government that would, among other things, protect the nation's citizens from the potentially destructive power of a central government. There was little reason for the framers to consider the relationship between private employment and personal rights. At the time, the number of private employers was relatively low, few had more than a handful of employees, and concern over working conditions (let alone privacy) was minimal.

And in fact, the framers of the Constitution would undoubtedly have been reluctant to interfere in the relationship between employer and employee because that was precisely the type of governmental interference against which they were revolting. So reluctant, in fact, were the framers to interfere with private relationships that they deferred action on the issue of slavery, a decision that would later cost the country dearly.

Over the years, employees have periodically raised constitutional claims in disputes with their employers, and courts at every level have routinely held that the U.S. Constitution simply does not apply to private employers. As we'll see throughout this book, what rights private employees do enjoy stem from state and federal statutes, and in some limited circumstances, provisions of various state constitutions (which can provide greater protections than the federal constitution).

The availability of constitutional protections is one area in which government employees have a modest advantage over private employees. If your employer is a government body, agency, or department, then generally speaking, the protections of the Constitution (and particularly the Fourth Amendment, which prohibits unreasonable search and seizure) do apply to you.

The freedom private employers enjoy from the provisions of the U.S. Constitution gives them tremendous latitude in how they handle their employees. The latitude is not absolute: Congress has recognized that employers sometimes treat certain employees unfairly, and has passed legislation designed to curb some of the worst abuses (i.e., the Fair Labor Standards Act, the Civil Rights Act, the Americans with Disabilities Act, and the Employee Polygraph Protection Act). Nonetheless, the freedom private employers enjoy from the boundaries imposed by the Fourth Amendment has allowed them to engage in extensive surveillance of their employees. With daunting regularity, technology is expanding the scope of that surveillance, and there is no end in sight.

## The Rationalizations for Workplace Surveillance

Despite the amount of workplace surveillance that takes place in this country, peering into the lives of their employees is not something that businesses undertake lightly: It's expensive, time-consuming, and inherently destructive of employee morale. It's reasonable to assume that businesses would not spend so much on surveillance technologies—Internet monitoring, closed-circuit television, drug testing, background checks, GPS systems, etc.—if they did not feel compelled to do so. A variety of interwoven factors, however, are driving U.S. companies to spending enormous amounts of time and money on employee surveillance. The bet is that the investment in increased surveillance will pay off by reducing employee theft and sabotage, increasing productivity, preventing lawsuits, avoiding violent incidents in the workplace, and preventing terrorist attacks.

## Minimizing Theft and Sabotage

To understand the rationale for employee surveillance, you need go no further than this figure: In 2001, employees stole an estimated $15.243 billion in inventory from their employers. According to the 2001 National Retail Security Survey (NRSS) Final Report, prepared by the Department of Sociology and the Center for Studies in Criminology and Law at the University of Florida in Gainsville, "There is no other form of larceny that annually costs the American public more money than employee theft." Based on the responses from retailers, the NRSS estimates that 45.9 percent of all inventory shrinkage is the result of employee theft, compared to the estimated 30.8 percent that results from shoplifting. The fact that retailers lost more than $10 billion from customer theft is also relevant, however, since a lot of employee surveillance is an accidental by-product of trying to stop customer theft or misbehavior.

The theft of consumer goods, of course, is only one of the theft risks that employers face. According to a study by the Santa Monica, California, think tank Rand Corporation, high-tech equipment has proven to be a very popular target as well, accounting for as much as $4 billion in losses during late 1998 and early 1999.

If the computers themselves aren't being stolen, then they're often being used to steal. The tremendous increase in the number of personal computers in the workplace and the enthusiastic adoption of the Internet by the business community has opened up enormous new security concerns. It's one thing to try to prevent the theft of things that must be physically removed from the workplace; it's another thing entirely to prevent the theft of information that can be downloaded to a floppy or Zip™ disk, e-mailed to oneself or a confederate, or even posted to a Web page for the entire world to see.

For the past seven years, the Computer Security Institute (CSI) in San Francisco, in conjunction with the San Francisco Federal Bureau of Investigation's (FBI) Computer Intrusion Squad, has conducted a survey of computer crime and security in the United States. Among the important findings of the CSI/FBI 2002 Report:

- Nine out of ten respondents were the victims of computer security breaches;

- Eight out of ten respondents suffered financial losses as a result of those security breaches;

■ Forty-four percent of the respondents had tallied the cost of the security breaches: They reported a total of $455,848,000 in financial losses;

■ The two most expensive categories of theft were intellectual property ($170,827,000) and financial fraud ($115,753,000); and

■ Three-quarters of all respondents said that their Internet connections were a frequent point of attack, while only a third listed their internal network systems.

It would be tempting but inaccurate to blame nonemployees for the computer and Internet security breaches that plague companies. In fact, experts estimate that 70 percent to 80 percent of all computer crime is committed by employees against their employers. In the CSI/FBI report, for instance, eight out of ten respondents reported that their employees had abused their workplace Internet connections in some manner, ranging from inappropriate use of the e-mail system to downloading pornography.[4]

Theft is only one of the perils faced by employers in today's high-tech world. Before computers, causing significant damage to an employer's property required time, energy, and typically the use of an accelerant like gasoline. Today, however, a few lines of software code can wipe out millions of dollars of intellectual property. For example, in 1996, Timothy Lloyd, a thirty-year-old network program designer at the Bridgeport, New Jersey, facility of Omega Engineering, Inc., was told that he was about to be fired. Outraged at the company's treatment of him, Lloyd wrote and planted a "logic bomb" that detonated three weeks after his departure from the company. The "bomb" destroyed Omega's main database, resulting in an estimated $10 to $12 million in lost sales and repair costs, and causing eighty other Omega employees to be laid off.

Companies are often reluctant to report insider attacks for fear of revealing vulnerabilities that might be exploited by others, or they're unwilling to go through the time and expense of actually prosecuting someone. There's little doubt, however, that employees pose the greatest threat to corporate computers.

## The Productivity Paradox

The next most-frequently cited justification for employee surveillance is the need to maintain or improve productivity. "An honest day's work for an honest day's pay"—that's the core agreement between worker and employer, whether payment is in bushels of wheat or stock options. How we determine "productivity" has changed somewhat over the years ("Kill the mastodon or you don't eat" eventually became "Get that report in on time or you're fired") but the basic issue remains the same. In a capitalist system, businesses that do not produce an adequate supply of goods or services, or whose costs routinely exceed their revenues, effectively starve to death.

The challenge that companies have faced over the last century is that many of the same technological innovations aimed at improving individual workplace productivity have carried with them the risk of wasted time and resources. Of course, a chatty coworker is more than sufficient to waste time at work, and doodling has been a reliable workplace diversion since the pencil was invented. But one of the great things about technology is that it makes the wasting of time so much easier.

Employers got their first taste of this phenomenon with the introduction of the telephone. It took less than fifty years for the telephone to make the transition from Alexander Graham Bell's crowded workshop to virtually every office desktop in the country. As it did so, it became the communication equivalent of the railroad, helping to accelerate the Industrial Revolution by dramatically speeding up (if not entirely inventing) the art of the deal.

From an employer's perspective, the chief benefit of the telephone was that it made it possible for employees to do more work in a shorter period of time. But this new technological marvel added something not typically found in more formal office communication—chitchat. To a limited degree, of course, businesses promote chitchat: They want their employees to develop personal relationships with the people with whom they regularly deal.

The challenge, of course, is balancing telephone chitchat with productivity. This was less of a problem in the early part of the twentieth century, when the number of residential telephones lagged behind business phones. By the late 1950s, however, more than 75 percent of the homes in America had their own telephone, and the office gradually stopped being the secluded domain of the man in the gray-flannel suit. *Leave It to Beaver*'s June Cleaver would never have called her husband Ward, asking him to stop and pick up a gallon of milk on the way home, but *thirty-something*'s Hope Murdoch Steadman saw nothing inappropriate in calling Michael to discuss everything from dinner plans to child crises. More than any other single technology, the telephone helped blur the lines between work and home.

Most employers recognize that as long as the number or length of personal calls is not excessive, attempts to ban them are bad for employee morale. Besides, the telephone offers only middling possibilities for wasting time. In most offices, it's fairly difficult to keep fellow employees or bosses from realizing that you're spending hours on the phone chatting with family or friends.

The same thing, of course, can hardly be said about the personal computer. To be fair, when they were first introduced to the office, personal computers posed little threat to employee productivity. The early PCs were fairly simple machines: stand-alone devices with limited storage space (the first IBM desktops didn't even have a hard drive), even more limited memory, and monochrome screens, none of which were particularly conducive to game-playing or other time-wasting applications. More importantly, their expense made most companies very conscious of how they were being used.

Games were not completely unavailable, of course—my college buddies and I spent a now-embarrassing number of hours playing *Oubliette*, a Dungeons-and-Dragons-type game that was very clever in its ability to create images on a monochrome screen. In addition, text-based games like *Adventure*, *Zork*, and *The Leather Goddess of Phoebos* also enjoyed a brief but intense period of popularity, but overall, the businesses that made early purchases of desktop computers could safely assume that they would in fact be used for business purposes.

By the early 1990s, however, simplicity had become a lost art. With the release of Microsoft's *Windows 3.0* (1990) and *3.1* (1992), businesses rapidly discovered that a perfectly functioning PC offered an almost limitless potential for frittering. Users could and still do spend hours tweaking color schemes and wallpaper, changing various settings, and installing utilities.

From a productivity point of view, the real footsteps of *Doom* could be heard in 1990, when Microsoft included a version of *Solitaire* in its release of Windows 3.0.[5] *Solitaire* has remained a part of Windows system releases ever since and may well hold the title as the world's most frequently played computer game. And *Solitaire* is merely the most obvious example of a huge universe of available computer games. Expert estimates vary widely on how much game playing takes place in offices around the country, but Apreo (formerly DVD Software), which produces a game-blocking program called *AntiGame*, recently claimed that workplace game playing now costs employers over $50 billion per year. On the Apreo website, Steve Watkins, an assistant vice president and director of information technology at Summit National Bank in Atlanta, Georgia, offers a typical comment:

> *AntiGame* is a great asset to our organization. . . . With its customizable database, *AntiGame* allows us to unobtrusively monitor users' workstations for unapproved software, games or otherwise, and clean the offending stations if deemed necessary. With about one hundred users spread over six locations from Georgia to California, *AntiGame* is a tremendous time-saving improvement over our former monitoring technique—visiting each workstation individually.

As the Internet becomes an increasingly important part of the workplace, however, game playing is losing its position as the chief time-wasting tool by employees. From an employer's perspective, having unmonitored Internet access on each desk is roughly the equivalent of installing a gazillion-channel television set for each employee. In part because of its sheer convenience, and in part because businesses tend to have faster Web access, employees are finding it difficult to resist the temptation to shop for presents, plan vacations, check out sports scores, trade stocks, buy and sell items on eBay, correspond with friends and family, read reviews, buy movie tickets, and so on. There were certainly noncomputer ways to do all of these things before the Internet; it's just that the Internet makes it so much easier and less immediately obvious to the employer.

Moreover, the very nature of the World Wide Web exacerbates the productivity problem. As any researcher knows (including yours truly), the lure of hypertext links is so seductive that it's easy to begin researching the finer points of wireless networks and wind up reading a Web page about the right kind of chiles for salsa. This type of research drift is problematic enough in a library; on a device where the next interesting thing is simply a click away, it can be a huge challenge to maintain focus.

## Minimizing Workplace Litigation

In truth, most companies recognize that an occasional personal e-mail or a little online Christmas shopping is not an enormous threat to employee productivity and, in fact, may help to improve workplace morale. Companies run into real trouble, though, when employees use the Internet to share racist or sexist jokes, or to access sexually explicit websites. Companies that fail to take steps to prevent that from happening face the threat of harassment suits based on the existence of a hostile work environment.

### Examples of Internet-Related Harassment Actions

- In 2001, nine female workers sued John Deere & Co. for discrimination and sexual harassment. They alleged, among other things, that coworkers printed out Internet pornography on company equipment during work hours.

- In 1996, financial giant Smith Barney, Inc. was sued by twenty-five female employees for sexual harassment and discrimination, based in part on messages and materials distributed across the company's computers. In 1998, the company fired two high-ranking stock analysts for violating the company's rules on the use of computers to distribute pornography.

- In 1995, just as the World Wide Web was growing in popularity, Chevron was sued by a number of female workers under the hostile work environ-

> ment theory. Among the evidence that the plaintiffs introduced was an
> e-mail message that was circulated on the company system entitled
> "Twenty-Five Reasons Why Beer Is Better than Women." That e-mail
> cost Chevron just under $100,000 per reason; the company settled the
> lawsuit for $2.2 million.

Lawsuits that allege the existence of a hostile work environment are an outgrowth of the landmark Civil Rights Act of 1964, a piece of legislation that resulted in the longest debate in the history of the U.S. Congress. Under Title VII of the Civil Rights Act, it is "an unlawful employment practice for an employer . . . to discriminate against any individual with respect to his compensation, terms, conditions, or privileges of employment, because of such individual's race, color, religion, sex, or national origin."[6] Not surprisingly, nearly every word in that sentence has been the subject of repeated litigation, as the employers and employees try to sort out the boundaries of permissible conduct.

Not long after the Civil Rights Act went into effect, courts concluded that discrimination did not have to be "economic" or "tangible" in order to be a violation of Title VII. Ruling for a woman, Teresa Harris, who had been subjected to gender- and sexually-based comments and other offensive behavior from her company's president, Justice Sandra Day O'Connor wrote: "When the workplace is permeated with discriminatory intimidation, ridicule, and insult that is sufficiently severe or pervasive to alter the conditions of the victim's employment and create an abusive working environment, Title VII is violated."[7] O'Connor went on to add that the Court was attempting to draw a line between conduct that causes a "tangible psychological injury" and conduct that is "merely offensive."

Not surprisingly, employees (and their lawyers) were quite pleased with the *Harris* decision. After the case was decided in November 1993, the Equal Employment Opportunity Commission (EEOC) saw an immediate rise in the number of sexual harassment claims, from 11,908 in fiscal 1993 to 14,420 in fiscal 1994, or an increase of more than 20 percent. Currently, approximately 15,500 sexual harassment claims are filed with the EEOC each year.

The cost of sexual harassment claims has also gone up significantly since Harris was decided. According to the financial services magazine *Treasury & Risk Management*, corporations paid about $1 billion on sexual harassment settlements and awards between 1992 and 1997. In 1998 alone, the average award for an employment claim was $550,000. And those figures, of course, do not include other related costs of sexual harassment litigation, such as lawyers' fees and litigation preparation.

Technology—especially the Internet—has dramatically increased the risk of hostile work environment claims. Fifteen years ago, an insensitive lout might tell a sexist joke around the water cooler or in the lunch room; if the conduct was pervasive and sufficiently long-lasting, it could serve as the basis of a hostile work environment claim, but the scope of the damages was likely to be relatively limited. Today, that same lout not only has access to thousands of offensive jokes and images, he (or she, to be fair) can distribute them around the entire company with a click of a button.

## Preventing Workplace Tragedies

Just after 11:00 A.M. on December 26, 2000, Michael McDermott stood up from his desk at Edgewater Technologies, a Wakefield, Massachusetts, Internet-consulting firm where he worked as a software tester. Having just been told that his car was being repossessed and facing garnishment of his wages by Edgewater for federal back taxes, McDermott pulled a rifle, shotgun, and pistol from a gun bag, and went on a shooting spree that resulted in the deaths of seven coworkers.[8] Just six weeks later, on February 5, 2001, a sixty-six-year-old former employee at Navistar International Corp. in suburban Chicago pushed past security, opened his golf bag full of weapons, and shot four coworkers. After wounding four other employees, William Baker then killed himself.

The two incidents were merely the latest in a string of high-profile workplace shootings. Overall, the Occupational Safety & Health Administration (OSHA) reported that in 2000, 674 workplace homicides occurred, and in 1999, violent (but nonfatal) assaults occurred 16,664 times. Put another way, during an average five-day workweek, nearly thirteen people are killed and roughly 320 are attacked at work.

Needless to say, employers have an interest in doing everything they can to minimize workplace violence. Apart from the pain and suffering that workplace violence causes, companies face significant liability issues arising from on-the-job attacks. Preferring to go after defendants with so-called "deep pockets," or at least deep-pocketed insurance policies, plaintiffs' attorneys have worked hard to develop new theories of potential corporate liability, including negligent hiring and negligent retention of dangerous employees. Increasingly, corporations are also being challenged on whether they had in place adequate security measures to prevent workplace violence.

Because of its high profile and the scope of the perceived threat, workplace violence may be the biggest single contributor to reduced employee privacy. As most employers correctly realize, the best solution to workplace violence is to prevent it from occurring in the first place. Unfortunately, the type of information that might signal that an employee is a potential threat is often among the most private—a history of physical or sexual abuse, serious domestic issues, profound financial pressures, psychological illness, etc.

Despite the potential invasions of privacy, workplace security consultants strongly advise employers to undertake the types of investigations that might root out such information. For instance, Michael McIntyre, a professor of psychology at the University of Tennessee in Knoxville and the developer of a test to identify the potential for workplace violence, says that he "recommends that employers do as much due diligence on the preemployment side as possible." While conceding that his test can't predict that someone will become a workplace shooter ("There aren't enough incidents to use as a basis for scientific study," he said), Professor McIntyre is confident that the twenty-five-question test developed by him and his colleague, Larry James, can successfully identify people with a propensity for "desk rage," the cubicle equivalent of "road rage."

The steps companies take to ferret out potential violence include putting increased resources into background checks and increasing their efforts to obtain medical and psychological records. Since health records are often difficult (but unfortunately, not impossible) to obtain, employers are administering more psychological and personality tests to applicants and existing employees in an attempt to locate potential time bombs. In addition, employers are also paying closer attention to how employees behave on the job, instituting tighter access controls, and even expanding their monitoring of employee off-hour activities.

Some of these measures have a relatively limited impact on employee privacy—even tracking where employees are in a particular building is not an enormous infringement on privacy. The problem with some inquiries—psychological and personality tests, for instance, or monitoring off-hour activities—is the seemingly tenuous relationship between the information gathered and a propensity for violence. The potential for abuse and misguided profiling is enormous: Should we watch more closely the National Rifle Association member with the cabinet full of guns? How about the bulky, bearded Hell's Angel member? The stereotypically angry, militant feminist? The Vietnam vet? The short, mild-mannered bookish type just waiting to avenge a lifetime of wisecracks and Randy Newman songs? The list, obviously, is endless.

## Preventing Electronic and Physical Terrorism

Before September 11, 2001, concern over terrorism in this country, particularly in the business community, was largely limited to the threat of cyberterrorism. Admittedly, there was some increased concern as a result of the first bombing of the World Trade Center in 1993 and the destruction of the Alfred P. Murrah Building in Oklahoma City in 1995, but to a large extent, those were viewed as aberrations. The perception of the country as Fortress America remained strong.

By contrast, concern over the growing threat of cyberterrorism—outside attacks on computer systems—had been growing steadily for some time. Even before the World Wide Web began skyrocketing in popularity in 1995 and 1996, businesses and government agencies had awakened to the unpleasant fact that the new international communications network could be used by hackers, competitors, foreign governments, grumpy employees, and precocious twelve-year-olds to do unpleasant things to their computer systems and critical data. The ongoing efforts to protect corporate computer systems diminished employee privacy in a number of ways, from the increased scrutiny given to workers when they are hired to the greater surveillance of all computer-related activity.

The phenomenon of hacking first hit the mainstream when Hollywood released *War Games* in 1983. In the film, the character played by Matthew Broderick shows off for a friend by using his computer to dial into the computer system at the North American Aerospace Defense Command (NORAD) and play computer games with the "WOPPER," the system's mainframe. In the process, he nearly triggers World War III. A commercial success (taking in nearly $80 million), the film helped stir public interest in the vulnerabilities of computer systems.

But to really grab the public's imagination, you need a hero or a villain. Hacking got its villain on July 4, 1994, when John Markoff reported on the federal government's efforts to capture hacker Kevin Mitnick. The front-page article in *The New York Times* breathlessly recounted Mitnick's exploits as a "phreaker" and hacker and said that Broderick's character in *War Games* was based on Mitnick, who had allegedly broken into the NORAD computer systems as a teenager in the early 1980s.[9] Both NORAD and Mitnick, not surprisingly, strenuously denied that the break-in ever occurred, but the article helped to establish Mitnick as the most infamous hacker in the country.

The online debate over Mitnick's guilt or innocence is passionate. At the time that Markoff's article was written, Mitnick was allegedly a fugitive from justice and carrying out an electronic crime wave resulting in tens of millions of damage to a variety of major corporations, including Motorola, Nokia, and Sun. However, during pretrial proceedings in 1998 and 1999, government prosecutors conceded that Mitnick had largely complied with the terms of his earlier probation, although they stood by their claim that the issuance of a secret arrest warrant did make the hacker a fugitive.

While it was apparently true that Mitnick was breaking into corporate computer systems, a similar disagreement arose over the amount of damage that he caused when he did so. The government asserted that Mitnick's activities caused corporations $80 million in damages, and as part of his plea agreement, Mitnick admitted to $10 million in damage. Mitnick's defenders, however, allege that he was the classic hacker—someone who broke into systems merely for the intellectual challenge of doing so, and not for economic gain. True hackers distinguish themselves from a "cracker," defined as "[o]ne who breaks security on a system, a term coined ca. 1985 by hackers in defense against journalistic misuse of hacker." ["Cracker," q.v., *The New Hacker's Dictionary* (Eric S. Raymond, compiler), Cambridge, Mass.: MIT Press, 1994.]

While acknowledging that Mitnick did not seek to profit from the material he copied from invaded systems, prosecutors nonetheless argued that Mitnick's activities diminished the value of the material he copied and made it easier for others to steal and sell the confidential material.

For his exploits, real or imagined, Mitnick earned the dubious honor of being the first hacker on the FBI's most-wanted list and became the subject of a nationwide manhunt. He was arrested on February 15, 1995, after a widely publicized investigation spearheaded by Tsutomu Shimomura, a computer expert at the San Diego Supercomputer Center. Following his arrest, Mitnick was denied bail (in fact, in a exceedingly rare move, he was even denied a bail hearing) and spent the next four years in jail awaiting trial. Just prior to the scheduled start of his trial in April 1999, Mitnick signed a plea agreement in which he pled guilty to five of twenty-five counts of fraud. He was sentenced to forty-six months in federal prison, and with credit for time served, was released in 2000.

Mitnick may or may not deserve the scarlet H that's been pinned to his chest, but there's no question that media reports about his alleged career and the exploits of hacker gangs like the Legion of Doom helped heighten public awareness about the potential for cyberterrorism. A 1998 report by the Rand Corporation warned of the potential for a "digital Pearl Harbor" and concluded because of the growth of network systems, "the U.S. homeland may no longer provide a sanctuary from outside attack." Congress also leapt on the cyberthreat bandwagon, with Senator Fred Thompson of

Tennessee declaring that an attack on the United States would start with attempts "to screw up our computers." (Unfortunately, 9/11 proved Senator Thompson wrong.)

The increased concern over electronic attacks has also led directly to sizeable increases in spending on cybersecurity measures. In 1999, the Aberdeen Group, a Boston Internet analyst firm, estimated that corporations spent $7.1 billion to guard against cyberattacks, and predicted that outlays would rise to $17 billion per year by 2003.

In addition to protecting themselves against cyberattacks, companies are also investing much more heavily on physical security. Even before 9/11, corporations were spending nearly $12 billion per year on security systems; in a survey conducted not long after the attacks, the corporate security firm Kroll Inc. found that the percentage of businesses rating physical security as a priority had jumped from 40 percent to 90 percent.

In general, businesses that spend money on physical security are trying to accomplish two separate objectives: to protect their employees and property from attack, and to make sure that their resources and systems are not infiltrated and used to attack other targets.

A seemingly inevitable by-product of the increased corporate security is a shrinking of employee privacy. In order to effectively protect their resources, businesses need to be aggressive about keeping track of who is on their property, what they're doing, and where they are.

As we'll see in the following chapters, the determination of who is on a business's property is currently the most intrusive part of employment. The largest increase in the amount of money that businesses are spending on security is for background checks of employees, with the result that more employees are being examined, more information is being gathered, and stricter standards are being applied. In many cases, relatively minor and seemingly irrelevant past infractions are causing a loss of employment or a failure to be hired in the first place.

## End Notes

1. Simson Garfinkle, *Database Nation* (O'Reilly & Associates, Inc., 2000), p. 4.

2. *Webster's New Collegiate Dictionary* (G. & C. Merriam & Co., 1977).

3. Samuel D. Warren and Louis D. Brandeis, "The Right to Privacy," *Harvard Law Review*, Vol. IV, No. 5 (December 15, 1890).

4. Press release, "Cyber crime bleeds U.S. corporations, survey shows; financial losses from attacks climb for third year in a row," Computer Security Institute (April 7, 2002). Available online at www.gocsi.com/press/20020407.html.

5. Ironically, the author of *Solitaire*, Wes Cherry, did not receive a single cent for

creating his Windows version of the game. "Some program manager in the Windows group saw it and decided to release it with Windows 3.0," Cherry said in an interview with journalist Charles Slocum. "[T]he condition was I did it for free (I was uncompensated other than the use of a computer they provided to work on it during my senior year of college). I probably could have negotiated some kind of one-time payment, but Microsoft really doesn't like to give per-copy royalties unless they absolutely need the technology." Charles B. Slocum, "Solitary Confinement," *Written by* (February, 2001).

6. 42 U.S.C. 2000e-2(a)(1).

7. *Harris v. Forklift Systems, Inc.,* 510 U.S. 17 (1993) (internal citations and quotations omitted).

8. "Workplace shooting suspect accused of killing seven victims in seven minutes," Court TV website, [n.d.]. Available online at www.courttv.com/trials/mcdermott/background.html.

9. A "phreaker" is someone who breaks into telephone systems, primarily by using equipment or even whistling to fake dial tones.

# CHAPTER TWO

# Applying for a Job in a Digital and Wired World

In the summer of 2002, an English theatrical newspaper, *The Stage*, ran an advertisement for the position of a hermit on a Staffordshire estate known as Shugborough Home. The successful applicant was expected to live in a damp cave on the estate grounds, give up bathing and shaving, and cut off all human contact. Duties were described as light: The only thing the hermit was expected to do was scare off occasional trespassers.

As it turned out, the hermit opening (once a familiar position on English estates) was merely a temporary position created to help promote England's National Heritage Week. The idea was the brainchild of artist Anna Douglas, who told applicants (and interested reporters) that the position was just a weekend gig. Nonetheless, Douglas was apparently stunned by the fact that more than one hundred people, including some from as far away as Pakistan, submitted an application to live in the cave.

Ironically, even applying for the position of hermit these days is not as anonymous as it undoubtedly once was. Each of the applications was put through a fairly intrusive and very nonhermit-like background check, similar to the background check that would be conducted if you were to apply for a position with most large American companies today.[1]

Most people understand and accept the fact that if they want to be hired for a particular job, they need to provide the prospective employer with a certain amount of information about themselves. After all, the employer's essential goal is to hire a well-qualified individual for that position, so you expect to provide basic background information, such as your identity, your experience, and your qualifications for the job.

What is less obvious is that hiring a well-qualified individual is only part of the employer's objective. Increasingly, employers are interested in hiring employees who will not expose the company to additional costs and liability. As a result, few employers feel that their hiring concerns are satisfied with the information that applicants themselves provide. In fact, job applications and resumés are merely a starting place for further inquiry, which can quickly turn into a highly invasive review of your personal life.

Here's how it works. Most employers, for instance, require you provide your Social Security number as part of your job application; as we'll see, the Social Security number has become a golden key that offers access to enormous amounts of personal information. Most standard job application forms also contain a release that, once signed, gives the prospective employer the right to obtain a wide variety of information about you. In some cases, the scope of the hiring investigation is mandated by federal or state law (school departments, for instance, are generally required to check all new hires for criminal records), but most employers conduct additional background investigations voluntarily, because they are strongly interested in making sure that they do not hire an employee who will increase their costs through negligence, misconduct, wrongdoing, or even bad health.

You have the right, of course, to refuse to provide your Social Security number or sign a records release, but that refusal will likely mean that you will not be considered for the job. The assumption, unfortunately, will not be that you are taking a principled stand to protect your privacy rights, but that you have something to hide. And to be fair, employers have often found the latter assumption to be correct.

## Creative Writing: Resumés and Job Applications

There are few head coaching positions in the United States more prestigious than that of Notre Dame. Football legends have coached and played at Notre Dame—Knute Rockne, George Gipp, Ara Parseghian, Joe Montana, and Lou Holtz, to name a few. In 1924, the famed sportswriter Grantland Rice immortalized members of the team as "the Four Horsemen," in a story that has one of the great opening lines in all of journalism:

> Outlined against a blue, gray October sky the Four Horsemen rode again.
>
> In dramatic lore they are known as famine, pestilence, destruction, and death. These are only aliases. Their real names are: Stuhldreher,

Miller, Crowley, and Layden. They formed the crest of the South Bend cyclone before which another fighting Army team was swept over the precipice at the Polo Grounds this afternoon as 55,000 spectators peered down upon the bewildering panorama spread out upon the green plain below.

Even Hollywood has jumped on the Notre Dame bandwagon, memorializing the legend of George "the Gipper" Gipp (played by former President Ronald Reagan) in *Knute Rockne All American* (1940) and the inspirational story of long-time benchwarmer Rudy Ruettiger in the 1993 film *Rudy*.

It was with no small fanfare, then, that in December 2001, Notre Dame announced the selection of George O'Leary, the head coach at Georgia Tech, as the next head coach for the Fighting Irish. O'Leary resigned his Georgia Tech position and participated in a glowing press conference in South Bend, Indiana. Within five days, however, he had sacked himself, leaving Notre Dame scrambling to find a replacement.

This abrupt reversal stemmed from an increasingly common problem: Some of the information on O'Leary's resumé turned out to be inaccurate. The biographical information handed out by Notre Dame listed him as a three-year letterman at the University of New Hampshire and the holder of a master's degree in education from New York University at Stony Brook. But when Jim Fennell, a reporter for the Concord, New Hampshire *Union Leader & Sunday News*, began to follow up on the local angle of a UNH player hitting the big time, he discovered that the former UNH coaches and players he interviewed did not remember O'Leary.

Fennell then learned that O'Leary had transferred to UNH for his last two years, that he had not played in any football games, and that he had not earned any varsity letters. When other reporters began checking items on O'Leary's resumé, it turned out that he had also not received a master's degree from Stony Brook. As the information became public, O'Leary resigned as Notre Dame's head coach.

While most of us do not have to worry about inquisitive reporters checking on our employment history, it should come as no surprise that employers and their human resource departments have caught on to the fact that not everything on a resumé is necessarily the entire truth. Even before the 9/11 terrorist attacks, nearly 70 percent of all employers were doing some sort of check to verify the information provided on applications or resumés. Since then, both the number of employers doing background checks and the scope of those checks has increased appreciably.[2]

In a tough job market, it's probably not surprising that applicants often take a little creative license with their work history. According to The Risk Advisory Group (TRAG), a London-based employee screening firm, over 50 percent of the resumés that they examined in 2001 had some type of error or exaggeration. The statistics for the United States are even worse: Hire-Right, an Internet-based background checking company, found that 80 percent of the 200,000 resumés they reviewed in 2001 were misleading in one or more ways:

- One in five listed fraudulent degrees.

- One in three contained inaccurate dates for previous employment.

- Two in five gave salary histories that were inflated.

- One in three had fictional or overblown job descriptions.

- Roughly one in four provided false references.[3]

What is a little surprising is the willingness of applicants and employees to take these kinds of risks, particularly in an era of nearly instant communication, online databases, and increasingly skeptical employers.

The consequences of false information on a resumé are predictably harsh. Of the firms interviewed by the *The New York Times*'s job market research team, 79 percent said that their policy is to terminate employees who are found to have falsified information on a resumé (and presumably, the percentage that decline to hire people with fraudulent resumés is even higher). The second-most common response, some form of internal discipline of the employee, was the policy of only 7 percent of the firms interviewed.[4]

Verifying the information that job applicants provide about themselves is obviously not much of an invasion of privacy. After all, if you're providing information to a prospective employer in an effort to get a job, the employer has a virtually unassailable right to make sure that the information you've provided is correct. If you tell a potential employer that you are a graduate of the Wharton School of Economics or have an advanced engineering degree from MIT, it's simple common sense for the employer to pick up the phone and make sure that you actually got a degree.

If that were all employers did, there would be far fewer privacy concerns for prospective employees. But few employers these days are satisfied with simply verifying the information you give them. Instead, they are increasingly motivated to obtain as much information about you as they can. And to do that, employers are turning to the private detective industry, which is happy to provide employers with as much help as they need (and can afford).

## Private Detectives and Employee Privacy

Most companies are able to handle the workload necessary to check out a job applicant's resumé—all that's required are some perceptive interview questions and a few phone calls. But conducting the types of background checks necessary to thoroughly investigate a potential employee can be far more time-consuming. Because relatively few companies find it cost-effective to maintain their own internal force of investigators and detectives, most rely to one degree or another on the private detective industry.

According to the United States Department of Labor's Bureau of Labor Statistics (BLS), approximately 39,000 people were working as private investigators in 2000. Roughly one-third worked for detective agencies, another third worked as store detectives, and the balance worked for a variety of employers, including hotels and law firms.

The requirements for becoming a private detective vary widely from state to state, although most jurisdictions require aspiring detectives to demonstrate investigative experience, provide evidence of relevant course work, and pass a licensing test. According to the BLS, the most stringent jurisdiction is California, where investigators need the equivalent of three years of experience, must pass a background check, and must receive a qualifying score on a two-hour written examination.

By contrast, in a handful of states—Alabama, Alaska, Colorado, Idaho, Mississippi, and South Dakota—there are no licensing requirements: All that the aspiring PI needs is fifty dollars' worth of business cards, a telephone, a ginned-up ID in a cheap plastic case, and a trench coat.

Over the last two decades, the nature of the private investigation business has undergone dramatic changes: Sam Spade, the trenchcoat-wearing, cigarette-smoking, love-'em-and-leave-'em private eye, whose bread and butter came largely from spying on errant spouses, has largely been replaced by the business-suited, Scotch-sipping, computer-toting security consultant, whose natural environment is more boardroom than barroom. Despite the tragic consequences this might have for American literature, it's been a phenomenal boost for the private detective industry: Multinational corporations tend to pay better than bitter soon-to-be-ex-spouses. In fact, *Fortune* estimated that the 2001 revenues for the private detective industry in the United States would be around $4.6 billion.

In particular, the merger mania of the 1980s accelerated the maturation of the investigative industry. The beginning of the shift can be traced with some precision to 1982, when Drexel Burnham Lambert helped spearhead a $25.6 million debenture offering for a company called Flight Transportation Corp. Just a few weeks later, the FBI knocked on Drexel's door and cordially informed it that the FBI had discovered that Flight Transportation was a sham corporation and had shut it down. Not surprisingly, offering debentures for a sham corporation, even unwittingly, makes the Securities and Exchange Commission a little annoyed. Drexel decided it needed some investigative help to prevent future debenture offerings from crashing and burning, so it went out and hired Jules Kroll to vet its business relationships.

A lawyer by training and described as a large man with a personality to match, Kroll has proven adept at publicizing his numerous successful investigations on behalf of various Wall Street firms. Like Alan Pinkerton a century before him, Kroll has successfully attracted large numbers of corporate clients by offering strict ethical standards and producing quick results. When ABC, for instance, approached various private detective firms and asked them to illegally bug a room, Kroll's was the only one that refused to do so.[5]

Even before the attacks of 9/11, which may have boosted the revenues of the private detective industry by as much as 20 percent, Kroll's was prospering. In 1999, the company reported that it took in $300 million in revenues. But even those kinds of earnings leave a lot of room in a nearly $5 billion industry for competitors. Pinkerton's, the best-known name in U.S. private detective firms, remains a significant player in the industry, taking in around $1 billion per year; Washington-based I.G.I. and New York-based Decision Strategies/Fairfax are also very well known in the corporate investigation field. And competition is coming not just from other private detective firms; not surprisingly, businesses in related fields have been eyeing the growth potential for private investigators and have begun setting up their own security divisions. In an April 1997 article, "The Detectives," *Business 2.0* reporter Kim Clark noted that several of the major accounting firms, including Coopers & Lybrand, Deloitte & Touche, and KPMG Peat Marwick, were busy hiring investigators to help them tap into the private investigation revenue stream.[6]

The other major force that is driving the private detective industry is globalization. In an era of rapid transportation and nearly instantaneous communication, it's safe to say that no economy is an island; the flapping of the exchange rate in Brazil can cause a hurricane in Europe. In a world where deals can be consummated across borders nearly as easily as across the street, it is becoming particularly important for businesses to hire investigators to help them check on the people with whom they're dealing.

Reflecting the increasingly international flavor of the investigative industry, Pinkerton's was acquired in 1999 by the Swedish security company Securitas. The following year, Securitas also acquired the United States' second-largest security firm, Burns International. Currently, Securitas claims to be the leader in the two largest security markets, Europe and the United States. The company employs over 200,000 people and has annual worldwide revenues in excess of $5 billion.

The purchase of the two largest U.S. security firms by a foreign corporation raises some interesting security and corporate intelligence issues, most of which appear to have gone unexamined. It's worth asking, for instance, how we'd feel if Pinkerton's and Burns International had been purchased by a Russian or Chinese company. Global politics aside, the salient fact for employees is that businesses are spending steadily larger sums of money on private detective services, and a significant portion of those expenditures are going to pay for increasingly detailed and invasive background checks of both prospective and existing employees.

# The Growing Scope of Background Checks

In April 2001, Kroll told *The Financial Times* that preemployment screening "will be the equivalent of what drug testing was in the 1980s."[7] Kroll's assessment and the undeniable rising popularity of detailed background checks both stem from the fact that from an employer's perspective, prevention is nine-tenths of the battle. As a practical matter, it is far less costly to do a thorough or even overly thorough background check on a potential employee than to deal later with the consequences of a lewd, dishonest, or dangerous worker.

In addition, employers are increasingly aware that a failure to conduct a thorough background check may be introduced as evidence of negligence if an employee injures someone on the job. The majority of states, for instance, now recognize the tort of "negligent hiring" under which an employer can be held liable for hiring someone with violent or criminal tendencies who should have been uncovered through a reasonable investigation. Even worse, from a workplace privacy perspective, there is a slow but steady trend in support of the tort of "negligent retention," in which an employer can be found liable for not immediately terminating an employee who may pose a risk to coworkers or the public.

As a result, employers are asking their human resource departments and private investigators to go after increasingly personal information on prospective employees in an effort to weed out potential sources of liability before they're hired. Here's a sampling of the information that's routinely sought by employers.

## Criminal Record Checks and Fingerprints

In theory, we believe in rehabilitation in this country. If you've committed a crime but have paid restitution or successfully served a prison sentence, then you've "paid your debt to society."

The reality, of course, is entirely different. A criminal record is a permanent black mark, a legal stigma to be dragged around like Marley's chains. Many states, for instance, require fingerprints and criminal record checks for applicants whose jobs deal with children or the elderly, and virtually all states now have a version of Megan's Law, which requires sex offenders to register their current location with the state so that the information can be provided to communities and neighborhoods.

Roughly a third of all employers will check to see whether you have a criminal record when you apply for a job. While the current cost of doing a reasonably thorough background check can run from $100 to $200, the cost of doing a basic criminal record check is often much lower, in the $20 to $25 range. Typically, an investigator will check the criminal record files of the county in which you currently reside, as well as those in which you recently lived. An employer is primarily interested in knowing if you've committed any crimes that involve violence (rape, aggravated assault, murder, theft, or drugs).

The technology for doing such checks efficiently still has limited capabilities. At the moment, there is no single, easily searchable database of state criminal records that is readily accessible by employers or private investigators. The National Crime Information Center (NCIC) maintains records of most felonies and some misdemeanors, but its use is limited to law enforcement personnel.[8]

Thanks to a $640 million upgrade, the FBI recently replaced the original NCIC with the NCIC 2000. In addition to containing the original database of wanted lists, rap sheets, names of missing people, and lists of stolen items, the new, far faster database also integrates both fingerprint records and mug shots. With the appropriate hardware and wireless connection, a police officer conducting a routine traffic stop can use a small reader to send a suspect's index fingerprint directly to the NCIC 2000, which can report back in minutes whether the fingerprint matches the print of a known fugitive.

Two weeks after the NCIC 2000 was launched, the Federal Bureau of Investigation also opened a new computerized database of fingerprints at its Criminal Justice Information Services facility in Clarksburg, West Virginia.[9] Known as the Integrated Automated Fingerprint Identification System (IAFIS), the system makes it possible for the FBI to search its collection of 39 million fingerprint records in just two hours. Before the installation of the IAFIS, it took the FBI up to twenty days to determine if a set of crime scene fingerprints matched another set in its records.

Lacking the better part of a billion dollars to implement similarly powerful systems, states are taking a much longer time to computerize their criminal records. However, the trends are unmistakable: Computerization of court records is steadily expanding, and as it does so, the time and cost required to do a criminal record check will continue to fall. Inevitably, the percentage of businesses that do criminal record checks will correspondingly rise.

Knowing that your prospective employer will do a criminal background check on you might make you uncomfortable, but it's hard to argue that it constitutes an invasion of privacy. In fact, most courts agree with the Massachusetts Supreme Judicial Court, which stated that "a convicted person has a low expectation of privacy in his identity by reason of the taking and storing of fingerprints, photographs, and other criminal records. . . ."[10]

While searching criminal records may not be an invasion of privacy, the potential impact of a positive response does raise an important public policy question. The Equal Employment Opportunity Commission, which is charged with enforcing the 1964 Civil Rights Act, has stated that job applicants cannot be denied employment simply because they have a criminal record, but it has also ruled that a business may take a person's criminal record into consideration and may refuse to hire if it has a "sound business reason" for doing so. Not surprisingly, businesses are typically given a fair degree of latitude in deciding what is a "sound business reason" for not hiring someone, and the steady rise in negligent hiring verdicts makes them increasingly cautious. The dilemma, of course, is that if a large enough number of employers take the position that it's better not to hire people with a criminal record, the process of reentering society will get steadily more difficult for hundreds of thousands of people.

## Motor Vehicle Records

Not surprisingly, state motor vehicle databases are rapidly becoming one of the most popular sources of information about potential employees. The amount of information contained in those databases is enormous: The Federal Highway Administration reported that in 2000, for instance, there were 190,625,023 licensed drivers in the United States. With varying degrees of accuracy, your state knows where you live, how tall you are, what color your eyes are, whether you need corrective lenses or other types of visual assistance, and how old you are. In addition, your driver's license contains a unique identifier (often your Social Security number) that is linked to an ever-growing record of your behavior behind the wheel.

In addition, as of 2001, there were roughly 133,600,000 registered automobiles on the road today, along with 87,000,000 trucks. Every time a vehicle is bought and sold, registered with the state, destroyed in an accident, or stolen, another piece of data is entered in a state motor vehicle database.

The value of these databases is obvious to employers looking to hire people as drivers: If you're in the habit of picking up speeding tickets or you have a suspended license, then you're probably not the best candidate for a driving job. With potential liability levels so high, employers are particularly concerned about arrests and convictions for driving under the influence (DUI), along with license suspensions or revocations.

A check of your driving record can reveal far more about you than simply your ability to obey traffic laws. Security specialists point out that a mismatch between the address you put on your job application and the address on file with the state motor vehicle department should be a warning sign for the employer. For instance, if your license was issued in a different state, an employer might wonder whether you applied for a new license in an effort to hide a bad driving record.

Of course, most jobs don't require driving. Nonetheless, a prospective employer may still be interested in your driving record because of what the employer thinks that it says about you as a person. An employer might conclude, for instance, that a DUI conviction on your driving record is an indication of alcohol abuse that could lead to other problems in the workplace. Even if your alcohol use has not risen to the level of addiction, an employer may simply conclude that your lifestyle is simply too dangerous or irresponsible for the company.

The absence of a driving record is almost as troubling to an employer as a bad one. Some people, particularly those who live in urban areas, don't drive, but employers have learned that some applicants have no license because they want to hide a bad driving record.

Since state driving records are public, there's no inherent basis for objecting to a potential employer's examination of your driving record. But obviously, this begins to raise some potentially troublesome issues. Is it fair for an employer to conclude that because you were once arrested for DUI, you're not suitable for a data entry position? How direct does the connection have to be between an earlier infraction and the responsibilities of the job for which you're applying? Could an employer decide that he or she is only going to hire teetotalers? Where should the line be drawn between acceptable criteria (e.g., no convicted child molesters working with children) and unacceptable discrimination (e.g., men only)? The battle between employers and employees over these types of questions is just beginning to be waged.

## Civil Litigation Records and Worker's Compensation Claims

Civil court records are also becoming a particularly fruitful source of information. If you've been involved in legal proceedings of any description, there is a potential treasure trove of information available to the determined employer or investigator. For instance, a search of the court records in your local jurisdiction will reveal if you have child support obligations, liens on your property, restraining orders for domestic problems, claims for worker's compensation, and a variety of other types of information.

Most of the documents in a court case are public records, which means that they're open to inspection by anyone who wants to take the time to view them. At the very least, the court will have on file the pleadings of the case—the complaint, the answer, and assorted motions that were filed during the course of the case—along with a copy of the verdict and any questions answered by a jury. The court may also have on file copies of depositions taken during the case, during which you may have been required to answer some highly personal questions. Similarly, trial transcripts are also sometimes available, which can be highly informative reading depending on the nature of the case and the answers that you gave under oath.

Over the last several years, the federal court system has grown steadily more computerized, making it relatively easy for investigators to do a national search for cases in which you may have been involved, ranging from criminal proceedings to bankruptcy. State court records, however, are still generally more difficult to search. In order to do an effective state court record search, an investigator must physically visit all of the courthouses where you may have been sued or filed suit against someone else, and actually check the indices that are maintained by each court clerk, and then go through the paperwork of any cases in which you were involved.

The majority of states forbid local governments (i.e., counties, cities, and towns) from selling public information at a profit, which means that court systems have little incentive to put their older records into a searchable online database. The cost of doing so is high, and while money has been budgeted in most jurisdictions to make current court records more accessible, the focus is generally on current information rather than historical records.

To help fill the perceived need for better searching capability of state court records and older municipal records, a new industry has developed to collect and compile local information into commercial databases. Most of these services are available on the World Wide Web for a relatively nominal fee. However, as courts receive more requests from businesses for copies of their records, they've begun to look at the potential privacy implications. Specifically, courts are wrestling with the question of whether different standards should apply for paper and electronic records. Courts are also very concerned about the highly personal information that can wind up in court files, information that may or may not have been relevant to the proceedings. Here too, technology and economic opportunity are outpacing the ability of the courts around the country to formulate a consistent privacy policy.

## Credit Reports

As we'll see in Chapter 4, credit card companies and credit reporting bureaus have been at the forefront of the computer revolution for the past half century. They have had and continue to have an enormous economic incentive to develop and maintain extremely fast networks and databases of personal information on virtually every consumer in the United States. As a result, credit reports have become among the most sought-after and easily obtained sources of personal information. That makes sense when you're filing an application for a mortgage or for a new car loan, but it makes less intrinsic sense when you're applying for a job, particularly one that does not involve the handling of money.

For a modest subscription fee to the right commercial database, an investigator can check the credit report header for a variety of basic information. For instance, if an employer wants more information about an applicant named Charles Franklin, an investigator can retrieve a listing of all of the Charles Franklins in the country or in a particular region, and the header of each credit report will show their full names, former and current addresses, Social Security numbers, and birthdates.

Under the provisions of the Fair Credit Reporting Act, an investigator should not be able to retrieve the full credit report for any of the Franklins. However, many prospective employers will require you to sign a form giving them permission to retrieve full credit reports from each of the credit bureaus. You can refuse to sign the authorization form, but your prospective employer can also refuse to consider your application. Currently, there is no legal protection for someone who is denied a job because they refused to permit access to their credit report.

## Health Records

If people get twitchy about a prospective employer reviewing their driving records and credit reports, they get positively apoplectic at the idea of their medical records being a routine part of a job application.

In general, it's not quite as bad as you might think, at least during the application process. There are no national or state databases of medical records, and most physicians, hospitals, and even health insurance companies have strict rules that prohibit the unauthorized release of medical information. That's not to say, of course, that the occasional records clerk or nurse's aide hasn't dined quite nicely on an investigator's dime, but such security breaches are more the exception than the rule.

Moreover, the Americans with Disabilities Act establishes clear rules regarding inquiries into medical history. Employers with more than twenty-five employees are barred from asking you about your medical history or requiring a physical exam during the application process. Once a job offer has been made, the employer may require you to take a physical, but only if a physical is required of every other employee hired for a similar job. And finally, if the job offer is withdrawn due to the results of your physical exam, the prospective employer must be able to prove that the exam showed you would have been physically incapable of performing the job for which you were applying.

According to a recent survey by the American Management Association, roughly half of all new hires in the United States are asked to undergo preemployment medical examinations. Doing so obviously makes sense if the job for which you are applying involves heavy physical activity of some kind, or is a job in which an illness could lead to catastrophic consequences (most of us would prefer not to have a bus driver with advanced coronary disease, for instance). But a large number of the jobs for which preemployment exams are done have no special physical requirements or risk to others, so it's unclear why an exam is necessary.

Moreover, even a relatively routine physical examination can provide a prospective employer with excessive amounts of private information. During the course of most exams, the doctor or her staff collects a fairly detailed medical history; a listing of medications that are currently being taken; an assessment of your vital signs (temperature, blood pressure, weight, etc.); and examines your skin, lungs, abdomen, and other areas of your body for obvious signs of illness.

In theory, the final report from a preemployment medical examination is supposed to be bare bones: Are you able to work, able to work with restrictions, or not able to work at all? However, anecdotal and survey evidence suggests that much more comprehensive reports are typically turned over to the prospective employer. And it can be very difficult to prove that you were turned down for a job because the employer didn't like the look of something in your medical exam results.

## Have You Been Googalized?

The phenomenal growth of the World Wide Web and the ease with which information can be posted online has created an entirely new, entirely free resource for conducting background checks on prospective applicants (or for that matter, prospective dates). Search engines like Google and AltaVista use software called "spiders" to crawl around the Web and create huge indices of the various pages that they read on their travels. While the spiders can't gain access to every Web page (by some estimates, even the largest search engine, Google, only indexes about 25 percent of all online material), the Web is so enormous that the search engines still read and index hundreds of millions of Web pages at a time.

If you enter the name of someone into a search engine, the chances are increasingly good that some piece of their life has stuck to the Web. Obviously, this type of search is going to be more useful if the person's name is relatively uncommon, but even with widely shared names like Smith or Jones, it's still possible to find useful information if you know the city or even the state in which your target lives.

The breadth of material that is available about people is stunning; try this type of search sometime on your own name and see what comes up. Have you created a home page to share news and photos with family? Bingo. Does your gardening club or bowling league put its newsletter online? There you are, proudly reporting on the success of your delphinias at the county fair. Have you been quoted in the local newspaper recently? The newspaper archive may well be reachable by the indexing spider.

Lawyers were among the first to spot the potential of search engines to turn up useful information about people. It is now common practice to run the names of a jury pool or potential witnesses through a search engine to see if any affiliations or activities turn up that might indicate potential bias. For instance, in a recent trial for damages resulting from smoking, the tobacco company's lawyers discovered that one prospective juror was listed on a website as a member of an active antismoking group; they were able to use that information to get the potential juror dismissed from the panel.

Other corners of the Web can also turn up potentially interesting background information. For two decades, computer users have been able to post messages on a huge range of topics to various newsgroups in a portion of the Internet known as Usenet. In the early days of the Internet, simply finding, let alone using the Usenet required some serious geek credentials. In 1995, however, a small company called Deja.com created a Web interface for the newsgroups, which made it far easier to read and post messages. By 2000, the Deja.com newsgroup archive contained 500 million postings and was over 1.5 terabytes (1,500 gigabytes) in size.[11]

In February 2001, Deja.com sold its Usenet discussion service to the Internet search engine Google Inc., which has since developed a new interface for the sometimes balky news resource. In addition to making the Usenet easier to access, Deja.com and Google have also made it possible to conduct detailed searches of the newsgroup archive. An investigator, for instance, can search for all of the messages posted by someone using a particular e-mail address, or in some cases, a person's actual name (since those are often included in a message's address line). Another popular search option, particularly for corporate espionage types, is to search for all of the messages posted from a particular domain name. For instance, if you're looking for leaks in the soft drink industry, you might do a search for all newsgroup messages posted from the domain "pepsi.com." There's no guarantee, obviously, that you'll find anything interesting, but it's often startling to see what messages people have actually posted from their employer's domain.

## Social Engineering and Pretexting

Despite the vast amount of information that is available for free or for a fee, employers are often most interested in information that is unobtainable by legitimate means or simply too expensive to purchase. When that situation arises, some private detectives will use a technique known as "social engineering" or "pretexting" in order to obtain the desired information. In the frequently asked questions file for the Usenet newsgroup alt.private.investigator, the term "pretext" is defined as follows:

> Pretext equals a nice way of saying a lie. Some PIs use this tool to find information about people. Can be very helpful, but can also land you in hot water. Never try to pass yourself off as a policeman or government agent. Many PIs will tell you that they do not believe in pretexting and have never done it before. That is a good example of a pretext.

Thanks to the success of some hackers in using this technique to obtain passwords and other confidential information, there are some in the hacking community (and among the journalists who follow them) who think that hackers invented social engineering as a means of worming information out of unsuspecting individuals. But long before there were computers to hack, private detectives—including Sir Arthur Conan Doyle's famous fictional detective, Sherlock Holmes—were making ample use of disguise and impersonation to work their cases.

Detectives today have a much easier time of it than Holmes. Successful social engineering and pretexting still require some ability to play a role, but the telephone eliminates the need for a physical disguise (which if nothing else helps to keep costs down). The nearly ubiquitous customer service department has become the private detective's best friend: It is staffed, after all, by people whose primary job description is to be helpful and provide information to anyone who calls.

In an effort to crack down on the practice of pretexting, the Federal Trade Commission filed a civil lawsuit in April 1999 against James J. Rapp, a Colorado investigator who allegedly used pretexting to obtain private information; later that same summer, Rapp and his wife were indicted on federal racketeering charges. (Colorado, where the Rapps were operating, has a state law that makes it illegal to impersonate someone else to obtain information.)

Rapp's company, Touch Tone Information, came under investigation when a raid of a Los Angeles private detective revealed that Touch Tone had provided him with assorted private information about members of the Los Angeles organized crime squad, which he had used to harass the department's detectives and even hijack pager messages in an effort to learn the identity of a confidential informant.

After the Colorado Bureau of Investigation (CBI) raided Touch Tone, company records revealed that Rapp had successfully obtained a wide variety of highly confidential information, including:

- Records on visits by *Ally McBeal* star Calista Flockhart to a Beverly Hills doctor during intense tabloid speculation that she suffered from an eating disorder

- Information about Diana, Princess of Wales, and her friend Dodi Fayed shortly before their death in Paris

- The phone records of Kathleen E. Wiley, one of the women who accused former President Clinton of inappropriate sexual advances

- Credit card records for John and Patricia Ramsey, the parents of slain six-year-old Jon-Benet Ramsey

- The credit card and phone records of Enis Cosby, the son of actor Bill Cosby, who was shot on the side of a Los Angeles highway in January 1997

- The unpublished phone numbers and phone records of victims of the Columbine High School shootings

The indictments helped shed some much-needed light on the practice of pretexting. At any given time, Rapp employed up to twenty "investigators," many of whom worked from their homes on a commission basis. The callers would do whatever they could to obtain the necessary information, ranging from false accents and fake tears to heartrending tales of domestic betrayal.

The notoriety surrounding the Rapp case helped spur the inclusion of antipretexting language in the Graham-Leach-Bliley Act, also known as the Banking Modernization Act of 1999. It is now a federal felony to obtain or attempt to obtain the private information of a customer of a financial institution "by making a false, fictitious, or fraudulent statement or representation" to the financial institution. It is also a felony to hire someone to obtain such information, knowing that the person will use a pretext to get the information. Violators can be sentenced to up to ten years in federal prison and fined up to $500,000 per offense.

Yet some investigators still strongly defend pretexting. In one impassioned article about the Rapp case, former federal agent Bill E. Branscum put it this way:

The FTC has adopted the position that obtaining information by pretext should be outlawed as an unfair and deceptive trade practice. To this I would say that shooting people is bad too but there is a time and a place for it.

. . .

The notion that the identity of your bank and your account number is some sort of secret worthy of all this hoopla is nonsense. Your bank sends this information to everyone who writes you a check as evidence that you cashed it. When you pay your property taxes, the tax office copies both sides of your check and that is generally public record. There are many, many examples of ways in which to obtain this sort of information.

Nevertheless, there is no doubt in my mind that the government is going to put the habeas haltus to the act of using pretexts to obtain financial information, the fastest, most dependable, and least expensive way to get it. As a consequence, debts will go uncollected—the big losers will be the big creditors (the number one consumer of this sort of information). Who do you suppose they will pass their losses on to?[12]

## The Baring of a Job Applicant's Soul

In addition to more traditional background information, employers remain enthusiastic about tests that purport to reveal something about a job applicant's personality and temperament. Ever since Sigmund Freud developed his theory of the subconscious mind and the role that it plays in our behavior, we've been fascinated by the idea that future behavior can be predicted based on the responses that people give to various test questions. While the validity of that idea is questionable, it has not stopped a wide range of organizations, from the military to private employers, from using tests in an effort to find the perfect employee.

According to the 2001 American Management Association employment survey, 26 percent of responding employers said that they used psychological testing for their job candidates. That figure was actually down four percentage points from the preceding year, which labor specialists attributed to a tight labor market.

The phrase "psychological testing" actually covers a fair amount of territory. The popular perception is that it's designed to make sure that you don't have any major mental illness that will threaten yourself, your fellow workers, or the business's customers. But the phrase also applies to tests aimed at gauging your cognitive ability, your ethical values, and your personality.

## Pyschological Exams

The U.S. military, not surprisingly, was among the first major organizations in our country to make extensive use of psychological testing. During World War I, the military created the Psychological Testing Corps to develop and implement psychological tests that could be used to assign soldiers to specific jobs.

After the war, the military's testing program came under heavy fire because of its pronounced racism. Studies revealed that eastern and southern Europeans consistently scored lower than northern Europeans, and African Americans consistently scored lower than Caucasians. These studies underscored one of the fundamental problems with psychological testing of any sort: The challenge of creating a test that fairly takes into account often profound cultural differences.

In the late 1960s and early 1970s, psychological testing fell further out of favor due to federal restrictions on asking prospective employees about certain forbidden subjects, including age, race, gender, or sexual orientation. There has been limited action in this area among the states: Only New York has a relevant statute, one that prohibits employers from requiring that job applicants or employees take psychological stress evaluator tests.

When lie detector tests were essentially banned as a hiring tool in 1988, psychological testing made a brief comeback, but it still suffers from a stigma of being associated with mental illness. Employers generally tell applicants that they are being asked to take a personality or aptitude test instead of a psychological exam.

In addition, psychological exams are governed by the same constraints that apply to preemployment medical exams. An employer can require you to take a psychological exam, but only if all other applicants for the same type of job are required to do so. The report that comes out of the exam is supposed to be limited to your psychological fitness for the job, and not include information about any nonwork-related psychological problems that you may have. A consistent problem, of course, is that when the employer is paying for the cost of the exam, there is a serious potential conflict of interest for the tester when the employer requests additional information.

# Lie Detector Tests

In his 1964 book *The Naked Society*, author Vance Packard described a scene in which he was invited to watch the administration of a polygraph test to a prospective salesman named "Bill." In addition to questions aimed at testing Bill's honesty and whether he intended to remain in his sales position for a reasonable period of time, the examiner also asked several questions (including a direct inquiry after the exam) that were intended to determine if Bill was gay. On the basis of little more than a hunch, Packard reported, the examiner raised a question about Bill's sexual orientation with his prospective employer (at a time when such questions could have devastating consequences) and suggested that further investigation or a second polygraph test might be useful.[13]

Packard made it clear that the ordeal to which Bill was subjected was not at all uncommon at the time. In the absence of any federal or state statute or regulation, employers were free to instruct polygraph administrators to ask job applicants virtually any question, regardless of how private or personal it might be.

At the time that Packard was writing, approximately three quarters of all polygraph testing in the United States was performed on employees or prospective employees. In 1987, the federal government's Office of Technology Assessment estimated that 2 million job applicants and employees were given polygraph tests each year. The following year, with the strong support of the American Civil Liberties Union, Congress passed the Employee Polygraph Protection Act (EPPA), which bans (with a few exceptions) the use of the lie detector device for screening new hires and only permits the use of the polygraph on existing employees if there is a "reasonable suspicion" of wrongdoing.

Even when an employer is permitted to give a polygraph test, the EPPA requires your employer to hand you a statement, which you must sign before the test can be administered, that explains the limits of the test:

- There are a number of topics about which you cannot legally be asked questions, including religious beliefs, sexual preference, racial matters, lawful activities of labor organizations, and political affiliation.

- You have the right to refuse to take the test.

- The employer cannot require that you take the test as a condition of employment.

- The employer must explain how the test results will be used.

- You have certain rights, which the employer must list, if the test is not properly administered.

- You have the right to stop the test at any time.

- You can request that questions not be asked in a "degrading or needlessly intrusive fashion."

The EPPA had a devastating impact on the commercial use of lie detectors and left employers scrambling for ways to find out the information that they were used to getting during the polygraph tests. The most popular option has been the growing number of personality tests, many of which skirt the lines of legality.

## Personality Tests

Despite serious questions about their effectiveness, personality tests are becoming a huge business. In a 2000 survey of human resource managers, for instance, the American Management Association found that 30 percent used personality testing during the hiring process, and some testing experts report that the percentage is now over 40 percent and rising. In 1999, the Association of Test Publishers estimated that the personality testing industry had total revenues of over $400 million. And as with so many other aspects of employment, the attacks on 9/11 have heightened interest in the use of personality tests to improve workplace security.

The unregulated nature of personality tests makes them ripe for abuse. While the Americans with Disabilities Act regulates the administration of psychological exams, there is no similar federal statute governing the administration of personality tests. The chief threat to employee privacy of personality tests is that they will be used to ask improper questions or gather otherwise private information. For instance, in 1993, the retail giant Target agreed to pay $2 million to settle a class action suit filed by job applicants for security guard positions.

The suit stemmed from a long screening test administered by Target, in which the retailer asked applicants over 700 true/false questions. The test, known as the Rodgers Condensed CPI-MMPI, contains questions that are often exceedingly personal, including: "I believe in the second coming of Christ," "I have had no difficulty starting or holding my urine," "I have never engaged in unusual sex practices," and "I believe my sins are unpardonable." About 30 percent of the 2,500 people to whom the test was administered were not offered jobs by Target, although it's unclear how much of a role the applicants' screening test answers played in the decision.

The class-action plaintiffs asserted that the screening test violated their privacy rights and violated the Wisconsin labor code, which forbids asking questions about a job applicant's sexual orientation. Target defended the use of the test, claiming that it successfully weeded out emotionally unstable candidates. In settling the suit, Target did not admit that it had done anything wrong, but agreed to discontinue its testing program for a period of five years.

There's a famous *New Yorker* cartoon by Peter Steiner that shows a hound sitting at a computer and saying to a canine buddy, "On the Internet, no one knows you're a dog."[14] At least one website, however, can fix that.

The growth of the World Wide Web has added a whole new wrinkle to the personality test: the online multiple-choice exam that can help you find, among other things, your inner canine. At Emode.com, an online test can help determine if you've got the personality of a German shepherd, a basset hound, a Saint Bernard, a chihuahua, or one of a half-dozen other dog breeds. Emode pegs me, for instance, as a Scottish terrier, which it says has the following characteristics:

> No bones about it, you're an adventurous Scottish terrier. Fearless, feisty, and always up for a challenge, you like having things your way. Some people might even label you stubborn or headstrong. But we know you're just ambitious and motivated. (Being misinterpreted is *such* a trial, isn't it?) Besides, your can-do attitude serves you well when facing challenges at work or in your personal life. No job is too big, and absolutely no obstacle is going to stand in your way. You're always ready, willing, and able to rise to the challenge. A loyal, caring friend, you choose your pals very carefully, then stick by them through thick and thin. Woof!

According to Emode's calculations, 5 percent of its members match this breed, and an estimated 7 percent of the world's population. Is the description accurate? Well, it's close enough, I guess (some might say spot-on), but then, the descriptions of the various breeds are all general enough that they can apply to a wide range of people.

In addition to its dog breed personality test, Emode offers a wide variety of other online personality tests, ranging from a test of your relationship IQ (I scored a genius-level 128, which all by itself raises serious questions about the validity of these tests) to identifying your inner rock star (I was hoping for Sting, but got Chris Isaak instead).

These are all pleasant online diversions, but whether they offer any meaningful insights into someone's personality is another question altogether. In fact, there's no indication that any employers are seriously basing their hiring decisions on whether you're a chihuahua or a Saint Bernard. But at the same time, the complete lack of standards for the use of personality tests makes this an employment tool ripe for abuse.

# End Notes

1. One important difference, however, was that the Shugborough Home estate cave was larger than most corporate cubicles.

2. Susan Bowles, "Background checks: Beware and be prepared," *USA Today* Careers Network (April 10, 2002).

3. Sally Richards, "Resume Fraud: Don't Lie to Get That Job!," www.hightechcareers.com, downloaded on 23 July 2002 from www.hightechcareers.com/doc699/nextstep699.html.

4. "Resume Padding Is Common, According to *New York Times*," *Business Wire* (May 29, 2002).

5. Kim Clark, "The Detectives," *Business 2.0* (April 1997).

6. Also cited in Clark's article was the accounting firm Arthur Andersen, which was then actively pursuing a piece of the private investigator market. Thanks to the recent Enron debacle, however, the now-defunct accounting firm has instead turned into a major source of income for corporate investigators.

7. Andrew Edgecliff-Johnson, "Corporate Security: Industry Comes Out of the Dark Shadows," *The Financial Times* (April 10, 2001).

8. Although it is illegal to do so, officers have been known to pick up some extra cash by running the names of applicants through the NCIC for employer friends or former colleagues.

9. Merely one of the many federal facilities that has wound up in a mountainous and sparsely populated state, thanks to the longevity and largesse of Senator Robert Byrd.

10. Landry v. Attorney General, ——— Mass. ——— (1999) (challenging constitutionality of DNA database).

11. Chris Oakes, "Usenet Sale: Sounds to Silence?," *Wired.com* (October 25, 2000). Downloaded from the Web on 27 October 2000 from www.wired.com/news/print/0,1294,39622,00.html.

12. Bill E. Branscum, "A Bad Rapp" (1999). Quoted from the website for Oracle International, P.A. and available at www.oracleinternational.com/articles/rapp.htm.

13. Vance Packard, *The Naked Society* (New York: David McKay Company, Inc., 1964), pp. 59–66.

14. Steiner, whose cartoon appeared nearly ten years ago in the July 5, 1993, edition of the *New Yorker*, was prescient. Public interest in the Internet did not begin to take off until two years later, when the World Wide Web helped make the Internet more accessible to the average user.

# CHAPTER THREE

# Identification: Your Name Is Not Enough

Once you have been hired, you will find that your employer has taken steps to make sure that access to company property is limited to people who are supposed to be there. As we've seen, corporate espionage and theft are major problems for companies and limiting access to authorized personnel is the first step in minimizing potential loss.

The first—and still the best—employee identification method is the simplest: visual recognition of employees by the people who work with them. In smaller workplaces, this is a reasonably practical approach: Employees get to know each other and can easily identify strangers. The ease with which our brains perform this routine task is astonishing. The average person is able to recognize and recall the face and name of hundreds of different people.

Obviously, however, visual recognition has its limitations as a corporate security measure. It doesn't take long for a business to grow to a size where such an approach is simply impractical. If a business has more than one location, or if there is a lot of turnover, an employer cannot reasonably rely on the ability of employees to know all of their coworkers. As a result, businesses spend an enormous amount of money—approximately $314 million per year as of October 2001—on various types of sign-in technologies designed to distinguish between those people who should have access to company property and those who should be kept out.[1]

## From Uniforms to Smart Card IDs

In many situations, the first means of identifying someone as an authorized employee is the uniform or clothing they're wearing. The concept of distinctive clothing for employees first gained prominence in the Middle Ages, when servants, soldiers, and even vassals would wear some mark of their liege lord. From the perspective of employee rights, one benefit of the growth of the merchant class and private employers was the freedom from wearing a lord's mark. Clothes might still mark your profession, of course—the leather apron of the smithy or the powdered wig of the attorney. But the use of clothing to identify people as employees of a particular company was still far in the future.

Today, when you see someone striding into a business dressed in a brown jumpsuit and carrying a package, you instantly think "UPS." A red-and-blue polo shirt and a thermal bag is the uniform for Domino's Pizza; taupe-and-pink are the colors of Dunkin' Donuts; and so on.[2] Emergency personnel—police, fire, EMTs—rely on their uniforms in large part to help identify them in a crowd, and of course, distinguishable clothing is particularly important in wartime. Commanders need to be able to quickly identify their own soldiers, and soldiers need to know who to shoot and who not to shoot.

As innumerable books and movies have demonstrated, of course, employee uniforms are hardly the most secure method of controlling access. Credible imitations can easily be bought from clothing supply stores, and actual uniforms are rarely kept under tight control. As a matter of fact, you can purchase uniforms from a number of companies, including UPS and McDonald's, on eBay.

Uniforms themselves would seem to have little impact on employee privacy. For the time being, at least, a uniform can't spy on you at work or report on what you've been doing outside of the workplace.

But even something as low-tech as a cotton polo shirt can be the starting place for potentially invasive scrutiny by your employer. In order to provide you with clothing that fits, your employer at least needs to know your size. And the more extensive the uniform, the more information that must be provided to your employer: A polo shirt, for instance, may only be issued in a handful of sizes (S, M, L, XL, etc.), but a jumpsuit or shirt-and-pants combination may require more extensive and revealing measurements. If your measurements change over time, you may need new clothing; for inventory control purposes, your employer is likely to keep a record of the uniforms that have been issued to you. That information offers general information about your health: sudden weight gain or loss, for instance, can indicate a variety of medical conditions.

Another alternative available to employers is to use a service that will track that information for them. A typical example is Gallagher Uniform, which services clients in the south central Michigan area. Gallagher offers employers a number of different reports for tracking uniforms, including a serial number report:

> A serial number report provides detailed bar code information on a specific person's garments. You can track the inventory and age of a person's garments, as well as the garments' delivery history. This report is helpful when an associate is terminated because it provides you with a quick view of their inventory and the serial numbers of their garments. Also if an associate thinks they have misplaced their uniform they can easily track the location of their garments by using this report. If you think you are missing a uniform just let us know, we can email or fax this report directly to you.

Another potential source of information, although slower to infiltrate the workplace, is the technology that can detect the dust and smells that cling to your clothing. A large number of airports and prisons in the United States, for instance, are currently using a device called the Ionscan Sentinel II, an explosive/drug detection machine designed and manufactured by Barringer Protection and Detection Systems.

The device (which looks like an overgrown metal detector) consists of a processing unit attached to a portal. If you step into the portal, gentle puffs of air are used to dislodge trace particles and vapors emanating from your clothes. Any trace substances are pulled into the processing unit, where they are tested and analyzed. In just eight seconds, the Sentinel II can detect over forty different types of explosives and drugs.

Although there are no reports of private businesses purchasing the enormously expensive machines, one of the applications identified for the Sentinel II by Barringer is "site security," which suggests a wide variety of potential applications. And one of the constants of technology is that the cost always goes down over time, which in turn makes the technology more easily available to a larger number of potential users.

One factor that may slow the adoption of the Sentinel II by private companies, however, is the potential uncertainty of its results. The sniffer's primary success is evaluating whether your clothing has been in the presence of something illegal; just because your clothing has been there doesn't necessarily mean that you have. Your roommate, for instance, may have borrowed your jacket without your knowledge and worn it to his job as an explosives expert for a highway construction project.

When it comes to airport security, the mere presence of trace amounts of drugs or explosives on your clothing is a reasonable basis for further investigation. But the use of a machine like the Ionscan to detect drugs in the workplace may be overkill, particularly given the cheaper and more reliable methods that are either already available or are now being developed.

## Sizing You Up: The Trend to Smart Uniforms

Admittedly, the information that can be gathered by tracking your uniform size over time is not particularly revealing. However, in the not-too-distant future, your uniform itself might reveal much more detailed information about your habits and your health.

In 1999, Kursty Groves, a student at the Royal College of Art in London, invented the Techno Bra, an undergarment equipped with a heart rate monitor, GPS locator, and wireless phone.[3] The purpose of the bra, Groves said, was to detect the jump in a woman's heart rate stemming from a domestic assault or rape, and to transmit the victim's location to the police or a friend. The bra would be able to distinguish between the heart rate increase resulting from a frightening attack and that caused by being startled, feeling angry at a careless driver, or becoming excited by a lover's embrace. As columnist Meredith Levinson wrote in the April 2000 issue of *CIO Magazine*, Groves's invention gave a whole new meaning to the phrase "tech support."

The Techno Bra is illustrative of the type of clothing that could potentially transmit a great deal of useful information about you to your employer, ranging from various health indicators to your specific location. As we'll see in later chapters, companies are showing tremendous interest in a variety of systems that enable them to track the precise location of equipment and personnel both on and off their property. It's not difficult to imagine corporate interest in clothing that can be positively identified as belonging to the company, particularly given the ease with which most uniforms can be duplicated. It's also not difficult to imagine that some companies might not tell their employees that the snazzy new uniform they're wearing is secretly wired to monitor their heart rate, respiration, body temperature, and a handful of other medical indicators, along with their precise physical location.

Such so-called "smart clothing" has already attracted attention from several "big-label" companies, including Adidas, Levi Strauss, and even Samsonite. Those companies were part of a group that helped fund an early research project run by the Brussels-based Starlab, a quasi-utopian experiment in advanced research. Founded by U.S. millionaire Walter de Brouwer in 1996, the one hundred or so scientists at Starlab were encouraged to develop interdisciplinary projects; one of them was "I-Wear," an effort to develop intelligent clothing. The project's head, Walter Van de Velde, envisioned clothing that someday would have circuits woven into the fabric, with the pattern of the circuits determining their capabilities.

As it turned out, even Utopia is vulnerable to economic cycles: The tech sector implosion cost Starlab some important investors, and the remaining supporters lost their enthusiasm. Despite the fact that Starlab crashed and burned, however, the concept of wired clothing has continued to attract attention. In April 2002, the German semiconductor manufacturer Infineon Technologies AG announced its first prototypes of smart textiles, including sensors that can be incorporated into clothing to measure heart rate, body temperature, and other health indicators. The devices will be powered by tapping into the heat differential between the human body and surrounding layers of clothing, and the data will be transmitted wirelessly to a wristwatch or a nearby monitoring device.

Similarly, the Georgia Institute of Technology's School of Textile & Fiber Engineering has been working for the last several years on a computerized shirt. Embedded in the fabric of the shirt (called the Georgia Tech Wearable Motherboard or GTWM) is a simple computer motherboard, fiber optic connections, and special sensors. Research on the shirt has been funded by the U.S. Navy; one application will be a garment that can detect if a soldier or sailor has been shot and can pinpoint the location of the wound for medical personnel. In addition, the shirt's sensors can monitor the wearer's heart rate, temperature, and respiration.

The initial market for smart clothing like the GTWM will be the military, hospital or nursing home patients, and athletes, but private employers will not be far behind. Given the potential liability if a school bus driver or airplane pilot has an ill-timed heart attack, school districts or airline companies will worry (with justification) that they could be found negligent for *not* requiring those employees to wear smart clothing, if there was any reasonable indication that the clothing could have given enough notice to prevent injury to others.

## Faking IDs

Given the events on September 11, 2001, it's more than a little disconcerting that so much of the nation's corporate security is based on a credit card-sized piece of paper decorated with a photo booth-style head shot and a company logo, all stuffed into a small lamination pouch. The point of the nearly ubiquitous photo ID, of course, is to make visual identification an ongoing process, enabling your fellow employees or your company's security staff to verify that the person wearing your badge is really you.

But as any movie fan knows, the basic photo ID is hardly the most secure technology in the world: It's exceedingly easy to alter an existing ID or manufacture a new one. In the 1993 film, *The Fugitive*, Harrison Ford, in his role as Dr. Richard Kimble, gave roughly 30 million people a virtual tutorial on breaching loosely kept security. First, Kimble sneaked into the basement of a hospital and stole a janitor's photo ID. Next, he bought a janitor's uniform at a supply store. Finally, he used a razor blade to peel apart the plastic covering of the stolen ID, inserted a snapshot of himself taken at a photo booth, and sealed the ID back up. The doctored ID and uniform allowed Ford to wander essentially unchallenged through the hospital's corridors.

Sound farfetched? Unfortunately, it's not. In November 2000, a drifter named Gary Lee Stearley was arrested for trespassing after he used a physician's assistant ID he'd created at a local printing shop to do eight hours of rounds at Mercy Hospital in Pittsburgh, Pennsylvania. Stealey told the court that he had pulled similar stunts in Florida and Washington State.

In the aftermath of the attacks on 9/11, the FAA ordered every airport and airline to validate all of their identification cards. To assist in the review process, the United States Justice Department launched "Operation Tarmac," during which eleven government agencies reviewed the employment records of over 20,000 people. Disturbingly, the probe resulted in the arrests of ninety-four workers at Washington-area airports on charges of fraudulently obtaining airport security badges. Other arrests on similar charges occurred in Baltimore, Phoenix, Las Vegas, Salt Lake City, and San Francisco.[4]

Despite the increased scrutiny, a con man named Edward Forrest successfully gained access to supposedly secure areas of the Los Angeles Airport less than two months after the terrorist attacks. Forrest had used a computer and scanner to create fake badges identifying him as an employee of Delta Airlines, the Federal Aviation Administration, the Defense Department, and the Air Force.[5]

Employers and security firms, of course, are acutely aware of the fact that if you're a do-it-yourself-type person, a five-minute search on the Internet can produce all the information you need to alter a basic photo ID. The vulnerability of the laminated pouch IDs led to the development and increasingly widespread adoption in the late 1980s of an ID card technology called digital printing. Although the process remains relatively expensive, digital printing produces ID cards that are far more difficult to alter. Digital printers are capable of taking high-resolution images, including photographs, and printing those images directly onto a solid plastic card or a piece of high definition film that is tightly bonded to the ID card.

ID manufacturers have come up with a variety of other techniques designed to make it more difficult to copy an ID and use it as a template for fake cards. Here are some of the leading techniques used by Datacard Group, one of the world's largest identification card manufacturers:

- Topcoats—a clear polymer or laminate can be used to coat the top of an ID card to make it more durable and hard to alter (In addition, Datacard can incorporate holographs into its topcoat that don't show up when the card is copied or scanned.)

- Microprinting—a high-resolution printing process for IDs can incorporate extremely small characters into the card's design (If a card is copied or scanned, the microprinting is either missing or blurred in the copy.)

- Ghost printing—the printing of a faint copy of an ID's main photo, usually as background to some personal information contained on the card (Any effort to alter the personal information damages the ghost image.)

- Iridescent inks—inks containing metallic or pearlescent particles that glitter as the card is tilted in the light (A copier or scanner cannot reproduce iridescent inks.)

- Rainbow (iris) printing—a printing process that subtly and gradually shifts the background color of a card from one side to the other (Copiers and scanners cannot accurately reproduce the color shift.)

- UV printing—the use of ultraviolet inks that can only be viewed using a long-wave UV light source (Copiers and scanners cannot reproduce UV inks.)

- Indented and embossed printing—a familiar feature of credit cards, embossing and indentation requires special equipment to reproduce accurately

- Computer-generated image modification—in digital printing systems, the computer can be used to embed images that can only be viewed with certain equipment, and which are not reproduced by copiers or scanners

- Holograms—the major credit card companies have been using holograms for a number of years (Like most of these other features, holograms are not easily reproduced by average office equipment, and they are similarly difficult to manufacture. The holograms themselves may be metallic and affixed to the card, or printed over the card's data in a semitransparent layer.)

By themselves, these new printing technologies have little direct impact on your privacy. Even with high-tech features, a standard employee photo

ID contains information that is public anyway, at least within the company for which you work—your name, the name of the company, your appearance, and possibly your employee ID number.

The privacy impact of a basic ID, however, cannot be measured solely by the information contained on the card itself. In a post-9/11 world, the issuance of even the most rudimentary employee ID is now raising far more serious privacy issues.

First, the days of the basic ID are clearly numbered, as security experts urge businesses to increase the amount of information printed on each employee ID. Some security experts are already recommending that encoded biometric information—fingerprints, iris scans, even DNA—be printed on plastic ID cards. Although a variety of encryption technologies can be used to protect biometric information, the collection and encoding of highly personal information on a card that can be fairly easily lost or stolen raises obvious security and privacy concerns.

Second, as the cards grow steadily more sophisticated and harder to duplicate, their value as a means of identification steadily increases. This in turn means that employers will only be willing to issue them after a particularly thorough background check. The U.S. Transportation Security Administration has already drawn up plans to issue a tamper-proof ID to all transportation employees who pass a very strict background check (a proposal that is discussed in more detail in Chapter 4). A possible extension of the program, which the TSA is still discussing, will be to offer faster boarding lines to passengers who are willing to undergo a similar background check and carry the TSA's ID.

Also on the near horizon are security IDs that can record and store large quantities of data. For instance, LaserCard Systems, based in Mountain View, California, manufacturers ID cards with optical memory built into the card. These so-called "LaserCards®" are capable of holding up to 2.8 megabytes of information. The types of employee information that could be stored is really limited only by the imagination of a company's HR department, but would typically consist of identifying information, including a photo and biometric details, along with computer network passwords, security access authorizations, job description, attendance and timeliness records, and so forth—in short, virtually anything an employer might find useful. The LaserCard Systems technology is already being used to replace "green cards" on the U.S.–Mexican border with "laser visas" that can be updated with information about each border crossing.

The basic picture ID, which has been around for more than a century, will hardly disappear overnight: It has the advantage of being both simple and inexpensive to produce. The speed with which employers adopt digitally printed cards, LaserCards®, and other sophisticated ID technology will depend in large part on how quickly prices fall and how important improved security is to the company in question.

## Name, Rank, and Serial Number: Smart Cards Get Drafted

In the early 1970s, inventors in Germany, Japan, and France filed patents for a new type of card, one with a microchip built into it. As is often the case, it was an example of a good idea getting ahead of the technology. It would take another decade before the semiconductor industry could manufacture the components needed to make a practical "smart card."

Once the technological hurdles were overcome, the next challenge was to find a use for the cards. The French led the way, adopting smart card technology for the French National Visa Debit Card and the French Telecom system. Largely because of France's leadership, smart cards have become enormously popular in Europe. They are, for instance, an integral part of the Global System for Mobile communications (GSM). There are over 300 million GSM phones in use in Europe, and each one has a slot for a smart card, which stores the cardholder's phone number, billing information, and list of frequently called numbers. Likewise, a number of national health systems (led by Germany and Austria) now rely heavily on smart cards to track health insurance information and other basic patient data.

The popularity of the smart card stems from its steadily improving capabilities. To the average user, a smart card looks like a traditional credit card, albeit slightly thicker because of the memory or microprocessing chip embedded in the center.[6] Currently, smart card memory chips are capable of holding 16,000 bits of data, and the microprocessing chips can hold 32,000 bits. That's not an enormous amount of information, but in both cases, the storage capacity is expected to rise dramatically; after all, IBM now sells a hard drive the size of a quarter that can hold a gigabyte of information.

What makes a smart card "smart" is the fact that the information it stores can be retrieved, verified, amended, added to, and processed, depending on the capabilities of the chip embedded in the card. Most cards communicate with the card reader in one of two ways—either through direct contact (usually a gold-plated dime-sized disc in the upper left-hand corner of the card), or via a tiny antenna built into the card itself (such cards are described appropriately enough as "contactless"). An increasing number of cards, known as "hybrid" or "combi" cards, are manufactured with both types of communication technology.

Smart cards have not proven as successful in the United States as they have in Europe (and increasingly, in Asia). Chase Manhattan Bank, Citibank, Mastercard, and Visa have all launched trial programs for smart cards, but the result was the same for each—not enough consumers used the cards to make it worthwhile to expand the program. In 1997 and 1998, for instance, Citibank and Chase Manhattan issued over 100,000 smart cards to residents on the Upper West Side of New York. In theory, consumers could transfer funds from their bank accounts to their smart card and use the card to make small purchases at 600 different area merchants. The banks found, however, that most people did not charge up their cards a second time. Without a large enough pool of consumers making purchases, most of the merchants dropped out of the program.

To date, no widespread consumer application for smart cards has developed in the United States. However, the retailer Target Corp. is taking another run at the introduction of a consumer smart card. Target has teamed up with Visa and smart card manufacturer Gemplus International S.A. to introduce cards that consumers can use both in stores and on their home computers. In September 2001, Target began mailing out 2.5 million smart cards to holders of Target store cards. With a planned launch of a loyalty program in the fall of 2002, the Target/Visa/Gemplus consortium is hoping that they can reach a critical mass of both consumers and vendors.

The Target smart card is currently being actively promoted on the Target site:

> When you look at Target Visa, you're actually looking at the future. Why? Target Visa has a built-in computer chip, called a smart chip, that's designed to add more convenience and benefits to everyday life. Today, you can use your Target Visa with an in-home smart card reader to access exclusive offers. And soon, you'll see exciting new smart chip features popping up online, in Target Visa account management, at your local Target store, and more! The chip makes the Target Visa smart.

For a limited time, Target is also giving away a smart card reader that consumers can plug into their computer so that they can use their smart card for Web purchases. Consumers who have the smart card reader will be able to download electronic coupons onto their smart card and redeem them at Target stores.

The only other organization in the United States that is enthusiastically adopting smart card technology right now is the Department of Defense (DOD). By the end of 2003, the DOD expects to have issued over 4 million 32-kilobyte smart cards to active duty personnel and authorized contractors. The cards will contain such information as each person's name, rank, serial number, and Social Security number. In addition, the DOD card will store three public key infrastructure certificates, which the bearer can use to log onto military networks, authenticate e-mail, and digitally sign electronic documents. In the future, when the 32-kilobyte cards are upgraded to 64 kilobytes, the DOD plans to include biometric identification data, which will allow the cards to be used to regulate physical access to military facilities.

The wholesale adoption of smart card technology by the Department of Defense offers a model for the growth of smart card use in this country. Economies of scale in production will help lower the cost of smart cards, and increased capabilities will make smart cards more useful as security devices. In addition to the increased capacity that is in the works, smart card manufacturers are also turning to multiplatform programming languages like Java, which will make it easier for the cards to work with readers produced by a variety of manufacturers.

When digitally printed IDs and smart cards routinely carry biometric information, they will help employers implement a two-prong security system, one that identifies each employee by something she has (the card) and something she is (fingerprints, for instance, or iris scan). But even more secure identification is in the works.

## Employee Tagging: Not So Much if but When

From a security point of view, even the most sophisticated ID card is potentially vulnerable: It can be lost, stolen, or even sold. Given enough time and resources, a determined individual or organization can replicate virtually any card on the market today.

One solution to the security problem will be to require the use of identification devices that can't be taken off (or at least not easily or painlessly). In February 2002, one Florida family—Leslie, Jeff, and Derek Jacobs—offered a glimpse into the future when they volunteered to become the first consumers to have radio-frequency identification (RFID) chips, known as Veri-Chips, implanted in their bodies. A Brazilian government official also announced that he would have a chip implanted as well. Believing that implantation of RFID-enabled devices could someday be a $70 billion per year business, VeriChip manufacturer Applied Digital Solutions (ADS) has even trademarked the phrase "getting chipped."

The Jacobs volunteered to have the chips implanted in order to provide emergency care givers with medical information. Jeff Jacobs is a survivor of Hodgkin's disease and lymphoma, and his son Derek is allergic to antibiotics. The theory was that in the event either Jeff or Derek became incapacitated, the information contained on the VeriChips could be used to save their lives.

ADS's hope to link the VeriChip to medical information was put on hold by the U.S. Food and Drug Administration, which advised the company that any medical application of the chip would require FDA clearance. The FDA's medical device chief, Dr. David Feigal, told the Associated Press earlier this year that one serious concern would be the accuracy of the records contained on the chip because outdated medical records could be more dangerous than no records at all.[7]

In a somewhat surprising move, however, the FDA granted ADS permission to market the VeriChip for "security, financial, and personal identification or safety applications." The approval came despite the public reservations of one FDA investigator, who told *Wired.com* that he was unaware of any device approved for human implant without a full FDA review.[8] Following the FDA's action, ADS moved quickly to begin marketing the VeriChip, offering a fifty-dollar discount to the first 100,000 people who signed up to "get chipped." The device itself costs $200, plus an outpatient fee to a doctor for injection and a ten-dollar monthly fee to ADS to maintain the records to which the VeriChip is linked.[9]

Applied Digital says that there is tremendous interest in South America, where kidnapping fears outweigh privacy concerns, for an implantable device containing both VeriChip and GPS electronics. Antonio de Cunha Lima, who is a Brazilian senator from Sao Paulo and a minister in the federal government, had the VeriChip implanted as a deterrent to the epidemic of kidnapping that is occurring in Brazil.[10]

In addition, the British government announced in November 2002 that it is considering using the VeriChip to track sex offenders, particularly once the device can be tracked remotely. The British government is also interested in the possibility that future versions of the VeriChip will be able to monitor heart rate and blood pressure; sudden changes could be an indication of criminal activity.[11]

Right now, VeriChips can't be used to trace a person's physical location; the radio signals from the current version of the VeriChip only travel a few feet. In addition, the device, which measures 11.1 mm by 2.1 mm (roughly the size of a grain of rice), is too small to contain the GPS electronics needed to track and transmit the bearer's location. The RFID can be used in conjunction with an external GPS device, but if the device is removed or turned off, then the tracking information stops. Engineers have not yet figured out how to put together an implantable device containing both VeriChip and GPS electronics, but ADS planned to have a prototype ready by the end of 2002. Estimates are that when they do, the final product will be roughly the size of an electronic pacemaker.

The security and identification capabilities of RFID will spur further human use through one of two ways: payment convenience or employment security. At some point, the argument will be made that having an RFID device embedded in your hand offers the possibility of an extremely secure, highly convenient cashless payment system. Imagine simply being able to wave your hand over a cash register and pay for your purchases by having the correct amount deducted from your account. You'll never have to worry about forgetting your wallet, signing a credit card receipt, or fumbling for change again.[12]

Of course, the electronic databases that currently track your major credit card purchases would then contain a record of *every* purchase you make, regardless of how minor and insignificant. It will be a treasure trove of data for prosecutors, litigators, and marketers (although hopefully not in that order). But we've already clearly demonstrated our willingness as consumers to trade pieces of our privacy for things as insignificant as a ten-cent coupon, so it's unlikely that the increased data collection will serve as a serious deterrent.

With RFID technology in its infancy, there have been no reports of companies demanding implantation as a condition of employment. Given the tremendous increase in concern over security following the attacks of 9/11, however, it's only a matter of time before the business use of implanted RFIDs becomes commonplace. To be truly useful, the RFIDs will undoubtedly contain some type of biometric information about the individual—iris or retina scan, or fingerprints—that can be compared against a central database. Otherwise it would be far too easy for someone to simply sell their RFID to a potential infiltrator.

But employees are likely to resist the implantation of an RFID far more strongly than they have resisted other methods of verifying their identity. Even though it might be convenient to have a security ID that can't be easily lost or left on the bedroom dresser, it's doubtful that people will readily acquiesce to company requests that they roll up their sleeves and hold out their arms. Few employees will be able to resist speculation that the implanted chip is capable of doing far more than simply controlling access to company property. Moreover, it will be hard to justify a routine requirement that employees accept RFIDs when less invasive and nearly as secure alternatives exist. Nonetheless, at some point in the not-too-distant future, some employer is going to see the VeriChip (or something like it) as the ideal solution to its security concerns.

## Identification Using Biometrics and Bioinformatics

Since all of the identification devices supplied by employers can either be lost or duplicated (with the possible exception of RFIDs), and since the demand for greater security has been growing steadily, businesses are increasingly interested in technologies that allow them to identify employees using distinguishing physical characteristics. Thus, they are turning to the field of biometrics—the science of measuring and distinguishing individuals based on physical characteristics.

Human beings are very good at distinguishing people by their physical characteristics. When we see someone in the distance, we can identify him instantly from his gait, height, hairstyle, and a dozen other physical characteristics, long before we can distinguish his face. When we pick up the phone, a single word can tell us who's on the line. Even in a crowd, the way people toss their hair or shrug their shoulders can unmistakably distinguish them from everyone else around them.

As each of us is formed in the womb, we take on various physical characteristics that make each one of us unique. We may share eye color with a sibling, our height with a parent, or even our face with a twin, but some things remain ours alone, regardless of how closely our external features match someone else. With the growing emphasis on security, businesses are implementing increasingly powerful (and intrusive) technologies to measure and record our unique characteristics, as part of the ongoing battle to definitively distinguish those permitted to be on company property from those who are not.

## The Measure of a Man

Not long ago, it was believed that each person had a unique combination of superficial physical characteristics that, if properly measured and recorded, would enable that person to be positively identified. In the late 1800s, a French anthropologist named Alphonse Bertillon created a system called anthropological signalment to record measurements of eleven specific features of a person's body.

When someone was arrested for committing a crime, Bertillon or one of his assistants would measure the length of the suspect's arms, the size of the ears and feet, the size and length of the head, and so on. Each measurement was recorded on an index card and filed according to whether the measurements was below average, average, or above average. After Bertillon's system was used to identify hundreds of suspects with previous criminal records, he was appointed the head of a newly created Bureau of Identification in Paris.

Bertillon calculated that the odds of any two individuals having eleven identical physical measurements at just under one in forty million. When photographs were added to the measurement files, the odds against a mistaken identification grew even worse. However, the signalment system was an inexact science. For example, ten policemen might measure the same person and come up with ten different sets of measurements. In addition, while the system worked well for smaller numbers of criminals and suspects, in large police departments, the challenge of storing, maintaining, and searching the Bertillon cards threatened to destroy the system's utility.

A well-publicized case of mistaken identity helped lead to the end of the Bertillon system, particularly in the United States. In 1903, a certain Will West was brought to the Leavenworth Prison in Kansas. His Bertillon measurements were taken and the files searched to see if he had previously been a guest of the U.S. Government. The records clerk found a card on file with West's measurements, along with a photograph that appeared to be of West. The records clerk concluded that West was a repeat offender, something that West strenuously denied.

After further investigation, it was determined that West was right—the Bertillon card and photograph were of a man named William West, who was already imprisoned at Leavenworth. The two men were identical in both measurement and physical appearance. There is disagreement about whether the two men were strangers or were actually twin brothers; in either case, the well-publicized confusion of the prison officials badly damaged the credibility of signalment as a means of accurately identifying people.

## Fingerprinting

A few months later, Leavenworth prison officials determined that there was one physical characteristic that Will West and William West did not share—their fingerprints. In 1904, Leavenworth replaced the Bertillon system with fingerprint records, and numerous other American law enforcement agencies followed suit. Twenty years later, Congress made its first appropriation to enable the United States Department of Justice to create a program to collect and maintain records of fingerprints and other criminal records.

Remarkably, the commercial use of fingerprints in this country dates back even further. In 1882, U.S. geologist Gilbert Thompson put his own thumbprint on wage chits and then signed across the print to prevent forgery. His is the first known use of fingerprints in the United States.

Apart from photo IDs, fingerprints are the oldest and most widely implemented biometric identifier.[13] Commercial fingerprint authentication systems have been in use for approximately fifteen years and are becoming an increasingly common feature in mainstream computer applications. A number of companies, for instance, have announced plans to include fingerprint scanning technology as a security device for laptops, keyboards, and mice.

There are two main types of fingerprint scanners: optical scanners, which take a picture of your fingerprint, and scanners that use a semiconductor-generated electrical field to make an image of your fingerprint. Not surprisingly, there are some practical challenges in getting a clean optical image: Fingerprint scanners have a tendency to get dirty, and users need to be educated on how to properly place their finger in order to get a successful read.

A scanner's ability to read a fingerprint can also be compromised if your finger is callused, worn, damaged in some way, or simply too moist (or too dry) to produce a good image. Scanning companies are attempting to circumvent these problems by developing an imaging chip that focuses on the living cells underneath the top surface of your finger. These cells reveal the same fingerprint pattern as the cells on the surface of your finger, but often provide a clearer image.

In addition, scanner manufacturers are incorporating a variety of sensors (temperature, pulse, blood flow, skin conductivity, etc.) into fingerprint scanning devices that will be able to detect whether the finger being pressed against the scanner is actually alive. The goal, obviously, is to prevent someone from trying to replicate your finger with a latex mold, or more horribly, cutting off your finger in an attempt to gain access to your office.

Successfully getting a clean image of your fingerprint is merely the start of the authentication. The real challenge is to correctly identify your fingerprint so that it can be compared against your fingerprint template. There are two main categories of fingerprint matching: minutiae based and correlation based.

If you look closely at your fingerprints, you'll see that they're made up of a series of ridges and furrows. Some of the ridges in your fingerprints come to a stop; others split into two separate ridges. Minutiae is the term used for the points on your finger where a ridge either stops or splits. A minutiae-based scanning system identifies and maps those points, and then measures the relative distance between them. That information is then compared to a database of fingerprints to see if there is a match with a fingerprint having an identical relationship among its minutiae. A correlation-based system, by contrast, focuses on the overall pattern of arches and whorls in each fingerprint.

Each method has its drawbacks. Minutiae-based systems are generally faster and more accurate overall, but require a higher quality fingerprint scan. Correlation-based systems handle lower-quality scans more easily, but require a reference point that is consistent from one scan to the next. If your finger is not in the correct position, it's much more difficult for correlation-based systems to get an accurate read.

The challenge for the developers of fingerprint scanning technology, as with other biometric devices, is to create a system that has a very low false rejection rate for a given false acceptance rate. An employer can ensure a low false rejection rate, of course, by having a high acceptance rate, but that makes the biometric system essentially worthless. Similarly, requiring a very low false acceptance rate has the tendency to push up the false rejection rate, which irritates users and motivates them to find ways around the security system.

The other factor that has slowed widespread adoption of fingerprint scanning is the long association of fingerprints with criminal investigations. After a hundred years of detective stories, movies, and television shows, we indelibly associate being fingerprinted with being a suspect. Most of us, undoubtedly, can see the scenario in our head—the fingerprint card on the desk and the pad of printer's ink (quick-drying and nonsmudging), the hand firmly grasping each of our fingers, rolling it first across the inkpad and then across the corresponding square of the stiff cardboard.

As people grow more familiar with biometric fingerprint scanning, some of those fears will die away. Nonetheless, it will be some time before people lose their discomfort over having a fingerprint stored in their employer's computer system.

Ironically, of all of the various biometric identifiers that are currently being researched and marketed, the fingerprint is probably the one that says the least about you beyond identifying who you are (the iris runs a close second). Physical changes in your body are generally not reflected in your fingerprint, so you don't give up any extra information (such as other health data) when your fingerprint is scanned. If you are nervous, having hot flashes, or perspiring for some other reason, it might be difficult to read your fingerprint, but once your finger is dried, your fingerprint itself remains unchanged. As we'll see, that's a considerable advantage compared to some other types of biometric data.

## Voice Recognition

Given our familiarity with using the voice to recognize each other, it's not surprising that voice verification is the biometric security tool that has the highest level of user acceptance. Weeks before we're born, we learn how to distinguish one voice from another, and researchers have determined that newborn infants can distinguish their mother's voice from the voice of another woman. As we grow older, we build an internal library of hundreds of different voices that we can quickly recognize, ranging from our family to friends to favorite musicians and actors. Anyone who's watched television during the last decade, for instance, can instantly identify the voice of James Earl Jones as he intones, "This is CNN." And the number of preschoolers who can instantly identify the voice of a certain purple dinosaur is frighteningly high.

Thanks in large part to the telephone and the recording industries, the human voice is probably the personal biometric that has been studied the most closely. As early as 1936, AT&T's Bell Labs invented the "Voder" (from "voice coder"), a device that enabled an operator to use a keyboard and foot pedal to produce recognizable speech. There is a wide variety of computer-driven speech synthesization applications on the market today, ranging from toys to telephone directory assistance, and while the words produced are nearly always recognizable as electronic speech, they are at least understandable.

It has proven much more difficult, however, to get computers to either understand what we are saying or even identify the person speaking. Until recently, the greater effort was devoted to developing electronic translators. Not long after the end of World War II, the Defense Department began work on the development of a mechanical language translator. Given the complexity of human language and the state of computers at the time, it's not surprising that the results were erratic at best. One perhaps apocryphal output from the DOD's device was to translate the English phrase "The spirit is willing but the flesh is weak" into Russian for "The vodka is strong, but the meat is rotten." Rumors flit about the Internet that the ultrasecretive National Security Agency (NSA), with its underground forest of Cray computers, is capable of doing effective real-time speech recognition and translation, but the expert consensus is that even the NSA is still some years away from successfully using computers to routinely translate and understand human speech.

Since identification is a much more limited task than recognition, there's been considerable more progress on it. The early leader in this field was Texas Instruments (TI), which developed voice-activated systems for U.S. Air Force pilots in the early 1970s. In the thirty years since, TI has been joined by researchers from corporations and universities around the world.

The consensus, after all of these years of study, is that even if two people say the same word, each individual's voice print—the frequencies and patterns of the sound that comes out of each person's mouth—is unique. One typical method for creating a voice print is to reduce each spoken code word into segments and identify the dominant tones for each segment. The tones for each segment are plotted on a table or spectrum, which makes up the individual speaker's voice print. The voice print can then be stored as a table of numbers, with the presence or absence of a dominant tone being marked by a one or a zero. Since all the numerical entries are binary, the entire voice print table can be expressed as a long binary code, which makes comparisons of a new voice print with stored voice print templates very fast.

There are two main drawbacks, however, to using voice as a biometric security device. First, voice authentication systems tend to have a fairly high false rejection rate. Ideally, a voice authentication system should be fairly sensitive, so that it can accurately record your voice and create your voice print. However, that also makes it difficult to eliminate background noise, which in turn impedes successful matches. (Humans also have difficulty sometimes identifying voices when there's a lot of background noise, but we have a lot more processing power than most computers to assist us in filtering out the noise and making a match.)

Also, unlike some other physical characteristics, your voice is highly changeable. Something as simple and as common as a cold can alter the timber, tone, and pitch of the voice, making it exceedingly difficult for a computer to make an accurate match. Voice print technicians also point out that even if an individual is healthy, it is difficult to say the code words in exactly the same way they were said when a voice print template was created. As a result, even the most sophisticated voice authentication system needs to have a little wiggle room built in; the company deploying it needs to make a decision about what confidence level it will require before authenticating a given speaker.

The requirement of a little wiggle room just to make the system function in a reasonable fashion makes voice authentication inherently less secure than other forms of biometric identification. While it may in fact be impossible to imitate another individual's voice exactly, there are some people who are very good at copying how others speak: The accuracy of Will Farrell's impersonation of President Bill Clinton on *Saturday Night Live*, for instance, was downright scary. Similarly, in theory an individual's voice could be fed into a voice print computer from an audio tape, an idea that showed up as a plot device in the 1992 movie *Sneakers*.

The vendors of today's voice verification systems, however, say that there's no way that a tape recording of a voice can be used to gain access to a secure facility. In testimony before the U.S. House Subcommittee on Domestic and International Monetary Policy on May 20, 1998, Dr. Steven F. Boll, the director of licensed products for ITT Defense & Electronics, said that his company had solved the "tape recorder threat." The ITT Speaker-Key system, Boll said, requires users to repeat back random numbers during voice verification; the system also uses a variety of other "anti-spoofing" techniques to foil impersonators.[14]

The employee privacy issues raised by voice authentication systems are relatively minor. Your voice, after all, is one of the most common ways that other people recognize you, so there's no great intrusion if your employer uses the same technique. In theory, voice identification systems are set up to discard each new recording once verification takes place, but certainly, it wouldn't be too difficult to alter the system to record the words spoken each time you used the system. But there would really be little reason to do so; while we do notice changes in other people's voices over time, the impression is usually subjective. Occasionally a medical condition will affect the voice and change its sound, but there are usually other indications long before the voice is affected. It would be very difficult for an employer to glean much information even from a decade of voice authentication entries.

## The Eyes Have It: Irises and Retinas

In 1985, *National Geographic* published one of the most famous photographs of the twentieth century: From the cover of the magazine, the face of a twelve- or thirteen-year-old Afghan girl stared out from underneath her dark red shawl, her eyes an unusual green color and her expression enigmatic. The portrait had been taken a year earlier by photographer Steve McCurry at the Nasir Bagh refugee camp in Pakistan during a five-minute photo session, but because he was working without an interpreter, McCurry never learned the name of the girl he photographed.

In January 2002, the National Geographic television show *Explorer* learned that the refugee camp was scheduled for demolition, and the producers decided to try to find the "Afghan girl." They began an arduous search that started at the camp and wound up in remote Afghanistan, where a woman named Sharbat Gula lived with her husband and three daughters. The host of *Explorer*, Boyd Matson, said that he knew he was on the right track even before he saw a photo of the now-grown Gula. "The second I saw the color of her brother's eyes, I knew we had the right family," Matson told *National Geographic* news reporter David Braun.

Although Matson was confident that he and his crew had in fact located the "Afghan girl," the show sent the two photographs out for analysis. The results, using the same iris scanning and facial recognition tools employed by the U.S. Federal Bureau of Investigation, confirmed that the two photographs were of the same woman.[15]

The verification of Sharbat Gula's identity illustrates how eye scanning may soon become the definitive workplace security tool. In certain instances, a rare color or shade of color can help link us to a particular family; Gula's brother, apparently, shared her unusual green eye color. But the eye has two other features—the pattern of the iris and the retina—which can be used to unequivocally identify each of us.

The iris is the colored portion of the eye surrounding the pupil. The basic color of our eyes—our irises, really—can change during the course of the day, depending on the light, our clothing, make-up, our mood, etc. What doesn't change is the unique pattern of light and dark regions contained in each iris. The pattern is formed in part by a tissue within the iris called the trabecular meshwork, which gives the iris the appearance of being divided by radial spokes. In addition, the pattern of each iris is marked by a variety of other features, including "rings, furrows, freckles, and the corona."[16]

Unlike most of our other physical characteristics, the pattern of the iris is not determined by genetic make-up; instead, the pattern has been formed during the eighth month of pregnancy through a process called "chaotic morphogenesis," i.e., random formation of tissue. Since there is no genetic influence on the development of the iris pattern, it not only differs from person to person (including identical twins), it also differs from eye to eye: The iris pattern of your right eye is different from the one in your left eye. In his book *Database Nation*, Simson Garfinkel reports that the odds of two individuals having the same iris pattern is roughly one in $10^{78}$ (ten followed by seventy-eight zeros); right now, the population of the entire Earth is less than $10^{10}$.

Equally important, from an identification point of view, is that the pattern of the iris remains unchanged (barring accident or surgery) throughout the course of your life. The consistency and potential variation in each iris pattern thus makes it an extremely powerful tool for identifying individuals.

The idea of using the iris for identification has been around for some time. Bertillon included detailed descriptions of the irises of criminals in his records, and in 1936, American ophthalmologist Frank Burch proposed the idea to an annual meeting of the American Academy of Ophthalmology. Even Hollywood got into the act in 1983, using iris identification as a plot device in the James Bond film *Never Say Never Again*.

It wasn't until 1985, however, that serious steps were taken to make iris identification a reality. Drs. Leonard Flom and Ara Safir raised the idea of creating a biometric tool based on the iris and obtained a patent for the idea in 1987. In 1990, the two ophthalmologists founded a company called IriScan to develop and market iris scanning technology.[17]

In the early 1990s, Flom and Safir began collaborating with Dr. John D. Daugman, a professor of neuroscience and statistical pattern recognition at Cambridge University in England, to develop the mathematical algorithms and software necessary to perform iris scanning. Daugman developed and patented a system for reading points of reference in the iris and converting that information into a 512-byte mathematical code, which Daugman calls an IrisCode™. As part of the encoding process, Daugman's algorithms draw on data taken from up to 266 points in each iris, compared to the thirty to sixty points of information drawn from other types of biometric examination. Since the stored IrisCode™ is a mathematical representation of the iris's pattern and not an image of the iris itself, a comparison of a recently photographed iris to all of the other IrisCodes on file can be done quite rapidly. Even average computer equipment can compare hundreds of thousands of IrisCodes™ per minute.

Using the iris as an identification tool has a number of advantages over other types of biometrics:

■ An iris scan does not require an individual to touch a special sensor, and in fact, can be done without the person's knowledge.

■ The eye is a self-cleaning organ, and protects the fully-enclosed iris from damage and environmental changes.

■ Enrollment of an individual in an IrisCode™ database is quick—generally less than half a minute—and subsequent identification checks take only one to two seconds.

■ It is very difficult, if not impossible, to duplicate the pattern of another person's iris. In addition, scanning devices are programmed to look for natural fluctuations in the pupil to screen out potential fraud.

If anything, our retinas offer even more precise indications of who we are than our irises. The retina is a thin membrane at the back of the eye that gathers the images that come through the pupil and passes them to the optic nerve, where they are transmitted to the brain for interpretation. The retina is fed by an intricate system of tiny blood vessels, which form a unique pattern on the surface of the retina of each person. The blood vessel pattern is complicated enough to provide between 320 and 400 different points of reference, which can be stored in a remarkably small (35 byte) data file.

Despite its various advantages, however, retinal scan technology is hampered by the fact that it is considerably more intrusive than iris scanning. In order to get a successful retinal scan, the individual being scanned must hold his or her eye motionless a half inch from the scanning device while five successive scans of the retina are performed. In addition, the retina is subject to the effects of aging and disease, both of which can change the pattern of a person's blood vessels. If the changes are great enough, the system will be unable to verify your identity.

The fact that the retina is highly sensitive to the state of your health raises concerns about possible medical discrimination stemming from the use of retinal scanning. "The retina does change its state with various clinical conditions," Professor Daugman said, "such as diabetes, glaucoma, dietary imbalances, high blood pressure, and even just aging. The retina is highly vascularized."[18]

By taking daily retinal scans over a period of time, an employer might gain some insight into the general state of your health. The space required to store the information captured by a retinal scan is so small that it would be a trivial matter for even the largest corporation to store months or years of its employees' retinal scans. An employer might pitch routine retinal scanning as part of the company's health benefits, but the greater temptation would be to use the information to surreptitiously identify employees who are likely to make costly health insurance claims.

Professor Daugman contrasted the retina's susceptibility to health changes with the immutability of the iris:

> There is no medical evidence that the iris (the tissue at the front of the eye, in front of the lens, behind the cornea) has any correlation with a person's state of health. Many people, journalists especially, confuse the iris with the retina (which is the imaging tissue at the very back of the eye, whose outputs go via the optic nerve to the brain).[19]

Despite the clear evidence that the iris is unaffected by general health changes, there is a branch of study called "iridology" or "iris analysis" that argues that a person's overall health, mood, personality, and future can be revealed by closely studying the iris. According to its practitioners, the iris is connected by thousands of nerve fibers to the brain and spine; changes in the body travel along these nerve fibers and are reflected in the appearance of the iris. If this were true, the routine use of iris scans would pose tremendous privacy concerns for employees. Daugman's assessment, however, is blunt:

> You might like to look at the "iridology" links from my website. This occult practice, rather like palm reading, believes that each point on the iris is connected somehow to a particular organ in the body. It is of course all just hocus-pocus, and therefore very popular, like religion . . .[20]

The notoriety of iris recognition technology received a considerable boost in the summer of 2002, when it was a major theme in the midsummer release, *Minority Report*. Throughout the film, we see the hero, John Anderson (played by Tom Cruise), having to deal with the fact that iris recognition technology has permeated American culture. As he walks down a mall corridor, for instance, interactive advertisements scan his irises, retrieve his identity, and change their pitch accordingly. Iris readers on the Metro system provide a log of his movements, and access to his workplace is controlled by similar authenticators. When on the run, Anderson seeks out a black market doctor who can replace his eyes with someone else's; he keeps his old ones in a small plastic bag, however, so that he can break into his former office.

It will be some time before iris scanning technology reaches the level portrayed in Steven Spielberg's film. As Professor Daugman points out, long-range iris recognition just isn't being done. "Iris imaging requires the consent and cooperation of the subject," he said, "because the camera must be within about a foot or two of their face, and they must look directly into it. So, it cannot be done surreptitiously, as can face recognition from several tens of meters away (except that all current algorithms for face recognition have terrible performance results)."[21]

It's taken two decades since the debut of iris scans in Hollywood (in *Never Say Never Again*, 1983) for them to become a viable and well-understood technology. It's worth keeping in mind that, in 2020, we may be staring Spielberg's vision of the future squarely in the face.

## Facial Recognition

From an athletic perspective, Super Bowl XXXV—held in Tampa, Florida, on January 28, 2001—was a rather unremarkable affair. The Baltimore Ravens, a defensive powerhouse during most of the season, completely shut down the offense of the New York Giants, and walked away with a 34 to 7 victory. Columnists complained about the quality of the quarterbacks and worried that the game signaled the arrival of a new period of defensive dominance.

The Ravens were not the only ones who had their minds on defense. Super Bowl XXXV may have been a dud on the field, but from a security perspective, the contest was groundbreaking. The game was used as an opportunity to test the speed and accuracy of a new facial recognition system. Every ticket holder who attended Super Bowl XXXV—roughly 72,000 people—had his face scanned, and the image was electronically compared to an image database of approximately 1,700 known criminals. The images were taken from state and federal law enforcement files and held pictures of individuals convicted of everything from pickpocketing to domestic terrorism.

The surveillance test was a collective operation of Raymond James Stadium officials, the Tampa police, and a consortium of hardware and software manufacturers led by Graphco Technologies, Inc., a leading developer of access and surveillance systems. In addition to monitoring the crowds at the stadium, Graphco also installed monitoring systems at the NFL Experience, the pre-Super Bowl fan exhibition, and in Ybor City, a popular Tampa tourist destination and nightspot area.

The Graphco surveillance installation was a complicated combination of hardware and software drawn from a variety of companies. Veltek International, a Shrewsbury, Massachusetts, manufacturer of closed-circuit television equipment, provided over thirty cameras and miles of fiber-optic cable. Viisage (located in Littleton, Massachusetts) provided *FaceTrac*, facial recognition software that it based on technology developed in 1987 by Professors Matthew Turk and Alex Pentland at the Massachusetts Institute of Technology (MIT).

MIT's technology uses an algorithm known as Principal Component Analysis (PCA) to analyze the features of each face and construct an *eigenface*.[22] An eigenface is created by taking your photo, locating your eyes as a reference point, and then expanding or contracting your head so that it is a consistent size with the other images in the database. The software then electronically removes clothing and hair from the image, leaving just your face. Next, the software eliminates brightness and contrast caused by lighting, leaving a flat, gray image of your face. In that image, however, certain features of your face will stand out, and those distinctive characteristics form your eigenface. Once the software has extracted your eigenface from your image, it can compare your eigenface with the others stored in its database and return a list of those that match within a preset degree of variation.

As each individual passed by one of the cameras in Raymond James Stadium, the features on her face were photographed and an eigenface was constructed. In turn, her individual eigenface was compared to the eigenfaces of the individuals in the law enforcement photo bank. For each comparison, the system listed the likelihood of a match; if the likelihood exceeded a certain preset limit (for instance, 95 percent), then an alarm sounded and the two photos were displayed side by side on a monitor. If no matches were found, then the image was discarded (although it would be a simple if space-consuming process to save the images for later examination).

In an interview with *Time* magazine following the Super Bowl, Viisage CEO Tom Colatosti was ecstatic that *FaceTrac* positively identified nineteen people in the law enforcement database. "It was a phenomenal success," Colatosti told Lev Grossman. "If you had told me the day before that we'd get one, that would be great. The fact that we caught nineteen, that's astounding."[23]

Actually, no one got caught. The police did not make any arrests based on *FaceTrac* identifications, and in fact, admitted that the surveillance test had educated them on the need to use "choke points" in conjunction with the facial surveillance technology. It's one thing to identify a wanted individual using a facial recognition system, but if that person disappears into a crowd before the identification is completed, the system's utility is limited.

The test at Raymond James Stadium also underscored the sensitivity of facial recognition systems. The accuracy of any facial recognition system varies tremendously depending on the lighting conditions, the angle of the person's face, how still the person is holding his head, and so forth.

In a report issued a year after Super Bowl XXXV, the American Civil Liberties Union strongly challenged the effectiveness of facial recognition systems. Using Florida's open record law, the ACLU obtained the operating logs for Tampa's facial recognition system. According to the department's records, during the two months that the system was up and running in Tampa's Ybor City, the system failed to successfully match a single individual with the photos in the police department's file of criminals. In addition, the ACLU found that the system made a significant number of false identifications, despite differences in age, weight, and even gender.

Viisage's chief rival, Visionics, has had similar criticisms leveled against it. The Visionics technology, called FaceIt, is based on a type of facial analysis called local feature analysis (LFA). Under the LFA approach, eighty different points on an individual's face are identified, and the relative distances between each feature are measured. Those points and measurements are used to create a numerical template, which can be compressed to a record just 84 bytes in size.

The advantage of LFA, according to Visionics, is that even if an individual's face changes (as it does when he smiles or frowns), the relative distance between the individual's features remains fairly constant. While the debate over which facial recognition system performs best is not likely to subside soon, Visionics did recently receive a boost from the Defense Advanced Research Projects Agency, landing a $2 million research grant aimed at improving its facial recognition technology for military and intelligence agencies.

Although government agencies have long been the primary purchasers of facial recognition systems, corporations are showing significantly more interest in the technology following the attacks on 9/11. In many ways, business use of facial recognition technology makes more sense than field use: All of the facial recognition systems in the works right now perform best when the image capture occurs under well-lit, full-frontal conditions, and businesses will be able to create those conditions as part of their security set-up. That will dramatically improve the recognition rate for whatever facial identification system is in use.

For employees, the privacy implications of facial recognition are minimal. As with voice and even fingerprints, the use of your facial image takes nothing away from you that you don't offer to the world already. In theory, a long series of facial images could reveal something about your physical or mental condition that you would rather not share with your employer, but again, the correlation between your facial appearance and your health is not particularly strong.

## End Notes

1. Robert Lemos, "VeriSign Inks Deal for Smart Cards," *ZDNet News* (October, 10, 2001).

2. In her influential paper, "Belated Feudalism," UCLA political scientist Karen Orren argues that the American workplace was actually a feudal institution well into the twentieth century. As journalist Corey Robin recently argued, the modern workplace—from its insistence on distinctive uniforms to its near-obsessive surveillance of employee activities—retains many of the trappings of feudal society. "Lavatory and Liberty," *The Boston Globe* (September 29, 2002) p. D1.

3. Groves has since moved on to become a special ventures manager for Pankhurst Design & Developments, Ltd., an engineering design firm in London, England.

4. John Solomon, "Operation Tarmac nabs 94 workers at Washington-area airports," *Boston Globe* (April 23, 2002). Downloaded from the Web on April 23, 2002, from www.boston.com/news/daily/23/airport_arrests.htm.

5. Eric Nadler, "Fake ID cards make airport infiltration too easy," *Detroit Free Press* (November 10, 2001) Downloaded from the Web on June 15, 2002, from www.freep.com/news/nw/terror2001/wid10_20011110.htm.

6. A "memory" chip is simply used for storing information; a "microprocessing" chip has the ability, albeit limited, to perform calculations on and manipulate the data stored on it.

7. Associated Press, "Tech company to sell ID-only computer chip implant," *Burlington Free Press* (April 5, 2002) p. 7A.

8. Julia Scheeres, "ID Chip's Controversial Approval," *Wired.com* (October 23, 2002).

9. Julia Sheeres, "Implantable Chip, On Sale Now," *Wired.com* (October 25, 2002).

10. According to estimates, in São Paulo alone, a person is kidnapped every thirty-five hours.

11. Julia Scheeres, "Brits Mull Chipping Sex Offenders," *Wired.com* (November 19, 2002).

12. A not insignificant fact is that the RFID can be implanted and used without any external indication of its presence. That alone makes it a more attractive solution than tattooing bar codes on people so that they can pay by being scanned. Remarkably enough, a patent has been issued for such a system. See United States Patent No. 5,878,155, issued to Thomas W. Heeter of Houston, Texas, on March 2, 1999. The historical, sociological, and psychological barriers to the implementation of such a system begs description.

13. A successful biometric identifier requires that an employer have the ability to compare some physical characteristic of the employee against a previously recorded example (or "template") of that characteristic. For instance, a photo ID allows a security guard to compare the employee's existing facial features against the template, i.e., the photo on the employee's ID. One of the great conveniences of the photo ID is that there's no need for a central database; each employee carries her template with her. It's only recently that computers have become powerful and flexible enough to create and maintain central libraries of templates for other types of physical characteristics, such as fingerprints, irises, and so forth.

14. The SpeakerKey system, which has gone through a couple of changes of corpo-

rate ownership, is now marketed under the trade name VoiceVault by a Dublin, Ireland-based company of the same name.

15. David Braun, "Behind the Search for the Afghan Girl," *National Geographic News*, updated March 21, 2002; accessed on the Web on June 28, 2002, at news .nationalgeographic.com/news/2002/03/0311_020312_sharbat.html. The Web page contains side-by-side copies of the two photographs, along with links to additional information about the search for Gula.

16. "Iris Recognition: The Technology," n.p., n.d. Downloaded from the World Wide Web on June 27, 2002, from www.iris-scan.com/iris_technology.htm.

17. In 2000, IriScan merged with one of its largest licensees, Sensar Corp. (a specialist in developing iris recognition components for automated teller machines and similar electronic delivery channels), and changed its name to Iridian Technologies.

18. E-mail to author, June 29, 2002.

19. Ibid.

20. The web page for John Daugman, Ph.D., O.B.E., is located at www.cl.cam.ac.uk/users/jgd1000/

21. E-mail to author, June 29, 2002.

22. The term is derived from the German prefix "eigen," meaning "own" or "individual."

23. Lev Grossman, "Welcome to the Snooper Bowl," *Time,* Vol. 157, No. 6 (February 12, 2001). Downloaded from the Web on June 15, 2002, from www.time.com/time/magazine/printout/0.8816,980003,00.html.

# CHAPTER FOUR

# We're from the Government and We're Here to Help

Every business, even those small enough for management to know and trust each and every employee, collects large amounts of personal information. Even if they do not need details about you for purposes of identification, businesses nonetheless collect personal information about you because they are required to do so by a wide variety of governmental agencies.

For the first century and a half of this country's history, the federal and state governments took a laissez-faire attitude toward employers and employees. Over a remarkably short time, however, a combination of economic events and political good intentions combined to spark the government's interest in gathering information about employees across the country. Beginning with an innocuous form the size of a postcard, the government's collection of employee data has mushroomed into an enormous enterprise that creates a library's worth of data each year and costs employers billions annually in compliance costs.

As we'll see over the course of this chapter, each of the legislative initiatives requiring businesses to collect and report employee information was motivated by an arguably valid public policy concern; taken collectively, however, they represent an ever-growing invasion into employee privacy, helping to create an atmosphere for further intrusions by businesses themselves.

## Death and Taxes: The Origins of Federal Nosiness

In a message to Congress in June 1934, President Franklin Delano Roosevelt outlined the goals and accomplishments of his administration in dealing with the nation's Great Depression. "Among our objectives," Roosevelt said, "I place the security of the men, women, and children of the Nation first. This security for the individual and for the family concerns itself primarily with three factors. People want decent homes to live in; they want to locate them where they can engage in productive work; and they want some safeguard against misfortunes which cannot be wholly eliminated in this man-made world of ours."

The "safeguard against misfortunes" that Roosevelt envisioned was a national system of social insurance, funded by employee contributions and administered by the federal government to ensure a stable and long-lasting source of funds for old age. On August 14, 1935, Roosevelt achieved his goal by signing into law the Social Security Act (SSA).

A main goal of the SSA was to address one of the myriad problems facing the country during the Depression—the steadily declining economic status of its elderly. For centuries, when people reached retirement age or got sick, they were cared for by their extended families, who usually lived within shouting distance. With the growth of social mobility (spurred by the intercontinental railroad), families began to split and move around the country. One consequence of that trend was that the Great Depression hit the older segments of the population particularly hard. In large part, the SSA was the federal government's effort to provide a basic social safety net for its more vulnerable older citizens.

From the moment that the Social Security Act was first proposed, the concept of social insurance and the mechanisms chosen to implement it became the subject of extensive debate. Most of those debates are outside the scope of this book, but two aspects of the Social Security Act are directly relevant to the issue of workplace privacy: the tracking of employee earnings to calculate benefits and the creation of a system of Social Security numbers (SSNs). In drafting employers to help the government collect not merely information about employees but also their social security contributions, Congress got a seductive taste of how useful businesses could be in the implementation of policy initiatives.

More importantly, the creation of the Social Security number unwittingly ushered in a new era of information tracking by the federal government. For the first time, Washington had a means—albeit flawed—to link individuals to a potentially limitless number of records. In the precomputer days of the late 1930s and early 1940s, there was no way to anticipate the extent to which the SSN would infiltrate American society, any more than there was a way to predict that a post-World War II baby boom would threaten the continued viability of the Social Security trust fund itself. Nevertheless, there is little question that the Social Security number has become our de facto national ID; along the way, it has become a powerful tool for facilitating other Congressional invasions of workplace privacy.

## Collecting Data for the Social Safety Net

Appropriately enough, the Social Security Act is itself a senior citizen—it first took effect sixty-five years ago. On January 1, 1937, employees began accruing credits toward old age insurance benefits under the terms of the Social Security Act.

In order for employees to receive payments under the SSA, it was necessary for the federal government to collect detailed information about their earnings. While this was not the first time the federal government had collected information about employee earnings (the government briefly instituted a system of payroll withholding in the nineteenth century), the system for collecting employee data under the Social Security Act has proven particularly durable.

Setting up the new program, in an era before computers, was a phenomenal logistical challenge. With the January 1, 1937, deadline looming, the newly created Social Security Board essentially hired the United States Post Office to help it distribute and collect the necessary paperwork. First, the Board mailed enrollment forms to the nation's 3.5 million employers; when the forms were returned, the Board assigned each employer a unique Employer Identification number (EIN). At the same time, application forms for a Social Security number were being sent out to employees around the country.

When employees returned their applications, their local post offices assigned them a number from a pool allocated by the Social Security Board to each post office. The completed application forms were then handed over to the nearest local Social Security field office, and then forwarded to the main record-keeping facility in Baltimore, Maryland. By June 1937, the Social Security Board had set up 151 field offices around the country and had assigned more than 30 million SSNs.

On the Social Security Administration website, you can view an image of the original SS-5, the form used by employees to apply for a Social Security number. The form required each employee to provide a variety of information:

- First, middle, and last name (Married women were instructed to "give maiden first name, maiden last name, and husband's last name.")

■ Address

■ Current employer's name and address

■ Age, date of birth, and place of birth

■ Sex and color ("white," "negro," or "other")

■ Registration number, if any, with the U.S. Employment Service[1]

■ The location and date where the applicant previously filled out an SS-5

Prior to the arrival of the SS-5, the only employees in the United States with direct experience in answering questions posed by agents of the federal government were those inducted into the military or suspected of a federal crime. But in just six short months, the U.S. government successfully collected information from 30 million people about their names, their race, where they lived, and for whom they worked.

At that time, employees had a choice: They could decide whether answering the questions was worth the prospect of receiving benefits after they retired. Today, as a practical matter, that choice no longer exists. When the Internal Revenue Service began using the Social Security number in 1961 as the taxpayer ID number, the SSN became a required element of any financial transaction, including employment. In theory, providing your Social Security number is a "voluntary" act, but in reality, the chances of your being hired without a Social Security number are fairly small. A typical view is expressed in the privacy policy on the USAJOBS website, a online resource created and maintained by the U.S. Office of Personnel Management:

> Giving us your SSN or any of the other information is voluntary. However, we cannot process your application, which is the first step toward getting a job, if you do not give us the information we request.[2]

The passage of the Social Security Act was a momentous event for our society as a whole, but it was also a pivotal moment in the relationship between the nation's employers and Washington, one that helped usher in an unprecedented era of data collection by federal and state governments.

## Executive Order 9397: The Birth of a National ID

The Social Security Act was not greeted with universal approval; there was widespread concern about the possibility that the Social Security number would become a national identifier and the uses to which it might be put. During the 1936 election, media mogul William Randolph Hearst published a story stating that Americans would be issued a steel "dog tag" with their names and Social Security numbers, and that they would be required to answer highly personal questions on the Social Security applications.

Hearst and his newspapers had a well-deserved reputation for outright fabrication when it suited the bombastic publisher's purpose, but in this case, there was a small kernel of truth. The idea of metal Social Security IDs had in fact been presented to the Social Security Board by the Addressograph Corporation, which was keenly interested in bidding on a contract to produce millions of metal tags. Although the Board categorically rejected the idea, Addressograph made up a sample tag for SSA Board member Arthur J. Altmeyer, who kept the tag as a souvenir, eventually donating it to the SSA's History Room.

Hearst may have been a semiparanoid yellow journalist, but his concern over the SSN ultimately proved correct. Just six years after the implementation of the Social Security Act, President Roosevelt issued Executive Order 9397, which established the Social Security number as the official method of identifying individuals by federal agencies and departments. Any federal agency needing to identify people was ordered to use their Social Security numbers, and the Social Security Board in turn was ordered to provide any Social Security numbers an agency requested.

As a result of Roosevelt's Executive Order, the SSN is now an essential element of our interactions with both federal and state governmental agencies. At least forty different federal agencies or programs require use of the Social Security number for individual identification, including the Internal Revenue Service (which began using the SSN in 1962), the Department of Defense (1967), Aid for Families with Dependent Children (1975), the Selective Service System (1981), and the National Student Loan Data System (1989).

Of the various federal agencies that have adopted the Social Security number as a sorting tool, it is really the IRS that has done the most to solidify the SSN as our national identifier. Under IRS regulations, everyone over the age of eighteen who earns income is required to have a Social Security number, and employers are required to use that Social Security number to report the payment of income. More recently, the IRS adopted regulations requiring parents to obtain Social Security numbers for children they claim as dependents on their tax returns.

Congress has made some half-hearted efforts to limit the use of the Social Security number as a national ID. In 1974, for instance, the reform-minded congressmen who were elected following the Watergate scandal adopted the Privacy Act (5 U.S.C. § 552a et seq.), which purported to regulate the handling of personal data by federal and state agencies, declaring that ". . . in order to protect the privacy of individuals identified in information systems maintained by Federal agencies, it is necessary and proper for the Congress to regulate the collection, maintenance, use, and dissemination of information by such agencies."

Despite Congress's professed concern over the widespread use of the Social Security number as an identifier, however, legislators have continued to require or permit its use. In addition to the programs mentioned above, half of which post-date the Privacy Act, Congress also adopted legislation in 1976 that specifically permitted states to use Social Security numbers as identifiers on motor vehicle registrations, tax reporting forms, and drivers' licenses.

In 1999, Representative Ron Paul (Texas) proposed the Freedom and Privacy Restoration Act, a bill that would bar the creation of any "uniform standard of identification," prohibit any federal agencies from using the same number to identify a particular individual, and bar the use of the Social Security number as an identifier.

The Subcommittee on Government, Information, and Technology of the House Government Reform Committee held hearings on Representative Paul's bill, but took no further action. Paul reintroduced his bill last year as the "Identity Theft Protection Act of 2001" (H.R. 220), and the proposed legislation was referred to the Subcommittee on Government Efficiency, Financial Management and Intergovernmental Relations, where it languished for the remainder of the 107th Congress.

Despite Representative Paul's efforts, the fact of the matter is that the Social Security number *has* effectively become a national ID, an outcome that is underscored by comparing today's SS-5 with the original. Unlike the 1936 edition, the current Social Security number application form makes no reference to employment at all, implying that its use is no longer limited to the original purpose of identifying an employee's contributions account to the Social Security Administration.

As an identifier, the Social Security number has some serious flaws:

- It's too short—although nine digits theoretically offer 999,999,999 different combinations, the Social Security Administration may run out of unissued numbers sometime around the end of this century.

- It's insecure—with roughly 450 million Social Security numbers having been issued since 1935, the odds are roughly one in two that any randomly generated nine-digit number is a valid Social Security number (and those odds can be improved by looking at the SSA's helpful table of the areas to which the first three digits have been assigned).

- It's inconsistently applied—the Social Security Administration does not automatically issue a Social Security number to everyone who is born in or enters the U.S., waiting instead for people to request a number.

■ It's not self-verifying—unlike more well-designed numbering systems, the Social Security number lacks a check digit, a number appended to the end of the string of numbers that verifies that the substantive numbers in the string are in fact correct.[3]

Efforts to create a consistent, well-thought-out national identifier were loudly shouted down in the late 1940s and 1950s. Within a decade, however, private businesses were computerizing their records and looking for some tool to help them identify individuals in their electronic files. Despite its obvious shortcomings, the SSN gained widespread use as an individual identifier because there was no other viable alternative when computers entered the workplace. A unique number is far more effective in distinguishing individuals than names (which have an annoying tendency to repeat, be misspelled, change through marriage or adoption, and so forth).

The consequences of our unplanned adoption of the Social Security number as a national identifier have been profound. Not only does the SSN serve as a handy tool for uncovering and tracking large amounts of information about nearly everyone in the United States, employees and nonemployees alike, but it has also given rise to the Digital Age phenomenon of identity theft.

If someone can learn the name and Social Security number of another individual, they can pretend to be that person for the purpose of obtaining credit cards and other financial resources. Identity theft has become a vast problem for the credit industry, banks, and individuals; in 2000 alone, Mastercard and Visa reported identity theft losses of $114 million, a 43 percent increase from the year before. Law enforcement, using a broader definition of identity theft, estimates that the payment card associations actually lost a total of $1 billion to identity theft in 2000.[4] The impact on the victims ranges from the annoying—the tedium of replacing credit cards, licenses, etc.—to the devastating—years of contesting huge bills and rebuilding personal credit.

The credit card companies' response to the increasingly vast problem of identity theft has been, to put it charitably, half-vast. Far too many card offers are sent willy-nilly through the mails, seeking only a name and Social Security number in exchange for a freshly printed credit card. Some preliminary steps have been taken to increase the level of identification required to issue a card (which in itself raises privacy issues), but it still remains disturbingly easy to obtain credit cards under false pretenses.

## Federal Income Tax Withholding

Next to our medical history, how much money we make (or don't make) is probably the most sensitive topic for most Americans. For the last ninety years, however, anyone who earns money in the United States has been required to report to the government how much she made in the preceding year and to pay the taxes that are due on those earnings.

For the first thirty years of the modern income tax (which began when the Sixteenth Amendment—authorizing an income tax—was passed in 1913), the government relied largely on the honor system. At the end of each year, Americans were required to calculate their taxes on the preceding year's income and make a lump sum payment of the amount due.

As the enormous cost of fighting World War II began to have an impact on the U.S. Treasury, a movement arose to withhold estimated tax payments from wages. This was not the first time that withholding had been used to collect taxes: In 1862, the cost of the Civil War led to the adoption of the first income tax in the nation's history, and Congress included a withholding provision to capture tax revenue at the source of wage payments. Congress repealed that tax in 1872. A withholding provision was also included in legislation that followed the adoption of the Sixteenth Amendment, but that provision was dropped in 1917 after it led to extensive criticism of the new taxation system. It was not until 1943, when Congress passed the Current Tax Payment Act, that the system of withholding that we know today first went into effect.

Unlike earlier attempts to impose withholding, the resistance to the Current Tax Payment Act was far more muted. The country was distracted by World War II, and advocates of withholding argued strongly that it would increase the collection of revenues. There's no question that it did so: By 1945, after just two years of tax withholding, collections had risen from $7 billion to $43 billion.

The biggest reason for the successful introduction of withholding, however, was that the essential framework for a withholding system was already in place. Thanks to the Social Security Act, the federal government had seven years' experience in operating a payroll tax system (even though the Social Security payments were called a "contribution" instead of a tax). In addition, in 1942, the U.S. government had instituted a "Victory Tax," a 5 percent surcharge on everything earned above $624. Employers were required to withhold the tax and make periodic payments to Washington.

Sixty years after its inception, tax withholding is a firmly established part of our governmental system. The fact that the government effectively gets an interest-free loan from each worker is the subject of numerous impassioned articles in conservative publications. Remarkably, however, little attention is paid to the fact that tax withholding, along with the Social Security system, has created an institutional machinery of inquisitiveness by the nation's employers (which now number more than 6 million). In order to comply with federal record-keeping and withholding requirements (at an estimated annual cost of $5,100 per employee), employers are required to collect and maintain extensive records for each employee. More importantly, employers are required to share those records with a wide variety of governmental agencies, few of which have a good track record for preserving private information.[5]

Without one significant invention, the impact of governmental reporting requirements and poor security on employee privacy would be minimal. But the digital computer has made it possible (particularly in conjunction with the Social Security number) to compile incredibly detailed profiles of individuals both in and out of the workplace. While a better-informed government is arguably one that can better plan and implement policy, it's reasonable to ask whether greater governmental efficiency is an acceptable trade off for markedly less workplace privacy.

## Data Collection

In 1890, the United States government was facing its first major data-processing crisis. Under the terms of the United States Constitution, the government is required to conduct a census of its citizens every ten years. The 1880 census, tabulated entirely by hand, had taken seven and a half years to complete, and census officials seriously questioned whether it would be possible to complete the tabulation of the 1890 census before the start of the next census in 1900.

Looming on the horizon, however, was a technological solution that would take the census into the new century, and usher in an era of unprecedented data collection and manipulation. As the tabulation of the 1880 census began, a young man named Herman Hollerith went to work for the Census Bureau. Hollerith was familiar with the use of punch cards by Frenchman Louis Jacquard to produce complex woven patterns in his mechanical looms, and Hollerith thought that a similar process could be used to speed up the tabulation of the census. Over the course of the next decade, Hollerith perfected his design and when his machine won a tabulation contest in 1890, Hollerith was awarded the contract to count the 1890 census.

In an era of microchips and flat-panel plasma displays, the design and operation of Hollerith's machine seems positively quaint. Census data collectors used traditional paper forms to collect information. Those forms were sent back to Washington, where the information on the forms was put onto dollar bill-sized cards, each of which had twelve rows and twenty columns of holes that could be punched out to represent the collected data. The cards were then fed into Hollerith's tabulating machine, which was equipped with 240 metal pins, one for each of the possible holes in the data card. When a pin lined up with a hole in the punch card, it would make contact with a tiny cup of mercury below the card, completing an electrical circuit, and increasing a corresponding dial on the machine by one notch.

As archaic as it seems today, Hollerith's tabulating machine represented a phenomenal advance in counting technology. Thanks to his invention, the 1890 census was completed in just two and a half years—despite a 13 percent increase in the U.S. population.[6]

The data punch card became a mainstay of government and private business for the better part of a century. Beginning in 1906, for instance, railroads across the country began using the punch card to maintain their operational records and run their businesses more efficiently. Four years later, Aetna Life and Casualty became the first insurance company to use punch cards and Hollerith machines to compile mortality statistics.

The success of the Hollerith machine in processing the census records for 65 million people made it abundantly clear to other federal agencies that punch cards could be used in a variety of different ways. During World War I, for instance, the U.S. Army used punch card technology to keep track of supplies, equipment, and personnel records (including both medical and psychological records). By 1933, punch card technology had become so pervasive in federal government operations that they were being used by Washington as checks—the Agricultural Adjustment Administration issued the first punch card check that year, and from its start in 1937, Social Security Administration checks were also punch cards.[7]

In this modern age of data storage, when the laptop computer on which I am writing this book can store approximately 37,000 copies of the finished manuscript, it's difficult to appreciate the sheer physical mass of the punch cards needed to hold records created by the implementation of the Social Security Act alone. According to a research note prepared by the Social Security Administration's historian, in 1937 it took 24,000 square feet of storage space to hold all of the necessary employee and employer punch cards and related paperwork. It turned out that there was no building in Washington with floors strong enough to hold the nation's Social Security records, so they were stored for a time in an old Coca-Cola factory in Baltimore.

## Snow White to the Rescue[8]

The physical mass of records stored on punch cards was only the beginning of the logistical problems. In the months and weeks leading up to the implementation of the Social Security system, there was widespread skepticism that the Social Security Board could successfully assign all of the necessary numbers and do anything meaningful with the huge amounts of information that it would be collecting. According to the Social Security Administration's own history, a French industrial expert who had been hired to advise the U.S. on the implementation of the Social Security Act flatly declared that the program could not be implemented.

The solution, appropriately enough, was provided by an economic descendent of Hollerith's Tabulating Machine Company called International Business Machines. At the time that the Social Security system was being implemented, IBM was headed by Thomas J. Watson, Sr. Anticipating the problems that would face the Roosevelt administration in setting up Social Security, Watson ordered IBM researchers to begin working on new machines that could handle the enormous workload. By early 1937, researchers had successfully completed work on the IBM 077 Collator, a machine capable of handling and enumerating punch card information at very high speeds. The Collator remained a staple of Social Security operations for the next two decades.

Some anonymous wag once remarked that "to err is human; to really screw things up requires a computer." If that's true, then a lot of the blame can be placed on the Social Security Administration and the Internal Revenue Service for the role that they played in spurring the development of the computer. Those two agencies were not solely responsible, of course: The military was consistently at the forefront of computing innovation, and many large private industries (the telephone company, insurance companies, banks, and so forth) helped underwrite extensive developments in computer technology. Nonetheless, the ongoing, massive data-processing demands of the SSA and the IRS provided computer manufacturers with a steady source of business.

In the decades before the introduction of the commercial mainframe computer, the collection of employee wage information was comparatively benign. The files maintained by the Social Security Administration and the Internal Revenue Service were fairly detailed and extensive, but there was no easy way for the information to be accessed and shared with other government or state agencies. That all changed once government and businesses made the shift from punch cards to electronic bits.

The second major data-processing crunch for the U.S. government occurred just fifteen years after the passage of the Social Security Act, in the early 1950s. By then, the Social Security Administration's punch card files had grown in size to 320 million, outstripping the ability of even IBM's increasingly advanced collating machines to handle the workload.

Fortunately for the Social Security program, the growth in its workload coincided with rapid advances in computer technology, particularly at IBM. In 1952, the company introduced the IBM 701, the first mass-produced computer and the first to use magnetic tape for storing data. Two years later, IBM released the 705 model, which would be the workhorse at the

Social Security Administration for years. The Administration took delivery of its first 705 in 1955 (with a whopping 20 Kbytes of memory!), and the advantages of magnetic storage quickly became apparent. Even in those early days of computer development, a single magnetic tape could hold the Social Security records for up to 60,000 people.

## The Best of Intentions: Public Policy Goals and Employee Privacy

Now that the infrastructure of computerized employee records is well established and businesses are familiar (if not happy) with the process of reporting employee information to government agencies, Congress is constantly tempted to use businesses as agents of public policy. In military circles, this phenomenon is known as "mission creep," i.e., the tendency for objectives and goals to expand over time beyond their original boundaries.

None of the individual information-gathering policies enacted by Congress are, in and of themselves, especially invasive of employee privacy. Of far greater concern is the cumulative effect of all of these various information-gathering requirements—after all, the value of any potential pool of data is based on its breadth and depth. As marketers are keenly aware, the more information that they have about a potential purchaser, the easier it is to tailor a sales pitch. The federal government, ostensibly, is not in the business of selling anything, but the ever-growing capability of governments and employers to compile increasingly detailed profiles of individuals is troubling.

In England, where the government has installed and watches an estimated 2.5 million surveillance cameras, citizens concerned about their personal privacy are told that if they've done nothing wrong, they've got nothing to fear. The critical question, of course, is who gets to define "wrong." We can't honestly kid ourselves about possible abuses of governmental power, as two recent examples painfully demonstrate:

■ *J. Edgar Hoover and the FBI.* During J. Edgar Hoover's forty-eight-year tenure as the head of the FBI, he oversaw the compilation of extensive dossiers on leading politicians, social activists, academics, actors, and anyone else who he thought merited scrutiny. While there is disagreement about whether Hoover or his associates actually used the dossiers for blackmail, there's no question that the compilation of these files involved serious invasions of personal and workplace privacy.

■ *Watergate.* On August 17, 1971, John Dean wrote a memo to Lawrence Higby, an assistant of White House Chief of Staff Bob Haldeman, in which he stated:

This memorandum addresses the matter of how we can maximize the fact of our incumbency in dealing with persons known to be active in their opposition to our Administration, Stated a bit more bluntly— how we can use the available federal machinery to screw our political enemies? After reviewing this matter with a number of persons possessed of experience in the field, I have concluded that we do not need an elaborate mechanism or game plan, rather we need a good project coordinator and full support for the project. In brief, the system would work as follows:

> Key members of the staff (e.g., Colson, Dent, Flanigan, Buchanan) could be requested to inform us as to who they feel we should be giving a hard time.

> The project coordinator should then determine what sorts of dealings these individuals have with the Federal Government and how we can best screw them (e.g., grant availability, federal contracts, litigation prosecution, etc.)

> The project coordinator then should have access to and the full support of the top officials of the agency or departments in proceeding to deal with the individual.[9]

The potential for misuse is far greater today than it was thirty years ago. The amount of employee information flowing from all corners of the country to Washington is steadily growing, and technological improvements are making it easier and easier for the government to store, evaluate, and cross-correlate the information it receives.

## Occupational Safety and Health Administration

As part of an erratic but ongoing effort to improve the nation's working conditions, Congress passed the Occupational Health and Safety Act (OSHA) in 1970. The central requirement of OSHA is that every employer engaged in interstate commerce (i.e., that uses the mails or makes interstate calls, which essentially means every employer) must maintain as safe and as healthy a workplace as is reasonably possible. It was Congress's goal to "preserve our human resources" in part "by providing for appropriate reporting procedures with respect to occupational safety and health . . . ."

Under regulations subsequently adopted by the Occupational Safety and Health Administration (also called OSHA), employers are required to provide the agency with complete details within eight hours of any workplace accident where the accident causes the death of a worker or sends four or more workers to the hospital. The report must include the names of any injured workers, the nature and extent of any injuries they suffered, the time and place at which the accident occurred, and the type and description of any machinery involved in the accident.

In addition, employers are required to maintain a log of work-related injuries or illnesses and to provide a summary of the log to employees at the end of each year. For each log entry, employers are supposed to record the name of the individual injured, her job title, the date of the injury or illness and where it occurred, a description of what happened, the outcome (death, time away from work, job transfer or restriction, or other), and the number of days actually spent away from work.

Many of the reports that are required by OSHA involve records dealing with medical conditions or exposure to hazardous materials. When that's the case, OSHA standards require that the employer use a Social Security number to identify the employee. In general, medical records are handled by medical professionals, who understand the importance of medical record confidentiality. However, exposure records are often collected and handled by people who are not traditionally considered medical professionals. That raises the potential for unwanted disclosure not merely of exposure records, but also of the employee's SSN.

Despite OSHA's extensive reliance on employee Social Security numbers, the agency has taken some steps recently to provide employees with greater privacy. In a set of rule changes that took effect on January 1, 2002, OSHA stated that:

- Employers are now prohibited from entering an individual's name . . . if the individual has suffered certain types of injuries or illnesses (i.e., sexual assaults, HIV infections, or mental illnesses).

- Employers are allowed to omit a description of a sensitive injury or illness if it would reveal the employee's identity.

- Employers are required to remove the names of employees from all forms before providing the forms to people without access rights under OSHA.

The new rules are certainly a step in the right direction for protecting employee privacy. But they do little to stem the flow of information from employers to the federal government and virtually nothing to cut down on the amount of information being accumulated by employers about their employees.

## The National Directory of New Hires and the Federal Case Registry

In 1995 and 1996, Congress and President Clinton wrangled over legislation aimed at reforming the nation's welfare system. The law that Congress ultimately passed and the President signed was called the Personal Responsibility and Work Opportunity Reconciliation Act (PRWORA) of 1996.

The main goal of the legislation was to set strict limits on welfare eligibility and to set up requirements for "workfare"—benefits for recipients that were contingent on employment. However, another important component of the new law was aimed at improving the ability of the states to collect child support payments from delinquent parents.

Obviously, there are few public policies more worthy than improving child support payments. Every year, state agencies struggle to collect $50 billion in back payments. In the fall of 1998, for instance, the U.S. Department of Health and Human Services estimated that only 22 percent of the back payments were actually being collected.

To accomplish the goal of improving that figure, the PRWORA required each state to create a State Directory of New Hires and a State Case Registry. Congress also used the new bill as an opportunity to expand the Federal Parent Locator Service (FPLS), a program operated by the federal government's Office of Child Support Enforcement. The FPLS was ordered to set up and begin operating a National Database of New Hires by October 1, 1997, and a Federal Case Registry a year later.

In a frequently asked questions memorandum prepared by the Administration for children and families, the "new hire" reporting requirements are described as follows:

New hire reporting is a process by which you, as an employer, report information on newly-hired employees to a designated state agency shortly after the date of hire. As an employer, you will play a key role in this important program by reporting all of your newly-hired employees to your state.[10]

Thus, within twenty days of hiring a new employee, each employer is required, at a minimum, to send the following information to the appropriate State Directory of New Hires: the new employee's name, address, and Social Security number, and the employer's name, address, and Employer Identification number. The state directory compares the data against records of outstanding child support orders. The employee's information is then transmitted to the National Directory of New Hires (NDNH). Eventually, everyone who is hired as an employee in the United States will be entered in the NDNH.

The potential of this information to be used for purposes other than originally intended was unequivocally demonstrated in February 2001, when Frank Fuentes, then the acting director of the Office of Child Support Enforcement, sent a letter to each of the directors of the State Directories of

New Hires. Fuentes explained that under the terms of a federal law passed in November 1999, the U.S. Department of Education was given permission to access the information contained in the NDNH in an effort to collect unpaid student loans and grant overpayments. "[The Department of Education] estimates," Fuentes wrote, "that quarterly matches with the NDNH can result in the collection of $500 million of delinquent debts over the next five years."[11] Fuentes went on to say that the Office of Child Support Enforcement will be looking to implement other uses of the NDNH database.

# Employee Privacy in an Era of Homeland Security

Even before the terrorist attacks in New York and Washington, the Federal Bureau of Investigation was working aggressively to keep pace with the law enforcement challenges posed by the rapid pace of technological developments. One of the FBI's significant goals is to develop closer relationships with businesses and corporations. While these closer relationships are proving valuable in the fight against cyberterrorism, an inevitable consequence is that the FBI is gaining unprecedented access to private employee information in the name of national security.

The FBI's role in responding to cyberattacks was formalized in July 1996, with the creation of the Computer Investigations and Infrastructure Threat Assessment Center (CITAC). According to the FBI's website:

> . . . the formation of alliances with both the public and private sectors was absolutely necessary to ensure a free flow of critical knowledge, as well as to coordinate responses to attacks on critical infrastructure components.

## InfraGard and the Coming "Digital Storm"

On February 26, 1998, using a $64 million appropriation from Congress, Attorney General Janet Reno and FBI Director Louis Freeh created a new multiagency group called the National Infrastructure Protection Center (NIPC, pronounced "nip-see"). According to NIPC's first director, Michael Vatis, the group was based at the FBI because of the need for the agency's investigative resources when an unauthorized intrusion is detected.

Later that spring, on May 22, 1998, President Clinton signed Presidential Decision Directive 63, which charged NIPC with the responsibility of assessing the potential for cyberthreats, conducting investigations, issuing warnings, and evaluating infrastructure vulnerabilities. As designed by Reno and Freeh, NIPC will employ more than 500 people around the country;

Vatis told *Wired* magazine in the fall of 1998 that "[a]t least half of our staff will come from the Secret Service, National Security Agency, CIA, NASA, Department of Defense, state and local law enforcement, Department of Treasury, Department of Energy, and the Department of Transportation."[12]

A central focus of NIPC has been to expand and build upon a program called InfraGard, which was developed by the Cleveland FBI office in the summer of 1996. On its website, the FBI describes InfraGard as follows:

> InfraGard is a cooperative effort to exchange information between the business community, academic institutions, the FBI, and other government agencies to ensure the protection of the information infrastructure through the referral and dissemination of information regarding illegal intrusions, disruptions, and exploited vulnerabilities of information systems.

By the beginning of 2001, all fifty-six FBI field offices around the country were running InfraGard chapters, and more than 518 private businesses had signed up. In order to persuade companies to participate, NIPC provides them with a secure website on which information is posted and secure e-mail for exchanging information about intrusions and threats.

The FBI is steadily increasing its capability for gathering, storing, and cross-matching the detailed information it receives from the business community. As an extension of its work with NIPC, the FBI asked Congress in 2000 to appropriate $75 million to upgrade the Bureau's information technology. Under a program dubbed "Digital Storm," the FBI is planning to replace all of its analog wiretap equipment with digital intercepts, running off of specially modified PCs. As the FBI makes the transition to digital technology, it will gain the ability to do keyword searches on thousands of pages of wiretap transcripts; currently, agents must wade through lengthy audio tapes or hard-copy transcripts. The upgrade from analog to digital technology will also improve the FBI's data mining capabilities for the information contained in its myriad databases.

## The USA Patriot and Homeland Security Acts

The relationships the FBI is developing with businesses through InfraGard and the data mining capabilities inherent in a program like "Digital Storm" have taken on a particular significance in the wake of the 9/11 terrorist attacks.

In an action that mirrors its reaction to the turbulence of the 1960s, Congress recently adopted sweeping changes to the rules governing government wiretaps. The changes were included in the "Uniting and Strengthening America By Providing Appropriate Tools Required To Intercept and

Obstruct Terrorism" Act, better known as the USA Patriot Act. Among its various provisions are a number of significant changes to how surveillance is conducted in this country:

■ *Government Agents and the Foreign Intelligence Sueveillance Act.* The Act permits government agents to use the Foreign Intelligence Surveillance Act (FISA) to intercept communications and engage in surveillance even if the primary purpose of the surveillance is a criminal investigation. The benefit to law enforcement is that the standards for obtaining authority to do surveillance under FISA are far less onerous than those applied to surveillance of U.S. citizens suspected of committing a crime.

■ *Law Enforcement and Access to Websites.* Although the parameters for doing so are still unclear, the Patriot Act apparently authorizes law enforcement to obtain access to a list of websites visited by an individual under investigation, as long as law enforcement agents can obtain a U.S. District Court order.

Most disturbingly for employees, the Patriot Act also gives the Federal Bureau of Investigation a virtually unfettered right to demand any records maintained by a business about an employee under investigation. Specifically, the law states:

> The Director of the Federal Bureau of Investigation or a designee . . . may make an application for an order requiring the production of any tangible things (including books, records, papers, documents, and other items) for an investigation to protect against international terrorism or clandestine intelligence activities. . . .

If a federal judge or magistrate approves the government's application, an order is entered without any advance notice to the business or employee, and the business is forbidden from telling anyone that the FBI has even made a request for an employee's records. Not surprisingly, it's unclear how extensively this provision has been used over the past year, but it's clear that from both a legal and practical point of view, the FBI's ability to compile data about employees is steadily expanding.

Following the election in November 2002, the recapture of the Senate by the Republican Party helped spur passage of the Homeland Security Act on terms more acceptable to President George W. Bush. Among the more controversial provisions of the Act is the creation of a project called "Total Information Awareness" (TIA). The goal of TIA is to build a massive governmental database containing, among other things, every commercial, consumer, and financial transaction, every academic grade, and the title of every book or video rented or purchased in this country. It's unclear just yet how much information will be drawn from employers, but the potential scope of TIA is not encouraging.

The program will be administered by the Information Awareness Office, located in the Defense Advanced Research Projects Agency and headed by former Reagan national security adviser John Poindexter.[13] The Homeland Security Act provides him with a $200 million budget to begin implementing Total Information Awareness.

In a column describing Poindexter's new role as the government's official Peeping Tom, columnist William Safire noted that the Latin motto at the entrance to the Information Awareness Office reads *Scientia est potentia* or "Knowledge is power."[14]

## The Nose of the Camel? The National Transportation ID

As we've seen, the debate over a national identification card has been percolating for more than half a century. The first serious attempt came in 1948, when the U.S. National Office of Vital Statistics proposed the adoption of a national birth certificate number.

The debate reached its highest pitch in the mid-1990s, during the lengthy and often fierce debate over the national health care plan spearheaded by then-First Lady Hillary Clinton (now a U.S. Senator). Included in the proposal was the suggestion that each person be issued a unique health care identifier, which could be used to track the provision of health care services to that person and facilitate the handling of records and payments. Although the original proposal was rejected by Congress, a somewhat more limited version was passed in 1996 under the awkward title of the Health Insurance Portability and Accountability Act (HIPAA). The concept of a unique health identifier survived in the HIPAA, and work continues on the design and implementation of an appropriate identifier.

As with so many other areas of security, the concept of a national ID received a boost from the terrorist attacks. Long before the dust had cleared, legislators were renewing calls for the creation of a national driver's license, an idea that had been included in at least three pieces of legislation in 1996: HIPAA, PRWORA, and the Illegal Immigration Reform and Immigration Responsibility Act.

In each of those earlier bills, language was included that instructed the U.S. Department of Transportation to work with the American Association of Motor Vehicle Administrators to develop standards for the driver's licenses issued by each state. Among the standards to be established was a system for assigning each driver a unique numerical identifier; under the terms of the legislation, the licenses would eventually become a national ID. However, legislation introduced by Senator Richard Shelby (Alabama) in early 2000 blocked implementation of the license number proposal.

But the concept is far from dead. The U.S. House of Representatives is considering a bill introduced by Representatives Jim Moran and Tom Davis (Virginia) called the "Driver's License Modernization Act of 2002" (H.R. 4633). Under the terms of the proposed law, each state would be required to create a driver's license that uses a microchip to store the license-holder's fingerprint or retinal scan. So far, there's no sign that H.R. 4633 is gaining any traction, but a more modest proposal in the works may prove to be a test case for a civilian national ID.

Not surprisingly, the 9/11 attacks focused intense scrutiny on the security of America's transportation system, and it is among the employees of that industry that a national ID card will find its first widespread use. The new Transportation Security Administration is in the process of creating a smart identification card that would be issued to every transportation worker who has access "to secure areas of the [U.S.] transportation system." The card will contain some type of biometric identifier, although no decision had been made as to which one to use.

In late August 2002, the TSA's website displayed a mock-up of a possible version of the transportation worker's ID card (known by its acronym, TWIC), using virtually every trick in the ID manufacturer's arsenal:

> ... the ID card would probably be the size of a credit card and include microprinting, an intricate background pattern, ultraviolet ink, optical devices, and a thick laminate to prevent tampering or counterfeiting. In addition to a worker's photo, which would be shot in high-resolution digital film, the card would include the holder's name, employer, an identification number, issue date, expiration date, and the agency's name and logo. The back of the card would feature a swipe strip, various bar codes, a microchip cavity, another optical image device, and a ghost image of the cardholder.[15]

Less than a month later, however, the mock-up was no longer available on the TSA website. One likely reason for its removal is that the TSA's program to implement a transportation worker's ID hit a serious roadblock when Representative Harold Rogers (Kentucky), the Chairman of the House Appropriations transportation subcommittee, ordered acting TSA chief James M. Loy to put a hold on the TWIC project.

The hold stemmed from Congress's strong interest in the creation of an ID for so-called "trusted travelers, those willing to undergo an extensive background check in return for being allowed to bypass lengthy security checks at the airport." The TSA's transportation worker's ID is supposed to serve as a model for the trusted traveler ID. However, in Chairman Rogers's view, the Department of Defense technology on which TSA is reportedly basing its ID is not yet sophisticated enough to support biometric identification, which is viewed as a critical element of a trusted traveler ID program.[16]

If and when the transportation worker and trusted traveler IDs are implemented—most likely within the next eighteen months to two years—they will establish a new standard for worker identification, both in terms of the structure of the cards themselves and the scope of the background checks required to obtain the cards.

# End Notes

1. The U.S. Employment Service (USES) was created by the passage of the Immigration Act on February 20, 1907. Originally a division of the Bureau of Immigration and Naturalization and later a bureau within the Department of Labor, the USES helped place immigrants in jobs around the country.

2. USAJOBS website, "Privacy Policy," n.d. Available at www.usajobs.opm.gov/privact.htm.

3. Garfinkel, *Database Nation*, pp. 20–21.

4. United States General Accounting Office, "Identity Theft: Prevalence and Cost Appear to Be Growing," (March 2002). Available on the Web at www.consumer.gov/idtheft/reports/gao-d02363.pdf.

5. In September 2000, in fact, the House Subcommittee on Government Management, Information, and Technology released its first report card on Computer Security in the Federal Government. In the committee's view, the government's overall grade was a D , and a number of agencies that routinely gather information about employees—including the Office of Personnel Management, Health & Human Services, Small Business Administration, and Labor—received failing grades.

6. Ironically, the 1890 census records no longer exist. A portion of the records were damaged by fire and water, and the remainder were destroyed by the Library of Congress in the mid-1930s.

7. For a fascinating overview of punch card technology and in particular, the history of the phrase "do not fold, spindle, or mutilate," see the article by Steven Lubar, " 'Do not fold, spindle, or mutilate': A cultural history of the punch card," *Smithsonian Institution* (May 1991). Downloaded on June 18, 2002, from ccat.sas.upenn.edu/slubar/fsm.html.

8. In the early 1960s, the computer industry was jokingly referred to as "Snow White" (IBM) and the "Seven Dwarves" (Burroughs, Control Data, General Electric, Honeywell, NCR, RCA, and Sperry Rand). Today, of course, IBM is better known by the nickname "Big Blue."

9. Although Dean was probably speaking generally, he was also referring specifi-

cally to a list of twenty individuals prepared for him by the office of Charles W. Colson. From Facts on File, *Watergate and the White House*, vol. 1, pp. 96–97.

10. "Frequently Asked Questions," U.S. Administration for Children and Families website. Downloaded on September 15, 2002, from the Web at URL www.acf .dhhs.gov/programs/cse/newhire/nh/q-apam2.htm.

11. Letter from Frank Fuentes to all State IV-D Directors (February 8, 2001). Available on the Administration for Children and Families website at www.acf.dhhs.gov/ programs/cse/pol/dcl-01–10.htm.

12. Niall McKay, "Cyber Terror Arsenal Grows," *Wired* magazine (October 1998). Viewed online at wired.com/news/news/politics/story/15643.html.

13. Poindexter was convicted in 1990 on five felony counts of misleading Congress and making false statements, but his conviction was overturned by an appeals court on the grounds that Congress had granted him immunity for his testimony.

14. William Safire, "You Are a Suspect," *The New York Times* (November 14, 2002).

15. Raphael Lewis, "Transport worker ID in the works," *Boston Globe* (August 24, 2002) p. A1. The Transportation Security Administration website can be viewed at tsa.gov.

16. David Bond, "TSA's Fresh Start Has a Price Tag," *Aviation Week & Space Technology* (September 16, 2002).

# CHAPTER FIVE

# Watching What You Say and What You Do in the Workplace

Few rights are as deeply treasured by American citizens as their freedom of speech. The deceptively simple guarantee of the First Amendment— "Congress shall make no law abridging the freedom of speech . . ."—is deeply ingrained into our national psyche. If you want to stand on a street corner and describe loudly and in great detail how your elected officials are a bunch of idiots, then you have the right to do so. And even if you prefer not to spend your lunch hour criticizing the government, you may be one of the millions who enjoys listening to late-night comedians take potshots at the nation's politicians or to the vigorous give-and-take (or demented ravings, depending on your point of view) of talk radio.

You might be surprised to find, then, that freedom of speech doesn't mean the same thing at work that it means on a street corner or on late-night TV. If you would like to stand up in the middle of the company cafeteria and describe loudly and in great detail how the managers and directors of your company are a bunch of idiots, you technically have the right to do so, but no matter how vigorously you wave the Bill of Rights, it won't do much to protect your job prospects.

Thanks to various federal and state laws, you do have some protection if you criticize your boss on the phone or in a private conversation—as a general rule, eavesdropping on private conversations is not permitted. But as we'll see, you have far less protection when you conduct conversations via e-mail, or post comments on Web newsgroups, bulletin boards, or chat rooms.

Even more disturbingly, you may no longer be able to assume that you are free from casual observation while you are at work; a large number of different technologies are being used to track where you go and what you do while you're in the workplace. Infrared technology, for instance, is increasingly used to track employee movements. And as the size and cost of cameras steadily shrink, the frequency of video surveillance by employers is steadily increasing. Only a few states have passed laws regarding surreptitious videotaping, and virtually all of them contain exceptions that allow employers to conduct video surveillance for business-related reasons, a phrase that is usually broadly defined.

## Is Your Cubicle (or Donut) Bugged?

When we think of wiretapping, our minds leap naturally to the image of a trench-coated FBI or CIA agent, hunched with earphones over a jumble of wires through which the bad guy's voice can be heard with startling clarity. There's some truth to that image (or at least there was), but the reality is far broader. While government agents obviously do conduct wiretaps, their efforts at surveillance are more closely monitored and subject to far greater restrictions than businesses, who have been able to listen in on the conversations of their employees with near-impunity for decades.

### Fading Telephone Privacy at Work

Over the last century, improvements in technology have dramatically changed our expectation of privacy when making a telephone call. In the early days of the American telephone system, private phone calls were virtually nonexistent. It was cheaper for the phone companies to install and operate shared lines, which in turn made them less expensive for consumers; as late as 1950, 75 percent of all of the phone lines in the United States were party lines, shared by as few as two families or as many as twenty-four.[1]

To listen in on your neighbor's phone call, all you had to do was pick up your receiver. This was often regarded as a "feature" rather than a drawback; long before the phone companies introduced three-way and conference-calling technology, party lines enabled a number of neighbors to share the local gossip. The inherent appeal of party line technology was demonstrated in the 1980s, when phone companies introduced multiperson chat lines. The forerunners of today's Internet chat rooms and IRC channels, the party lines were best known for making it possible for teens to run up sometimes phenomenal phone bills.

In the latter half of the twentieth century, our privacy expectations regarding phone calls changed. The installation of advanced switching technology made it possible to dial numbers directly anywhere in the country without the assistance of an operator, who might be tempted to listen in. In addition, as the cost of telephone lines and equipment steadily dropped, the number of single-user lines increased, and consumers proved increasingly willing to pay for them. Over the course of a generation, we came to expect that a telephone conversation was as private as a face-to-face chat in our living room.[2]

Our privacy expectations regarding phone calls have been reinforced by the actions of the Supreme Court and Congress. After more than forty years of decisions upholding wiretapping because it did not involve a physical invasion of space, in 1967 the Supreme Court reversed itself in *Katz v. United States*,[3] holding that the constitutional protection from search and seizure protects people, not places. If we make a telephone call, the Court said, under circumstances that indicate a reasonable expectation of privacy, then government agents cannot intercept it without a warrant. Congress's Omnibus Crime Control and Safe Streets Act of 1968 was more of a mixed bag from a privacy point of view: While it did permit governmental agents to conduct wiretaps for the first time since the passage of the Communications Act in 1934, it also imposed strict requirements on the issuance of wiretap orders.

To a large degree, we have extended our expectation of privacy for phone calls to the workplace. For example, when we pick up the phone to make a call, we assume that no one is secretly listening in on an extension. In fact, one recent privacy poll found that 81 percent of us believe that employers have no right to monitor our phone calls at work.[4]

But employers do have a right to monitor our phone calls, so long as the monitoring is within "the ordinary course of business," which is why we so often hear the phrase, "This call may be monitored to ensure quality service" or some similar variation. Your employer can also monitor your phone calls when you give either explicit or implied consent. However, if your employer determines that you are making a personal call, he or she is supposed to stop any monitoring. As some commentators have pointed out, however, that loophole can give an employer 2–3 minutes of lawful eavesdropping. And not surprisingly, there is unequivocal evidence that some employers do not hang up at all.

In its 2001 annual survey of workplace monitoring and surveillance, the American Management Association estimated that 12 percent of the major U.S. corporations periodically record and review telephone calls, while 8 percent store and review voice mail messages. A far higher percentage (43 percent) monitor the amount of time that employees spend on the telephone, and check the phone numbers that have been called. Employers are motivated primarily by the impact excess phone calls can have on productivity, but also by concerns over the quality of customer service, possible loss of trade secrets, and security issues.

Tracking the phone numbers that an employee calls can be as simple as reading the monthly phone bill; a slightly more aggressive step involves installing a pen register, which records every number dialed from a particular phone. However, as computers and phones become increasingly integrated, more and more employers will be able to use PCs and software to track employee phone usage and produce detailed reports of all telephone activity.

According to Telemate.Net, one manufacturer of telephone monitoring software, over 20 percent of all workplace calls are personal. The company sells a software product called *Telemate™ Call Accounting* that a company can use to track all of the data generated by the company's telecom resources. The software allows management to identify "the calls and call patterns placed by individuals, teams, departments, and the organization." This software produces reports that:

- Identify call volume, topics, destinations, sources, length, frequency and peak calling times.

- Track account activity and build a marketing prospect/customer database.

- Classify phone numbers to identify potential productivity distractions.

- Integrates electronic calling card and DISA usage data to detect access code theft or fraud.

- Identify inbound callers to spot abuse or incorrect routing of 800 calls.[5]

Employers are particularly interested in such software because it helps them avoid concerns about the improper interception of employee telephone calls under the Omnibus Crime Control Act and the Electronic Communications Privacy Act; all the software does is analyze patterns of phone usage.

## Employer Bugs and Wiretaps

One significant aspect of the 1968 Omnibus Crime Control legislation was that Congress excluded switchboards and other types of business equipment from the definition of "interception devices." The practical effect of that exclusion was that for another twenty years, businesses were able to continue their nearly century-long practice of listening in on workplace conversations[6] without fear of violating the new federal wiretap laws.

In the last fifteen years, there have been some efforts–most notably the Electronic Communications Privacy Act–to restrict the amount of eaves-dropping that employers can do to their employees. Although the Act continues to favor employers, the threat of both civil and criminal liability has probably cut back on the amount of corporate eavesdropping that occurs.

Not surprisingly, however, there are no reliable figures on how many employers in this country are using hidden bugs and secret wiretaps to listen to their employees and their customers. In most states, it is illegal to record a conversation without the consent of all participants. The Granite Island Group, a Boston-based technical surveillance counter measures firm, offers a list of the signs that you may be bugged:[7]

- People seem to know your activities when they shouldn't.

- Your AM/FM radio has suddenly developed strange interference.

- Electrical wall plates appear to have been moved slightly or "jarred."

- The smoke detector, clock, lamp, or exit sign in your office or home looks slightly crooked, has a small hole in the surface, or has a quasi-reflective surface.

- Certain types of items have "just appeared" in your office or home, but nobody seems to know how they got there. Examples include clocks, exit signs, sprinkler heads, radios, picture frames, and lamps.

- You notice small pieces of ceiling tiles or "grit" on the floor or on the surface area of your desk.[8]

## Magstripe Cards

Currently, the most widely available and heavily implemented technology for tracking employee movement is the same familiar magnetic strip (or "magstripe") found on the back of the country's more than 1.4 billion credit cards. Magnetic strip technology, which has been around since the early 1970s, is now commonly integrated into employee IDs.

The typical magstripe is a thin strip of plastic film containing thousands of small (1/20-millionths of an inch) magnetic particles. Using a magnetic field, the particles in various sections of a magnetic strip can be oriented to the North or South Pole. Once information has been recorded on the strip, it can be deciphered by a magstripe reader.[9]

Typically, an employer will issue IDs that encode certain information on the ID magstripe, such as an employee's name, ID number, security level, and so forth. Depending on the level of security in place at the company, the employee will have to swipe her ID through a magstripe reader in order to gain access to the parking lot, the front door, and/or various internal doorways. The magstripe readers are typically wired into a network, so that when an employee swipes her card, the information in the strip can be verified by a central database. In addition, most such systems are specifically designed to record the date, time, and identity of each person who goes through a business's various checkpoints.

One drawback to a card reader system is that information about employee movement is collected only when the employee swipes his card. That limits the amount of information and level of detail that an employer can collect. An employer could set up a system that required employees to swipe their cards to go in or out of every door, but doing so has obvious practical difficulties, including cost and inconvenience. In addition, the hassle of constantly swiping an ID card would undoubtedly spur an employee rebellion. Magstripe cards have a number of other drawbacks. The physical process of swiping a magnetic strip tends to wear it out, which means that the strip eventually needs to be replaced. Exposure to a magnetic field can scramble or erase the data. And the structure for storage of data is well known, and the raw materials and software necessary to produce magstripe cards are readily available (thanks largely to the fact that the same technology is used on credit cards, which are a lucrative target), so they are all too easy to duplicate

The main concern for employers who use card readers (magstripe or otherwise) to monitor access and movement is the phenomenon of "tailgating," when one employee swipes his card and other employees pass through without swiping theirs. Some businesses have gone so far as to make "tailgating" a forbidden practice, and there's a growing industry of companies that market devices specifically designed to prevent tailgating. For instance, Designed Security, Inc., in Bastrop, Texas, offers a product called the ES520 Tailgate Detection System, which sounds an audible alarm or sends an alarm signal to a guard station if more than one person tries to pass the system on a single card swipe.

A challenge facing any employer who installs a security system is that employees often won't use it or will try to get around it. But security continues to be a critical issue—employers want the ability to know where their employers are and where they've been. As a result, employers are showing strong interest in tracking systems that require a minimum of employee participation. Until RFID technology becomes widespread, the leading candidate for more effective employee tracking is the incorporation of infrared technology into employee IDs.

## The Heat Is On

Each morning when I go into the kitchen to turn on the teakettle, I pick up a small plastic box and press a bright orange button in the upper left-hand corner. Fifteen feet across the room, a shelf-top stereo system powers up and Vermont Public Radio begins providing me with the day's news and weather. The same technology is familiar to anyone who has purchased a television in the last twenty years—the infrared remote control, a device now widely blamed for robbing us of the eighteen calories per hour we would burn by actually getting up off the couch to change television channels.

Infrared remote controls, first introduced in the early 1980s, were a big improvement over earlier designs, which used wires physically connected to the television's dials, pulses of light, or ultrasonic signals. (The early designs all had serious drawbacks. Wire remotes were slow and sometimes made people trip; photovoltaic remotes don't work well in sunlight; and ultrasonic remotes often make dogs howl.)[10] Today's infrared remote control devices make use of a discovery that occurred 200 years ago, when Sir Frederick Herschel used a prism to split light into its component colors and measured the temperature of each color. He observed that the temperature increased as he progressed through violet, blue, green, yellow, orange, and red, and that the very highest temperatures were just beyond the red section of the spectrum. He concluded that there were invisible rays beyond red that behaved like visible light. Herschel coined the phrase "calorific rays" for the invisible beams, they later became known by their current name, infrared rays.[11]

Despite our inability to see infrared rays directly, Herschel's discovery has proven to be immensely valuable. Infrared cameras pointed out into space allow us to peer through interstellar dust clouds. Other cameras pointed earthward use the infrared portion of the spectrum to monitor the environment, track weather around the globe, and even discover centuries-old footpaths and prehistoric settlements. On Earth, thermal imaging cameras are used in a wide variety of applications, including the maintenance of mechanical systems, the testing of personal computer circuit boards, search and rescue efforts, and medical diagnosis.

## The Active Badge System

The development of the infrared LED in the early 1960s has given rise to a huge number of applications, the most familiar of which is the remote control, and in 1989, researchers at the Cambridge University Computer Laboratory in Cambridge, England, began work on a system that incorporated infrared LEDs into employee identification badges.[12] After roughly four years of work, their research resulted in the development of the "Active Badge."

The basic concept of the Active Badge is straightforward. Employees are given a special identification card equipped with an infrared LED that sends out a unique code every fifteen seconds or so. If the card is within six meters of an infrared sensor (mounted on a wall or ceiling), the code is read by the sensor. The sensor is connected to a network of other sensors, all of which are linked to a central station. The central station periodically retrieves data from each of the sensors and uses the information to compile a map of each badge's current location.

As careful readers have already noted, the most obvious limitation of the Active Badge system is that it tracks badges and not people; it only tracks people if they actually wear or carry the badges, and more specifically, the badges that have been assigned to them. In the view of the designers of the Active Badge, the fact that you can take the badge off is one of the system's advantages:

> There will always be some days when for whatever reason somebody does not wish to be located. This is easy to solve because the system tracks badges and *not* people. Anybody in this situation can easily remove their badge and leave it on a desk. The Active Badge system will now be fooled into concluding that person is somewhere where they are not. This kind of escape mechanism is not an undesirable system feature and may be an important factor in making this system acceptable for common use.[13]

Technically speaking, when an Active Badge is put in a drawer or an employee's pocket, it slowly goes to sleep (as a power-saving measure). The sensor network will continue to display the badge's last known location, but the likelihood of finding the badge at that location (displayed as a probability on the Active Badge information screen) will steadily decrease.

The question for employees is how well such disappearances from the sensor grid will be tolerated by their employers. In a work environment where there is a strong management expectation that employees will wear their Active Badges, periodically taking off the badge and "disappearing" from the sensor system will undoubtedly be perceived as negative behavior. Companies can (and sometime do) impose a requirement that employees wear an Active Badge at all times, but with a technology that immediately raises so many privacy hackles ("Let's see, George, it says here that you spent a total of two hours yesterday in the second floor restroom—are you feeling ok?"), employers are taking a more persuasive approach.

The chief benefit that employers offer in exchange for wearing the Active Badge is a more efficient workplace. The Active Badge system makes it easier to receive phone calls while moving around a building and makes it easier to locate coworkers. Call-routing, of course, is only one of the Active

Badge's capabilities. The Active Badge system was designed with the following commands:

- WITH—a list of the other badges in the same area as the target badge

- LOOK—a list of badges currently located in a particular area

- NOTIFY—an alarm that goes off when a particular badge is picked up by the sensor system. (NOTIFY was designed to make it possible to deliver an urgent message to someone who had been out of the building and had just returned. It could be easily modified to sound an alarm when a particular badge enters an area where it is not authorized.)

- HISTORY—a log of the badge's location over a period of time

When the Active Badge was first developed, the period of history recorded was limited to a single hour, and the information was stored in dynamic memory, not archived to permanent storage. Back in 1992, storage was still quite expensive: roughly $4 per megabyte. By the summer of 2002, you could buy a 160-gigabyte hard drive for $229.98. One hundred sixty gigabytes will hold a lot of Active Badge data.

## Infrared Badges at Work

By 1997, nurses in over 200 hospitals were wearing infrared badges. The manufacturer, Executone Information Systems, called its version the Infostar® Infrared Locator System, and described it as "an infrared-based, wireless locating system to help healthcare staff quickly find people and equipment."

More recently, the lead in infrared badge technology has been assumed by Versus Technology, based in Traverse City, Michigan. Versus has been particularly aggressive in integrating telephone systems with the badge technology. Its PhoneVision™, Versus says, makes it possible for callers to "'see' (through the telephone) the location of the person [they] are trying to reach":

> By wearing a lightweight badge which emits infrared signals containing location data, the individual's location is instantly available. The location information is received by the system and is accessible to users through the telephone. By simply entering the person's extension, PhoneVision™ identifies the exact location of a person at that point in time. Once a person is located, the user may choose to ring the nearest extension, hear a list of others at that location, or automatically be forwarded to voice mail.[14]

The chief benefit of its infrared badge system, Versus claims, is the ability to locate staff members quickly, improving staff efficiency and enhancing patient care. In addition to locating specific individuals, the Versus system can also be configured to display the badges of various groups in different colors, so that administrators can see at a glance the locations, for instance, of all the nurses or all the cleaning staff.

In addition to locating individuals, the Versus PhoneVision™ system is also designed to locate equipment. Any piece of equipment can be rigged with an infrared tag containing a unique code:

> Simply dial into the system, enter the equipment's ID number, and PhoneVision™ will automatically identify its location. If desired, you may also choose to hear who is with the equipment or hear what other equipment is at that location.

There's some concern on the part of employees, and nurses in particular, that systems like PhoneVision™ will increase the tendency of management to look at them as merely bipedal pieces of equipment. Certainly, an infrared badge increases the granularity of the data available to an employer, i.e., the level of detail about each employee's activities during the course of the day. Employers argue that the additional information will help them evaluate internal processes to make them more efficient, and that the system will also help reduce ambient noise (since employees can be located quickly without having to be paged). Nonetheless, employees are concerned that the accumulated infrared badge data will be another tool to help employers demand additional work or deny salary increases.

## Wash Up, Doc?

The next time that you're sitting in your doctor's office, ask yourself this question: Has she washed her hands since examining her last patient? Better yet, ask your doctor that question: The odds are less than one in three that she has.

How about the harried waitress who plucks your morning toast out of the toaster at the diner, or the prep cook who makes your midday Caesar's salad? According to the U.S. Food and Drug Administration, as many as 1,400 people die each year as a result of food poisoning that can be traced directly to poor restaurant hygiene. The chances that you might get sick are frighteningly higher—roughly one in fifteen Americans in any given year will spend a miserable day or night that a little soap and water could have prevented.

From the outset, employees have been concerned that the infrared badge technology can reveal private and potentially embarrassing information, particularly about time spent in the bathroom. That concern seems almost quaint today, given the fact that infrared badge technology is being integrated into systems that are specifically designed to monitor employee hygiene habits.

You might think that the bathroom is the last bastion of privacy, a scrutiny-free zone that even employers can't invade. That may once have been true, but the potential for ruinously expensive litigation is pushing employers to overcome even the most basic concerns. Even if no one actually dies, a wave of food poisoning can ruin a restaurant; likewise, a malpractice suit resulting from the death of a patient due to poor hygiene can cost a hospital tens of millions of dollars. When numbers like that are tossed around, employers have a hard time justifying a continued respect for employee privacy.

In the spring of 1997, a New Jersey-based company, Net/Tech International, Inc., introduced the Hygiene Guard system for use in food service and health care facilities. The system uses sensors in employee restrooms, including sensors on soap dispensers and faucets, to make sure that employees engage in proper hygiene. The first system was installed at the Tropicana Casino and Resort in Atlantic City, with others soon following at Georgetown University Hospital and the Willam Beaumont Army Medical Center in El Paso, Texas.

Like other infrared sensor systems, the restroom sensors are tied into a central network that maintains a log of each employee's adherence to proper hygiene procedures. If an employee leaves the bathroom without washing up, an entry is made in the employee's log on the main computer. The Hygiene Guard system can also be programmed to cause an employee's badge to start flashing if he fails to wash up properly. Data from the various logs can be sorted and printed out in a variety of ways, and preformatted reports are available that can be reviewed with specific employees or posted on an employee bulletin board.

A variant on the Hygiene Guard system is produced by a Weymouth, Massachusetts, company called UltraClenz, which manufactures the Pro-Giene system. UltraClenz works with employers to establish an appropriate hand-washing schedule, and then issues each employee an infrared badge that beeps and flashes each time the employee is supposed to wash his hands. When the employee goes into the restroom, sensors in the sink faucet, soap dispenser, and towel dispenser record whether the employee has actually used them. It's not a system designed to make employees feel particularly dignified:

> The system instructs the employee on each step in sequence by both voice capacity as well as a LCD read out. The time interval for each function is determined by you and consists of the following functions; wetting hands, applying soap, lathering hands for a full twenty seconds,

rinsing hands, and drying with a towel. The individual is recognized as having completed a protocol hand wash that is recorded and time stamped.

Pro-Giene will also, on a real-time basis, recognize employees who have or have not successfully completed the procedure or who may be overdue for their scheduled wash.[15]

Given the limited attention that Congress has paid to employee privacy rights in general, it's not particularly surprising that there is no "Freedom from Employer Bathroom Monitoring Act." As we've seen, employer monitoring of our most basic communication—speech—is permitted when it is in the "ordinary course of business." While courts have shown some sympathy for the idea that certain spaces, even on business property, are off-limits to surveillance (e.g., bathrooms and locker rooms), it's hard to argue that the prevention of contamination and illness are not part of the "ordinary course of business" in a hospital or restaurant.

## Cameras, Cameras, Everywhere, and Not a Spot to Think (or If You Can See the Empire State Building, We Can See You)[16]

In one of the more depressing developments of the late twentieth century, the same nation that gave us the Magna Carta also provided one of the most starkly Orwellian views of citizenship. In the mid-1990s, Conservative John Major based his campaign for reelection as British Prime Minister in part on a promise to install more video cameras in public spaces. Major promoted his proposal with a highly successful slogan: "If You've Got Nothing to Hide, You've Got Nothing to Fear." Following an upset victory over Labor leader Neil Kinnock, Major kept his promise and began a program (later aggressively continued by Tony Blair's Labor government) that has made Britons the most heavily watched and supervised people in the Western hemisphere, if not the world. In an October 2001 *New York Times Magazine* cover story, legal scholar Jeffrey Rosen (the author of *The Unwanted Gaze*) said that according to some estimates, there are more than 2.5 million surveillance cameras in Britain, and the average Englishman is photographed by over 300 different cameras each day.

Thanks to an absence of a constant physical threat like the Irish Republican Army and the strong protections laid out in the Bill of Rights (our list of written freedoms is noticeably absent from the English legal system), the use of public surveillance cameras has been slower to catch on in the United States. In 1997, for instance, Josh Quittner wrote in *Time* magazine that the average New Yorker could expect to be photographed by surveillance cameras a mere twenty times per day.

That estimate is now unquestionably low. Industry analysts predict that roughly $5.7 billion worth of surveillance cameras will be sold in the United States in 2002, a figure that is certain to rise steadily in the years to come. A large number of communities around the United States are starting to install the types of closed-circuit television systems that are so popular in England, and facial recognition software companies are reporting boom times.

As Rosen pointed out in his article regarding camera systems in England, the growth of public surveillance technology in the United States presents this country with a stark choice:

> The promise of America is a promise that we can escape from the Old World, a world where people know their place. When we say we are fighting for an open society, we don't mean a transparent society—one where neighbors can peer into each other's windows using the joysticks on their laptops.[17] We mean a society open to the possibility that people can redefine and reinvent themselves every day; a society in which people can travel from place to place without showing their papers and being encumbered by their past; a society that respects privacy and constantly reshuffles social hierarchy.
>
> The ideal of America has from the beginning been an insistence that your opportunities shouldn't be limited by your background or your database; that no doors should be permanently closed to anyone who has the wrong smart card. If the twenty-first century proves to be a time when this ideal is abandoned—a time of surveillance cameras and creepy biometric face scanning in Times Square—then Osama bin Laden will have inflicted an even more terrible blow than we now imagine.[18]

Thanks largely to considerations of size and space, the United States may never experience the level of public video surveillance already being practiced in Britain. The real privacy threat in this country lies not so much in the existence of the surveillance cameras themselves (although that's bad enough) but in how and where they are deployed. Public surveillance systems are typically announced with large signs reading "CCTV in use" or something similar, in part to comply with constitutional requirements or public expectations (i.e., that the government will not conduct secret surveillance of us), and in part to oversell the capabilities of the surveillance system itself. (In his trip to England, Rosen found that a number of the CCTV systems in operation claimed more working cameras than were actually installed.)

In contrast to the general public, U.S. employees are already spending the better part of each day within range of visual surveillance systems that are not constrained by constitutional limitations.

Corporate security camera systems pose a much greater privacy threat to society as a whole and employees in particular because they are more consistently monitored (companies have both the resources and the financial motivation to do so), are more widely implemented, and are more frequently hidden. Nor are these new developments—Vance Packard identified the same issues back in 1964, when he included the rise of video surveillance by companies in his book *The Naked Society*. One New York company president, Packard said, had a hidden camera installed in a fake humidifier in the corporate board room so he could monitor meetings at which he was not present. Packard also quoted one installer of closed-circuit television systems as saying that "three-quarters of the name department stores in New York use television."[19]

The percentage of retail outlets that use video surveillance remains high. According to the University of Florida's 2001 National Retail Security Survey, nearly 75 percent of the retailers surveyed used live closed-circuit television (CCTV) as a loss-prevention system, and just under a third use visible, simulated CCTV (i.e., fake cameras).[20] Overall, the American Management Association reported last year that 15 percent of employers conduct general videotaping of their employees, although 38 percent said that they videotaped employees for security purposes.

As with other technologies, the main impediment to the widespread implementation of video surveillance systems has been cost, with the priciest components being the cameras, the monitors into which the cameras are hardwired, and the personnel required to operate and monitor the cameras. That impediment is rapidly vanishing: Camera costs are falling steadily, and more importantly, the images the cameras produce can now be fed directly into an office network or even onto the Internet. Thus, any computer can serve as a monitor, and a single individual can monitor dozens of cameras. In addition, images can be stored on a hard drive for later review, further minimizing the need for someone to do real-time surveillance.

## The Technology of Surveillance

The telescreen received and transmitted simultaneously. Any sound that Winston made, above the level of a very low whisper, would be picked up by it; moreover, so long as he remained within the field of vision which the metal plaque commanded, he could be seen as well as heard. There was of course no way of knowing whether you were being watched at any given moment. How often, or on what system, the Thought Police plugged in on any individual wire was guesswork. It was even conceivable that they watched everybody at the same time. But at any rate they could plug in your wire whenever they wanted to. You had to live—did live, from habit that became instinct—in the assumption that every sound you made was overheard, and, except in darkness, every movement scrutinized.[21]

In the nightmarish world created by George Orwell in his classic book *1984* perpetual surveillance was a given—the omnipresent telescreen was warning enough that you might be under the critical eye of the Thought Police. If Orwell were writing today, he might well equip his watchers with the latest in hidden video technology, on the theory that people are more likely to engage in illegal or subversive behavior if they don't think they're being watched. (Interestingly, as we'll see in more detail in Chapter 10, that's precisely the argument that various management and business groups have made in fighting workplace privacy legislation.)

The advances in camera miniaturization are truly startling. It's now possible to purchase a Sony CCD camera that is only 1.65 by 1.50 by .91 inches in size for less than fifty dollars.[22] The camera comes equipped with everything you would need to connect the camera to a television, VCR, or computer monitor. There is a host of companies on the World Wide Web that offer appliances such as lamps, clocks, air cleaners, smoke detectors, radios, and computer speakers with hidden cameras built in. In short, there is virtually no place where a video camera cannot be hidden these days.

At the same time that cameras are shrinking in size and cost, their capabilities are expanding. In early 1999, researchers at Johns Hopkins University announced that they had developed a low-power integrated chip with the ability to recognize and follow motion captured by a video camera. When hooked up to a motorized platform for tilting and panning, the chip would enable a video system to track and record the movements of an individual without human assistance. For instance, researchers say, when used in a video phone system, you would no longer have to sit still in front of the camera when talking on the phone; the chip would enable the camera to follow you as you moved around the room.[23]

If your employer is at all concerned that you might be suspicious about an extra wire sticking out of the back of an alarm clock or desk lamp, wireless versions of all of the products mentioned above are readily available. The cost is slightly higher, of course, since a transmitter needs to be incorporated into the hidden camera package, but the recent surge of interest in video surveillance is driving costs steadily downward.

## The Security Guards Keep Smirking at Me

It's one thing when companies make no secret of their video surveillance of their employees, or even conduct hidden surveillance for strictly business purposes (something the courts have generally endorsed). It's entirely another when businesses become electronic Peeping Toms. There's a fairly thin line between legitimate surveillance and prurience, and it's all too easy for businesses (or more typically, rogue employees) to cross it, as in these examples:

- In January 2001, Suzanne Collard filed suit against her employer, Health Education Corp., when she discovered that company-provided massages were being videotaped. After a massage in the lunch room, Collard spotted a video camera hidden among food boxes on top of the refrigerator and discovered that it was attached to a running VCR. The tape showed full frontal nude shots of her after she had undressed, and then images of her being massaged.

- In a September 1998 *Village Voice* article, Mark Boal reported that in a California Neiman-Marcus, a female employee discovered that male employees were watching a women's changing room through a hidden camera in the ceiling.[24]

- In 1998, workers discovered that the Sheraton Boston Hotel was secretly videotaping the locker room of its male employees. The hotel paid $200,000 to settle claims by five workers captured on tape.

- At Salem State College in Massachusetts in 1995, an employee discovered a video camera hidden in an office closet. College officials told Gail Nelson, a secretary who used the office, that the camera had been installed to capture images of anyone sneaking into the office after hours. In fact, the camera captured all activity in the office, including shots of Nelson changing into exercise clothes at the end of the day. Nelson sued, alleging invasion of privacy and emotional distress; the College argued that she had no expectation of privacy in the office and that the videotaping did not violate any laws.

A number of factors are contributing to an increase in workplace voyeurism. First, as we've already seen, technological advances are making cameras cheaper, smaller, and more powerful, which means that more employers will use them.

The second factor driving workplace voyeurism is the growing popularity of hidden surveillance in general. While visible video surveillance remains the more popular option, hidden video surveillance is steadily catching up.

A third factor supporting hidden surveillance is the lack of legal restrictions on the activity. Only a few states have adopted legislation aimed at curbing video voyeurism, and even fewer have addressed the issue of voyeurism in the workplace. There have been some court decisions that have held that employers may not make audio- or videotapes of employees in areas of the business where employees have a reasonable expectation of privacy, but when employers make it explicitly clear to employees ahead of time that they have no reasonable expectation of privacy, then surveillance is generally permitted.

## X-Ray Vision

If you took a poll of fourteen-year-old males around the country and asked them which of Superman's powers they most would like to have, odds are that x-ray vision would win in a landslide. Sure, being able to fly would be neat, and being able to leap tall buildings in a single bound might be exciting, but x-ray vision—now how cool would that be?

Lacking the positive benefits of interstellar mutation of our genes, however, our eyes remain stubbornly stuck in the visible light spectrum. But where nature has failed us, technology is stepping in.

In 1998, Sony Corp. answered the silent prayers of thousands of adolescents (most disguised as forty-year-olds) by inadvertently introducing x-ray vision to the consumer market. Sony released a line of video cameras with a feature called NightShot, an infrared option similar in some ways to military night vision technology, that allowed camera users to shoot footage at night. According to Sony spokeswoman Dulcie Neiman, "[NightShot] was intended for such nighttime activities as a baby sleeping, or children out on a Halloween night, or carolers at Christmas time."[25]

But Sony apparently forgot to test what would happen if the NightShot option was activated during the daytime. It turned out that when the Night-Shot technology is used during the day in conjunction with an infrared black filter, the video camera can effectively see through the top layers of thin clothing. This discovery proved particularly attractive to voyeuristic beach-goers, since the NightShot technology is especially effective at seeing through wet bathing suits. NightShot images quickly became a popular subcategory on voyeurism websites.

Despite the fact that a NightShot-equipped video camera retailed for between $700 and $1,500, news of the NightShot technology's hidden capabilities caused a sharp rise in the sale of Sony video cameras. Dismayed by the unwanted publicity, Sony announced that it was discontinuing sale of the cameras until it could figure out how to eliminate the x-ray capabilities of the NightShot technology. The company ended up modifying NightShot so that when it is activated during the day, the video camera simply shows a blank white screen. However, like mushrooms after a rain storm, numerous websites and online postings have popped up to offer helpful advice on how to get around the Sony fix.

Prurience aside, the nearly miraculous ability of x-rays to peer through otherwise solid objects has made them a popular field of study for security firms. One of the chief drawbacks to traditional x-rays, of course, is their tendency to damage the tissue through which they pass, resulting in either genetic mutations or cancers. The tremendous potency of x-rays makes their use in medical situations a reasonable trade-off for the risk, particularly now that we've figured out how to guard ourselves against the worst of exposure risks. But medical x-rays are an impractical tool in the fight against terrorism, since few travelers would be willing to subject themselves to repeated full strength x-rays just to fly from Boston to New York.

Thus, when it came to adopting x-ray technology for security work, less proved to be more. A low-power x-ray beam, it turns out, penetrates only a few millimeters into the body and is reflected outward. A detector can collect the back-scattered x-rays and construct a remarkably sharp image of the object reflecting the x-rays.

One of the leaders in this area of research is American Science & Engineering, Inc. (AS&E), a Billerica, Massachusetts-based company that has specialized in the development and production of scientific instruments for the last forty-five years. In November 1999, AS&E installed its first Body-Search device at O'Hare International Airport in Chicago. The $125,000 machine consists of a twelve-foot-tall, rectangular cabinet, with a scanning panel and platform at one end and a viewing screen and controls at the other.[26] Screening agents instruct passengers to stand on the platform, and the x-ray image of their body is displayed on the viewing screen. If the screening agent sees something strapped to the traveler's body, he is asked to submit to a more thorough, hands-on search.

The images produced by the back-scatter x-ray are startlingly clear. In addition to showing any contraband, the x-rays make it possible for a screening agent to see virtually every detail of the traveler's body, even to the point of determining whether a male traveler has been circumcised. Privacy advocates, needless to say, are horrified. As David Banisar, the deputy director of Privacy International, told the Associated Press, "This is a very intrusive thing. It has been installed with very little discussion . . . about whether this is a good idea or not."[27]

Government-run facilities remain the chief buyers of the BodySearch machine; by August 2000, AS&E's device was in use at five other airports—Atlanta, Houston, Los Angeles, Miami, and New York's JFK—and six prisons across the U.S. To date, the only private organization reported to have installed the BodySearch was a gold mine in South Africa. Given the increase in security concerns in this country, however, it is unlikely that the machine's price (roughly $200,000) will pose much of a barrier for larger businesses.

As prices for back-scatter x-ray technology inevitably fall, the question will be how many employees will be required to stand naked, even briefly, before their employer each day?

# End Notes

1. Although the number is microscopically small, party lines are still in use in remote areas, although their continued existence is threatened by the Internet, which doesn't share nicely with other types of services on POTS (plain old telephone service) lines.

2. Ironically, technology is shifting that expectation again. A large number of mobile phone users are willing to forego privacy in exchange for the convenience of making phone calls in subways, cafes, restaurants, movie theaters, and other public places.

3. 389 U.S. 347 (1967).

4. "Employee Monitoring, Investigations, and Privacy Rights," Jackson Lewis LLP, n.d. Available online at http://www.jacksonlewis.com/publications/articles/20010923/default.cfm.

5. "Telephone abuse," Telemate.Net website. Available online at http://www.telemate.net/product/callaccounting/telephoneabuse.asp.

6. The practice of listening in on employee conversations for "quality assurance purposes" began as early as the 1920s.

7. Following the impeachment of President Clinton, that small detail caused Linda Tripp some serious problems; her recordings of her conversations with Monica Lewinsky violated the Maryland eavesdropping law, since she did not have Lewinsky's consent to make the recordings.

8. For a complete list, see "Warning Signs of Covert Eavesdropping or Bugging," Granite Island Group website. Available online at www.tscm.com/warningsigns.html.

9. The process is essentially the same as the one used to record music on an audio-cassette tape.

10. "History of the Remote Control," n.p., n.d. Available online at www.modellbahnott.com/tqpage/ihistory.html.

11. "Infra-" is a prefix from the Latin word meaning "below"; infrared rays have frequencies that are below those of red light. By comparison, ultraviolet rays have frequencies that are higher ("ultra-") than violet light. Herschel is scheduled to be honored for his discovery in 2007 with the launch of the Herschel Space Observatory, an infrared-based telescope being operated by the European Space Agency.

12. One of the fascinating aspects of the World Wide Web is that it enables people to demonstrate their unquestionable expertise on incredibly arcane subjects. One of the premier examples of this phenomenon is Craig S. Johnson's LED Museum,

which is devoted to the history and taxonomy of light emitting diodes (ledmuseum
.home.att.net/ledleft.htm). Mr. Johnson claims to have spent 11,000 hours over
the last thirteen years to creating and maintaining his website, and there is utterly
no reason to disbelieve him.

13. Roy Want, Andy Hopper, Veronica Falcao, and Jonathon Gibbons, "The Active
Badge Location System," *ACM Transactions on Information Systems*, vol. 10,
no. 1 (January 1992), pp. 91–102.

14. Versus Technology, Inc., "Phone Vision™," n.d. Available online at www.versus
tech.com/phonevis.htm.

15. "Pro-Giene System," UltraClenz, Inc., n.d. Available online at www.ultraclenz
.com/index.html.

16. Richard Pollack, employee for Metro Networks, quoted in an article by David M.
Halbfinger, "Spread of Surveillance Cameras Raises Prospect of Prying Eyes,"
*The New York Times* (February 22, 1998).

17. An idea espoused by writer David Brin in detail in his book, *The Transparent
Society: Will Technology Force Us to Choose between Privacy and Freedom?*
(Cambridge, Mass.: Perseus Publishing, 1999).

18. Jeffrey Rosen, "A Cautionary Tale for a New Age of Surveillance," *New York
Times Magazine* (October 7, 2001).

19. Vance Packard, *The Naked Society* (New York: Van Rees Press, 1964), pp. 77,
85–86.

20. Richard C. Hollinger and Jason L. Davis, *2001 National Retail Security Survey
—Final Report*, University of Florida Security Research Project (2002). Available
online at web.soc.ufl.edu/SRP/NRSS_2001.pdf.

21. George Orwell, *1984* (New York: Penguin Books, 1981), pp. 6–7.

22. "CCD" stands for charge-couple device.

23. Kristen Philipkoski, "'Eye' Chip Tracks Movement," *Wired.com* (April 10, 1999).

24. Mark Boal, "Spycam City," *The Village Voice* (September 30, 1998).

25. Chris Reidy and Hiawatha Bray, "Camera can bare too much; Sony calls halt to
shipments," *Boston Globe* (August 13, 1998).

26. David Heinsmann, "Customs Agent at Chicago Airport Get Better Look with Body
Scanner," *Chicago Tribune* (November 23, 1999).

27. Lisa Lipman, "Airport Searches Reveal More than Passengers Know," Associated
Press (August 21, 2000).

# CHAPTER SIX

# Hardware, Software, and Spyware

Computers have revolutionized our workplaces in ways that earlier genera tions could not have imagined. Among the most significant changes is the remarkable extent to which an employee's activities can now be measured and monitored. The electronic signals that flow from one part of a computer to another, and from one networked computer to another, can all be measured, tracked, and recorded. In a remarkably short time, your employer can develop a highly detailed profile of exactly how you have been spending your day.

## Feeling the Electronic Lash

Roughly 2,500 years ago, Greek shipbuilders perfected one of the most fearsome vessels for ship-to-ship fighting that the world has ever seen—the trireme, a narrow-hulled vessel with outriggers for stability and a massive ram on the prow for slamming into enemy ships. The trireme had one large square sail and a few smaller sails, but for power, it relied primarily on the strength of 170 rowers. The dearth of sails was hardly an impediment: Maritime scholars estimate that a trireme could go from zero to its top speed of about twelve knots (approximately fourteen and a half miles per hour) in just over thirty seconds.

The modern day office is slowly becoming the equivalent of the Greek galley. While there's no whip-wielding taskmaster at the front of the room (at least in the more well-known companies), the pace of work is enforced by a far more relentless observer—software that monitors the number of keystrokes each employee makes during the course of the day, and/or records the keystrokes themselves.

Keystroke counting, surprisingly, is not an invention of the computer age. Long before computers appeared on office desktops, a management theorist named Frederick Taylor developed the concept of "scientific management," in which he argued that a company's economic success depended on the regular and objective measurement of each employee's performance. Taylor's concepts proved enormously popular with business owners, leading to the invention and implementation of a wide variety of employee-monitoring devices, including keystroke monitors for typewriters.

The only thing that early keystroke monitors had to measure was how fast a typist could type—the paper in the typewriter produced a record of which keys were struck. Today, some employers are still concerned with how quickly their employees type—the industry standard today for a good typist or data entry person is approximately 12,000 keystrokes per hour, or 200 keystrokes per minute. However, the majority of employers today are concerned not merely with productivity but also with the possibility of stolen secrets and hostile work environment lawsuits. As a result, companies are far more interested in software that can record the actual keystrokes made during the course of the day by each employee, along with a record of websites visited, programs used, and in some cases, the actions and movements of each employee's mouse.

The 800-pound gorilla in the keystroke-monitoring jungle is WinWhatWhere, a Kenniwick, Washington, software company that produces *Investigator*, a multifeatured computer monitoring program. First released in 1997, *Investigator* was developed by Richard Eaton, a programmer who came up with the idea when he wrote a program to help himself track down bugs in his software. Since then, he has sold more than 200,000 copies of *Investigator* to suspicious spouses, concerned parents, businesses, and even the FBI.[1]

*Investigator* not only records every keystroke made on the computer, it also maintains a record of dialogue boxes and takes periodic screen shots of what's being displayed on the computer. The software can even be configured to take secret photos of the computer user if the PC is equipped with a Web cam. By recording each keystroke made by a computer user, *Investigator* can effectively record every e-mail (sent or unsent), Internet relay chat, or instant messenger session that takes place on the computer.

*Investigator* could be monitoring activity on your office computer right now, but chances are, you'd never know if it's running or not. Eaton designed the program to be hidden in plain sight: An icon may appear in the system tray, but the various modules that make the program operate periodically change their name to make them more difficult to find. Similarly, the files that are used to hold the data that *Investigator* collects are given arbitrary names and dates so that they can't be easily located.

Even if you know that *Investigator* is running on your office computer system, you may not realize the extent to which it is actively reporting on your activities. *Investigator* can be configured to surreptitiously send its collected data by e-mail to your boss on a regular basis or wait until it discovers certain preset keywords ("boss," "pornography," "kill," or the name of an unreleased product).

Although it is perhaps the best-known keystroke monitoring program, *Investigator* is just one of the dozens of monitoring applications on the market. For instance, Scalable Software, a Houston, Texas, software company, produces *The Survey Suite*, which takes a slightly different approach to this issue. According to company literature, instead of monitoring keystrokes, *The Survey Suite*:

> "[d]etails the time the employee spends using Windows applications, e-mail, and the Internet, and provides the employee with easy-to-understand reports so that he/she can better manage their time."

The focus of *The Survey Suite* is on the amount of time you spend actually interacting with the programs on your computer rather than on what you are actually typing. It can be particularly useful for keeping an eye on telecommuting employees, because the software is designed to run locally on an employee's PC and then transmit the results of its observations to a central database. *The Survey Suite* gathers its information during the course of a day and then transmits it to the central server whenever a network or Internet connection is opened.

A company that installs a keystroke or software monitoring program may have to deal with employee morale issues, but there are no legal barriers to the use of such programs. The information gathered by such programs is not "in transit" within the meaning of the Electronic Communications Privacy Act, so its collection does not constitute an "interception." More importantly, whatever expectation of privacy employees might have with respect to their actual keystrokes or the time they spend in each program is generally outweighed by the legitimate concerns of business, or rendered nonexistent by company policy.

In addition to the privacy issues, an employer's use of these types of programs (particularly those that focus on counting keystrokes) can raise serious health concerns. Various studies have linked keystroke monitoring to a variety of physical ailments, including carpal tunnel syndrome. There's also growing concern that a high level of electronic surveillance is contributing to a growth in employee psychological problems.

There are no specific figures regarding how many companies use software to count or record keystrokes. These types of surveillance programs are either not being studied or the usage statistics are reflected in the three-quarters of American companies that do at least one type of electronic surveillance. It can be safely assumed, however, that as the cost of installing this type of program falls (right now, it's in the ballpark of ten to fifteen dollars per employee) and the data mining capabilities of business computers increases, the percentage of employees whose every keystroke is recorded will continue to grow.

Perhaps the only serious disincentive to increased keystroke monitoring is that the same keystroke evidence that companies gather to analyze potential misconduct by their employees can be used against them in litigation. As many companies have learned to their dismay with e-mail, archives of electronic data can be a mixed blessing.

# The Privacy of Computer Files

As we saw in Chapter 1, equipping employees with high-powered personal computers poses tremendous productivity issues for employers. Much of this problem has to do with the flexibility of computers: A PC is just as happy running the software for the latest role-playing game as it is running a spreadsheet. And even if an employer successfully limits its PCs to business applications, the PC itself makes no distinction between a word-processing document that contains an assigned market analysis or the latest chapter of your Great American Novel. The temptations for misuse are legion.

It should come as no surprise, then, that surveys show that roughly four out of ten employers periodically search the electronic files on their employees' computers. Companies are looking for a wide range of forbidden materials, ranging from unauthorized software (games, shareware, bootleg copies of programs) to files indicating a lack of productivity (personal work, pornography, offensive jokes, etc.). Lost productivity, of course, is only one reason for this type of search; increasingly, employers are also looking to see if an employee has files on his or her computer that should not be there, indicating a possible involvement in corporate espionage or outright theft.

## The Growing Frequency of Searches

There are a number of tools your employer can use to ferret out inappropriate files on your computer. The simplest tool is the Mark I eyeball. It's amazing how many people store games, jokes, and copies of their personal website in directories on an office computer or network server labeled "games," "jokes," and "my website." Even given the fairly large hard drives in most computers today, it doesn't take long for an experienced system administrator or computer tech to look at a computer's directories and identify evidence of possible misuse.

Nearly as easy to use is the search utility included as a standard tool in most operating systems. A basic search utility can be used to look for files with particular names, files with specific extensions (for instance, the ".jpg" in the file name "bikini.jpg,"), or even for files containing certain words. The main drawback to using the operating system's search utility is that it's not particularly easy to automate; a human being generally has to run it in order to look for potentially offending files. Not surprisingly, there are dozens of software products on the market that allow network administrators and management to automate the search process.

The most common type of search is to look for files containing certain words. For instance, at the Coca-Cola headquarters in Atlanta, network administrators might periodically check to see if any employee's computer files or e-mails contain the phrase "secret formula" or "secret ingredients." Of course, this can be a tedious process: For any moderately large corporation, the number of potential keywords can be huge.

It's slightly easier and more efficient to search for files with extensions that are associated with specific types of materials. An employer who is concerned that you might be looking at Internet pornography can search for files ending in ".jpg" (the extension of the most common compression format used to save photographs on the Web) or ".mpg" (the extension for the most common video compression format). As we'll see later in this chapter, if you're looking at those types of materials on the World Wide Web, copies of the images or movies you've viewed may remain on your hard drive even if you haven't deliberately saved them.

Not every file extension is associated with a particular type of material. For instance, while the files that run computer games generally end in ".exe," the ".exe" extension also covers most of the programs that are designed to run on a Windows-based computer. A search for ".exe" will bring up a list of nearly every program on the computer. The employer can always search for games by name, but with thousands of games on the market, that process could be a little tedious.

Sensing a need seven years ago, a company called Apreo (formerly DVD Software, Inc.) released *AntiGame*, which as the name implies is specifically designed to prevent game-playing. The Irvine, California, company claims that its current version, *AntiGame Plus*, is capable of detecting over 20,000 different games. In addition, purchasers can create their own library of banned programs, and *AntiGame Plus* will search for those as well. Recently,

Apreo has begun offering software that will perform the same functions for peer-to-peer programs and MP3s.

From an employer's perspective, *AntiGame Plus* offers two key benefits. First, in a networked environment, a company's computer technicians can use the program to scan your computer from a remote location; you will most likely be completely unaware that *Antigame Plus* is checking your hard drive for the latest version of *Warcraft 3: Reign of Chaos*.

Second, simply changing the name of a game to something innocuous like "spellcheck.exe" will not fool the surveillance program. *AntiGame Plus* is able to see through such deception by searching your hard drive for data strings, called signatures, that it associates with specific games. (It's the same technique used by antiviral software to identify viruses on your computer disks.) Even if you change the name of the file containing a game's program, the content of the program remains unchanged, and that's what *AntiGame Plus* is programmed to identify. On systems with a full-time Internet connection, the *AntiGame Plus* software can update its library of game signatures automatically.

Once *AntiGame Plus* has identified a game or other banned program, it can either delete the program and its components, or send a notice to the network administrator with a list of the games that it found on each computer. Apreo states that there are currently 1,200 organizations around the world that use its detection software. The company has recently started marketing a companion program, *SoundJudgment*, that searches out and destroys MP3s and peer-to-peer file-sharing programs.

Even Congress became involved—albeit briefly—in the issue of using business computers to play games. In July 1997, Senator Lauch Faircloth (North Carolina) proposed a bill, the Responsive Government Act, that would have required that games be eliminated from all government computers and would have banned the government from purchasing computers with games preloaded.[2] On a unanimous vote, the Senate agreed to attach Senator Faircloth's bill to that year's Treasury and General Government bill, but his proposal was stripped from the conference committee report and never became law. To the extent that Congress has paid any attention to computer games recently, it's mainly been in the context of online gambling or the marketing of video games to children.

## Computer Forensics: Why It's So Hard to Escape Your Past

One of the major goals of the software industry over the last fifteen years has been to create operating systems that are easier to use than the dreaded DOS C:> prompt. The chief strategy in making systems "user friendly" has been to incorporate features that emulate elements of a real office: The main part of the screen is referred to as the "desktop," information is stored in "files," which in turn are put in "folders," and deleted information is dragged to either a "trash can" (Macintosh, which Steve Jobs borrowed from Xerox PARC) or a "recycle bin" (Windows, which Bill Gates borrowed from Jobs).

Perhaps the most enduring myth is that when a file is put in the trash can or recycle bin, it's actually removed from the computer system. But just like in the three-dimensional world, throwing something in an electronic trash can is only the first step in the process of deleting it. All too often, material that you think you've "deleted" may still be somewhere on your hard drive. The practical consequence is that this type of material can frequently be recovered by your boss, a private investigator, or a federal or state prosecutor. This tendency of information to linger in the nooks and crannies of computers has proven to be a tremendous boon for lawyers, in particular, offering them a powerful new source of evidence for litigation.

The difficulty in cleaning information from a computer (and the ease with which it can be recovered) stems from two main factors. First, as most of us are painfully aware, one of the by-products of a consumer-oriented society is that stuff expands to fill available space. Anyone who's moved recently, or who's cleaned out an elderly relative's home, can attest to the remarkable amount of stuff that somehow accumulates over the years.

Over the last twenty years, we've undergone the electronic equivalent of moving from our first student apartment to a Beverly Hills mansion. In the early 1980s, a 10-megabyte hard drive would cost you about $3,000; by the summer of 2002, even the most basic $1,000 computer was routinely equipped with a 30- or 40-gigabyte hard drive. Thanks in large part to growing consumer interest in music and video editing, hard drives of 60 or 70 gigabytes are increasingly common.

In addition to the computer's internal hard drive, we can also choose from a bewildering variety of external storage media, including:

- The soon-to-be-obsolete floppy disk (1.2 megabytes per disk)

- Zip disks (100–250 megabytes per disk)

- CD-ROMs (640 megabytes per disk)

- Jazz disks (one gigabyte and up)

- Flash memory sticks (one gigabyte and up)

- External hard drives (5 gigabytes and up)

On the immediate horizon are burnable DVDs, which will initially allow us to store 7 to 8 gigabytes of information per disk; anticipated advances in technology will increase the per-disk capacity of DVDs to over 30 gigabytes; and 50-gigabyte disks are not much farther down the road.

The most immediate impact of all of this storage space is the steady accumulation of vast amounts of *digital* stuff—huge, feature-laden programs (also known as bloatware); enormous quantities of songs, pictures, and increasingly, videos; installation files for various programs; assorted temporary files generated by the operating system; and so on. Thanks to the ongoing advances in storage capacity, computer users have little incentive to clean off their hard drives. It's as if you hired a contractor to expand the size of your basement every time it got full so you could keep going to flea markets to collect more stuff.

But even if you wanted to keep your computer's hard drive uncluttered, the computer operating system that you use was written to make it very difficult to successfully eliminate unwanted material.[3]

## The Durability of Electronic Data

In the late 1970s and early 1980s when Bill Gates and Paul Allen were first working on what would eventually become MS-DOS (the Microsoft Disk Operating System), designing an operating system was a tremendous challenge, given the extremely tight constraints on processor speed, memory, and disk space. When a computer user instructed her PC to save a file, DOS carved the file into small chunks and stored each chunk in a separate sector on a floppy disk, beginning with the first available sector and continuing until the entire file was saved. A separate file on the floppy disk known as the File Allocation Table (FAT) was then updated with the name of the file and the number of each sector containing data for that file.[4] To retrieve a file, DOS went to the File Allocation Table, looked up the name of the file, went to each of the listed sectors, and put the data together.

When the time came to add another new file to the disk, DOS checked the File Allocation Table to find the first available sector of space. DOS then continued storing the file sector-by-sector. Remarkably enough, nearly twenty-five years later, that's still the basic process used by Windows-based computers to store files.

Given the hardware limitations at the time, Gates and Allen decided that when a user wanted to delete a file, it would take DOS too long to wipe out the data contained in every sector. It would be easier, they realized, simply to delete the first letter of the file name in the File Allocation Table. For instance, if you instructed a computer running DOS to delete a file named "resume.txt," the entry for that file in the FAT would be changed to "?esume.txt." When DOS next looked for free disk space and saw a file name with a question mark at the beginning, it would know that the sectors associated with that file were available for storing new data.

The significance of the programming choice made by Gates and Allen is that when you delete a file on your computer, all of the data associated with that file remains intact on the hard drive or disk; the only thing that is altered is the file name.

Eventually, some or all of the data associated with a deleted file gets overwritten by new files. As is the case with so much of life, however, timing is everything. How quickly a sector in a deleted file gets overwritten by new data depends on a variety of factors, including how frequently you use your computer, the size of the disk containing the sector, the types of programs that you store and run using that disk, etc. On a floppy disk, available sectors may get overwritten in an afternoon; on a 70-gigabyte hard drive, a given sector may not get overwritten for months. And as long as information from a "deleted" file exists on a disk, it can be retrieved.

Recent versions of Windows have added another step to the deletion of computer files. Today, when you delete a file, the system first stores the file in a system directory called the recycle bin. If you decide to recover a file from the recycle bin, you simply open the directory, highlight the file, and choose "restore" from the menu options. The operating system returns the file to its original location. If you wish, you can instruct Windows to "empty" the recycle bin. Windows then changes the first letter in the File Allocation Table for each of the deleted files. Again, the data in those files does not vanish in a puff of smoke. Instead, it remains on your hard drive until it is overwritten by new data.[5]

The fact that files or fragments of files continue to lurk on computer hard drives after they've been "deleted" has given rise to an entirely new field of investigation known as computer forensics. Prosecutors and defense attorneys alike have discovered the powerful impact that recovered computer files can have. Juries are often very impressed by embarrassing e-mails and memos that are magically recovered from the hidden recesses of a computer hard drive.

Even when no criminal violations have occurred, employers are using computer forensic techniques to assess what an employee has been up to, or how much damage a discharged employee might have done before he left. The detective agency Kroll Associates reported in 1997 that employee investigations of computer files had risen a steady 30 percent per year over the preceding three years. Given the amount of valuable information that can often be recovered from an employee's computer, it's not uncommon for private detectives to conduct "midnight raids" of a target cubicle, in which they sweep up any potential evidence, from the employee's Rolodex to her computer.[6]

Because of the value that recovered files can have, two competing software industries have developed: one that focuses on the recovery of such materials, and one that focuses on their complete and utter destruction.

In the recovery field, the industry leader is *EnCase*, a computer forensics product created and distributed by Pasadena-based Guidance Software. In the five years since the program was first released, *EnCase* has become the preferred file recovery tool of more than 7,000 businesses and government agencies around the world. The expensive software—$1,995 per license for government and educational facilities, $2,495 for the private sector—has a wide range of capabilities, but its most salient features are its ability to produce an exact, sector-by-sector replica of a hard drive and then analyze that hard drive for any deleted materials. Among other things, the software maintains the time stamp that Windows attaches to each file, which makes it possible for investigators to construct detailed chronologies of activity that took place on the computer.

What *EnCase* seeks to preserve, other programs seek to permanently destroy. The current industry leader among bit-burners is *Evidence Eliminator*, a program manufactured by the aptly named Robin Hood Software, Ltd., in Nottingham, England. The main function of the software is to sift through and eliminate unwanted data from all of the nooks and crannies where information about your computer use might linger. Once it has done so, then *Evidence Eliminator* writes over every unallocated or empty sector with a string of zeros, which will foil most conventional recovery efforts. The program can also be instructed to overwrite deleted material and empty space according to Department of Defense specifications, which require overwriting with zeros, then ones, then a random character, with each step repeated up to seven times.[7]

In the right setting, a program like *Evidence Eliminator* can be a powerful tool for protecting your privacy. However, it's important to recognize its limitations as a tool for protecting your privacy in the workplace. First, *Evidence Eliminator* and similar programs are likely to be considered unauthorized software, and their discovery on your computer may raise red flags with your boss. Second, many of the mechanisms available to your employer for tracking your computer activity would be unaffected by *Evidence Eliminator* or any other type of antiforensic tool—they will not, for instance, prevent your employer from viewing e-mail you send, monitoring your Web activity, or even recording your keystrokes.

And lastly (and this is the most common misunderstanding regarding antiforensic software), if you forget to delete a particular image or file, *Evidence Eliminator* will not know that you wanted it deleted, and it will remain on your hard drive.

## The Legality of Searches

Employers are often interested in conducting searches of the physical space in which you work. The rules governing such searches depend on the type of employer for which you work. If you work for a public employer, the employer's ability to search is restricted by the Fourth Amendment prohibition against unreasonable search and seizure. Under the leading case, *O'Connor* v. *Ortega*, the first question is whether a public employee had a "reasonable expectation of privacy" in the area being searched.[8] If the answer to that is yes, then the next question is whether the search itself was reasonable under the circumstances. Specifically, courts look to whether the search was reasonably calculated to further the employer's interest in supervision, control of the workplace, and efficiency.

The same general principles are applied to employer searches of the computer equipment used by their employees. One recent case, *Leventhal* v. *Knapek*, illustrates the difficulty that even public employees have in successfully protecting their computer files from searches by their employers.[9] An employee named Gary Leventhal, a principal accountant with the New York Department of Transportation, filed suit after his computer was searched during an investigation into his alleged use of company time to conduct non-DOT business.

Investigators found a hidden directory on Leventhal's computer and some files that indicated that Leventhal was preparing tax returns on DOT time. Leventhal challenged the search, arguing that his Fourth Amendment rights against unreasonable search and seizure had been violated. The U.S. Court of Appeals for the Second Circuit agreed with Leventhal that he had a reasonable expectation of privacy with respect to the contents of his computer. However, the court also found that the DOT was justified in beginning its investigation of Leventhal, and that the search of his computer files was reasonable in scope.

As we saw earlier, the Fourth Amendment does not protect people who work for private businesses from actions taken by their employers. However, some states do offer employees either constitutional or statutory privacy rights, and all states recognize lawsuits claiming an invasion of privacy. Typically, courts have recognized that private employees do have a reasonable expectation of privacy in areas that are typically set aside for the employee's personal use, including lockers, desks, office space, mail received at work that is marked "personal," and even computer files.

The problem for private employees (and to some extent for public employees as well), as the Second Circuit pointed out in *Leventhal*, is that an employee's reasonable expectation of privacy largely vanishes if their employer specifically notifies them that they have no expectation of privacy. As a result, more and more lawyers are recommending to their business clients that they have their employees sign policy statements that clearly delineate the boundaries of their privacy rights at work.

Moreover, if your employer has a reasonable basis for suspecting you of misconduct, then even if you do have an expectation of privacy in the files on your computer, your employer can override that expectation in order to protect its property interests.

## The Privacy of E-Mail

Since the widespread adoption of the Internet by the general public, electronic correspondence has grown to staggering levels: The research firm The Gartner Group estimated that in 2001, more than 5.5 *trillion* e-mails were sent worldwide, or roughly 15 billion messages per day. The research analyst group International Data Corporation predicts that by 2006, the *daily* e-mail count will quadruple, to something in the range of 60 billion messages. By contrast, the U.S. Postal Service handled roughly 200 billion pieces of mail for all of 2001.[10]

E-mail is rapidly becoming the predominant form of business communication. The advantages are self-evident: speed, convenience, low cost, ease of use, the elimination of phone tag, and so forth. But e-mail is, to put it mildly, a double-edged sword: Indiscreet workplace e-mail writers are, to borrow a cliché, the road kill of the information superhighway. Hardly a week goes by without new stories of employees who have been fired as a result of management disapproval of their workplace correspondence. According to the American Management's Association's most recent annual workplace survey, roughly one-half of all employers in this country periodically review their employees' e-mails, and one-third of all businesses have fired someone for inappropriate use of company e-mail or improper Web surfing.

To understand the role that e-mail is playing in employment and the ease with which it can be monitored, it's useful to take a closer look at this incredibly popular form of communication.

### Searching Electronic Mail

Much of the misconception regarding e-mail privacy stems from the way it mirrors the characteristics of other types of communication: It's a written communication, which implies the privacy of first-class mail, and it's person-to-person and virtually instantaneous, which suggests the privacy of a telephone conversation. Unfortunately, e-mail lacks the privacy protection given to either form of communication.

To begin with, the mere fact that an e-mail is a written communication from one person to another person (or a group of people) accords it no particular protection. Only letters that are sealed, stamped, and deposited in a U.S. Postal Service mailbox are entitled to the privacy protection offered by federal law. Since e-mail doesn't remotely conform to postal regulations, it has roughly the same privacy protection enjoyed by postcards, and no one would rationally consider a postcard sent through the mails to be a private document. But when it is mailed in a sealed envelope, even the raunchiest "You're Turning Forty" birthday card has more legal protection than the most sensitive or profound e-mail.

Telephone calls also offer employees greater privacy protection than e-mails. The Electronic Communications Privacy Act (ECPA), which Congress adopted in 1986, divides electronic communications into two categories: stored communications and communications in transit. Electronic communications that are in transit are entitled to roughly the same protection accorded voice communication—that is, an employer cannot intercept them or record them (subject to certain exceptions). But unlike voice communication, which is almost always live, e-mail is almost always stored in one fashion or another.[11] As long as an employer is searching a stored collection of e-mail, it can poke and pry at will.

The potential storage sites for your e-mails are myriad. Every e-mail program contains an option to copy the messages you send to a "sent" folder on your computer, and most computer users either purposely choose to have their messages saved or are oblivious to the fact that the program is doing so automatically. As we've seen, assuming that you've been given notice of the possibility of searching, your company can search the files on your computer at its discretion, and that includes the contents of your "sent" folder, your inbox, your "draft" folder, and anything else that it thinks might be interesting.

Even if you don't save copies of your e-mail on your computer, the normal operation of a corporate network creates other storage opportunities. When you click "send" on your office network computer, for instance, your e-mail program typically forwards your e-mail to the network mail server, which breaks the message into packets and sends them over the Internet toward their destination. For the purposes of the Electronic Communications Privacy Act, the e-mail's arrival at the network mail server is the equivalent of an airport layover. Even if the retransmission of your e-mail is virtually instantaneous, its brief stop in the network mail server constitutes "storage" for the purposes of employer investigation and review.

In some workplaces, incoming and outgoing employee e-mail is stored on a mail server, which the company copies each evening onto another hard drive or backup tape. Tape archives are typically kept for a finite period of time (usually thirty days or so), but it's not uncommon for e-mails that are months or even years old to be retrieved from archives. How long a particular company maintains its electronic archives depends on its own retention policy; companies need to balance a number of competing concerns including data integrity and protection, the ability to review the electronic behavior of their employees, and the legal exposure they risk by having months and months of electronic materials on file.[12]

## E-Mail Firings and Other Tales of Electronic Woe

Undoubtedly, Michael Smyth never intended to carve himself out a permanent place in the battle over workplace privacy rights. Nonetheless, his name is inextricably linked with one of the first federal court decisions regarding the privacy of e-mail. In October 1994, Smyth, a regional operations manager for the Pillsbury Company in Philadelphia, received some e-mails from his supervisor on his home computer. The e-mails originated on an internal e-mail system set up and maintained by Pillsbury, and Smyth's responses traveled across the same system on their way back to his supervisor.

During this e-mail exchange, Smyth ridiculed Pillsbury's sales management, threatened to "kill the back-stabbing bastards," and referred to a holiday party at Pillsbury as a "Jim Jones Kool-Aid affair." A company executive who reportedly saw a copy of that message in an office printer undertook a thorough review of all of Smyth's e-mails, and on February 1, 1995, Smyth was fired by Pillsbury "for transmitting what it deemed to be inappropriate and unprofessional comments over defendant's e-mail system." Smyth sued to regain his job, arguing that Pillsbury had explicitly promised that all e-mails would remain privileged and confidential. In fact, the District Court found that Pillsbury had also promised that e-mails "could not be intercepted and used by defendant against its employees as grounds for termination or reprimand."

The court agreed that Pillsbury had broken its promise to Smyth, but held that he had no claim against the company nonetheless.[13] Its language starkly underscores the limited privacy rights that employees have in their e-mail messages:

> . . . unlike urinalysis and personal property searches, we do not find a reasonable expectation of privacy in e-mail communications voluntarily made by an employee to his supervisor over the company e-mail system notwithstanding any assurances that such communications would not be intercepted by management. Once plaintiff communicated the alleged unprofessional comments to a second person (his supervisor) over an e-mail system which was apparently utilized by the entire company, any reasonable expectation of privacy was lost . . . even if we found that an employee had a reasonable expectation of privacy in the contents of his e-mail communications . . . we do not find that a reasonable person would consider the defendant's intercep-

tion of these communications to be a substantial and highly offensive invasion of his privacy . . . by intercepting such communications, the company is not . . . requiring the employee to disclose any personal information about himself or invading the employee's person or personal effects. Moreover, the company's interest in preventing inappropriate and unprofessional comments or even illegal activity over its e-mail system outweighs any privacy interest the employee may have in those comments.

Far more than the telephone, e-mail underscores the tension between an employee's work and his personal life. While most employees would agree that it would not be appropriate to spend large amounts of time making personal phone calls in the office, it's more difficult to see the harm in dashing off a few quick e-mails to family and friends. From the employer's perspective, however, personal e-mails are more problematic than personal telephone calls: The time required to send even a "quick" e-mail adds up over the course of the day, and even more distressingly, an inappropriate e-mail can later play a starring role in litigation against the company.

It was precisely those types of concerns that have led hundreds, if not thousands, of companies to fire employees for improper use of e-mail. Here are just a few examples, drawn from mid-1999 to late 2000:

■ In Michigan, Dow Chemical fired twenty-nine employees and suspended forty-two others for sending pornographic or "violent" images over the company e-mail system.

■ After a review of its employee e-mail archives, *The New York Times* fired twenty-three workers for distributing pornography and dirty jokes by e-mail.

■ Xerox fired twenty-two people from its Virginia office for sending offensive e-mails.

■ The St. Louis brokerage Edward Jones & Co. fired eighteen employees and warned forty-one others about sending pornography across the company e-mail system.

By now, employers can rely with confidence on the long line of court decisions that have resolved the tension between the company's property and employee privacy interests in favor of businesses. Whatever common law interests in privacy you may think you have in your electronic communications are superseded by the fact that your employer owns and operates the system over which the e-mail travels.

# The Privacy of Web Surfing

At the end of each business trip or family vacation, when you've lugged your weary self home, the first cold dash of reality is unpacking. Out from the luggage come the travel-worn clothes, souvenirs, unsent postcards, flight-surviving paperbacks, purloined toiletries, amusement park stubs, credit card receipts, local coinage, and tourist maps. This motley collection of stuff offers a good idea of where you went, the food you ate, and what you did while you were away.

Each time that you travel the World Wide Web, you bring back precisely the same type of post-travel tidbits, albeit in electronic form. It's a little more difficult to view the remnants of your Web journeys; the trade-off, however, is that the record of the journey maintained by your computer is far more detailed than anything that comes out of your suitcase.

## The Lure of Office Web Surfing

The popularity of Web surfing in the office can be traced to one main factor: Even today, the Internet connections in most offices are far faster than the connections that most employees have at home. That helps to explain why graphics-intensive sites like sports news, stock trading, and pornography see strong surges in activity beginning at 9:00 A.M. East Coast Time.

As we saw in Chapter 1, Web surfing by employees raises two main concerns for employers: productivity and liability due to the dissemination of inappropriate materials. Without adequate discipline, the World Wide Web can be a tremendous time sink; no other medium comes close to matching the Internet's depth of materials, interactivity, and sheer distractive potential.

Ironically, nonproductive Web surfing can be a problem for adult companies as well. Juli Stone, the director of sales and marketing for Falcon Foto, one of the largest providers of content for adult websites, has had to contend with employees who don't spend enough time surfing porn sites. "People have gotten into trouble at our office," Stone said, "for visiting nonporn sites too often. One guy was fired for spending all day monitoring his auctions on eBay." Falcon Foto doesn't have a written policy regarding Web use, Stone reported. "It's easy enough to walk around the office and see what everyone is doing," she said. "If they're not looking at a porn site, they're not working."

The other concern is that unfettered Web surfing carries a real risk of liability for employers—there is a simply staggering amount of offensive material online, the vast majority of which can be downloaded and redistributed throughout a company with a few clicks of a mouse. A company that does not take steps to limit or discourage the distribution of offensive materials runs a serious risk of litigation alleging a hostile work environment.

## Log Files, Browser Caches, Packet Sniffers, and Filters and Monitors

A company that wants to monitor your Web surfing activity has an almost endless number of options for doing so, and for doing so without your knowledge. In reality, many companies tell their employees they are monitoring Web activity in the hope that advance notice will cut down on the problem; some say they monitor but actually don't; the majority, however, monitor in one fashion or another without any notice to their employees at all. Currently, there is no legal requirement for an employer to tell its employees that it is monitoring Web surfing activity.

A company's Web surveillance options fall generally into one of the following four categories:

1. Log files and cookies

2. Browser caches

3. Packet sniffers

4. Filters and monitors

Each of these various monitoring techniques offers an employer valuable insight into how you're spending your time on the World Wide Web; taken together, they can form a devastatingly accurate picture of your surfing habits.

■ *Log Files.* Log files are the readily visible lists of resources that you've visited online. The two most popular browsers—Netscape *Navigator* and Microsoft's *Internet Explorer*—maintain log files to help make your journeys in cyberspace more convenient. *Navigator,* for example, has a drop-down button that reveals a list of the various sites that you've visited recently. *Navigator* also maintains an extensive history list as part of its normal operation. The history list shows every website that you've visited recently, broken down day by day (you or the network administrator can set the number of days to be recorded). If your network administrator wishes to do so, she can quite easily look at your drop-down list or your browser's history file and get a pretty good idea of what sites you've been visiting.

■ *Browser Caches.* Browser caches are less readily accessible than log files, but the information that they contain is far more detailed and potentially damaging. A browser displays Web pages on your computer screen by downloading all of the components of the Web page (images, banners, text, buttons, etc., each of which is a separate computer file), storing the files on your computer's hard drive, and then putting them back together on your screen so that you can view the page's information. The directory (or directories) in which the pieces of the various Web pages are stored as they are downloaded is called the browser cache.

Although the files contained in the browser cache are only fragments of larger Web pages, it's not difficult to get a pretty good sense of the pages from which they were drawn. Depending on your browser settings and the size of your computer's hard drive, your cache directory may contain hundreds or thousands of files used to make up complete Web pages, ranging from buttons and banners to text to images—basically, anything that you've viewed recently on a Web page. In addition, the cache directory tracks the address of the Web page from which something was downloaded, the date it was first accessed, the date it was last accessed, and so on. Given the sheer amount of information available, it's not surprising that browser caches have become a particularly popular source of investigation for company managers, prosecutors, and litigation attorneys.

■ *Packet Sniffers.* When information (an e-mail or Web page, for instance) is sent from one computer to another across the Internet, it is broken into multiple units called "packets." Each packet is electronically stamped with the information needed to deliver the message to the intended recipient and reconstruct the data when all of the packets arrive at their destination. By breaking messages and data into packets, the Internet can work more efficiently (computers can balance workload by sending packets along different routes) and protect itself from damage (if one computer system goes down, packets can be routed around the failed system).

A "packet sniffer" is a computer program that is installed on a computer that sends and receives Internet traffic. It looks at each packet that goes through the system, and if the packet contains certain words or phrases, the program saves the packet for further review. Most if not all of the Web monitoring or filtering programs discussed below are packet sniffers. If the software is installed on your computer, it will only look at the traffic between your computer and the Internet. If the software is installed on your company's main gateway computer or Internet service provider, then the software can be configured to look at every packet flowing in and out of your company.

■ *Filters and Monitors.* Most employers would rather that inappropriate materials never show up on your computer in the first place. There are two main approaches that businesses can take to restrict inappropriate Web surfing: Announce that they are monitoring online activity and hope that employees will regulate their own behavior, or install one of the myriad filtering programs designed to actively block access to inappropriate materials.

One of the current leaders in workplace filtering software is Websense, Inc., a San Diego-based software company that markets a server-based filtering program by the same name. Websense is actively working to create and dominate a new industry sector, "employee Internet management" (EIM). Websense claims that there are more than 17,500 organizations using its software, including Compaq (now Hewlett-Packard), General Motors, American Express, Blue Shield, Calvin Klein, IBM, and Pepsi, and that on any given day, nearly 7 million employees "are managed with the company's software."

*Websense* works by intercepting Web page requests from each browser and comparing the website address to the addresses listed in a database of over 3.5 million websites. The websites contained in the database are organized into thirty-one categories; companies that install the software can choose which categories of sites the software should block. Among the categories most typically blocked are:

- Adult material, including adult content, nudity, sex, sex education, and lingerie and swimsuit

- Drugs, including abused drugs, prescribed medications, supplements/unregulated compounds, and marijuana

- Gambling

- Illegal/questionable, covering sites that provide instruction in or promote criminal activity

- Racism/hate

- Violence

Employers can also choose to block other types of sites, ranging from general entertainment to shopping to job search information. *Websense* also provides filtering to premium customers for three different groups of materials:

- Productivity management, which blocks advertisements, freeware/shareware downloads, instant messaging, message boards and clubs, online brokerages and trading, and pay-to-surf sites

- Bandwidth management, which blocks Internet radio and TV, streaming media, peer-to-peer file sharing, personal network storage and backup, and Internet telephony

■ Malicious websites

In theory, *Websense* or one of its dozens of competitors can be implemented in such a way as to have relatively little impact on employee privacy. The software's sole function, for instance, could be to block access to forbidden websites. But in these days of stunning computing power, virtually unlimited storage space, and nearly instantaneous communication, restricting filtering software to simply blocking sites is like using grapes only to make jelly. There's just so much more you can do with them.

In addition to blocking access to forbidden sites, *Websense* also contains a module called the *Websense Reporter*, which enables employers to track the types of websites being visited by employees, list the amount of time that employees spend surfing, determine whether Web access policies need to be changed, and calculate the cost to the business of nonwork-related surfing.

Using a program like *Websense* can pose some risks for employers as well. One of the components of the *Websense* suite is the *Webcatcher*, which automatically adds sites to the filter database, depending on the surfing habits of a company's employees. Over time, a utility like *Webcatcher* could enable Websense to develop fairly detailed information about the activities of its customers and their employees. In addition, the records maintained by a utility like the *Websense Reporter* could prove useful in corporate litigation. For instance, records indicating that some of a company's employees were spending hours each day surfing adult websites might well support a claim that a hostile work environment exists.

## Hardware Monitoring Tools

Although the vast majority of tools for monitoring Web activity are software based, there are a few hardware solutions available to the suspicious employer. For instance, the website e-bugging.com offers the "PC Monitor," a hardware-only monitoring tool. The PC Monitor is a small device, approximately two inches long and one-half inch in diameter, containing a microcontroller and a fixed amount of nonvolatile memory.[14] Installing the PC Monitor takes less than a minute: All that's required is to unplug the keyboard cable from the back of the computer, plug the PC Monitor into the keyboard port, and then plug the keyboard cable into the PC Monitor.

Once installed, the PC Monitor records every keystroke made on the keyboard, up to the limits of its memory: 8Kb (forty-nine dollars), 32Kb (ninety-nine dollars), or 64Kb ($159). Since each keystroke takes up one byte, the largest PC Monitor can store roughly 64,000 keystrokes, which is about how many keystrokes it took to write this chapter.

The PC Monitor is easy to use without the employee's knowledge. Since all of the Monitor's electronics and monitoring are self-contained, it does not cause any unusual hard drive or CPU activity, and few computer users would think to check the back of their computer every time they sit down to use it. It's remotely possible that someone could stumble across the contents of the PC Monitor's memory by accident, but with a sufficiently secure password, the chances of that happening are fairly small.

Another popular option for employers who wish to monitor their employees' Web surfing is to use a hidden video camera pointed at an employee's monitor. Depending on the layout of the workplace, an employer could configure the video set-up so that a number of monitors could be viewed at the same time.

Improvements in wireless technology will also make monitoring employees' Internet use easier. In the not-too-distant future, most personal computers will come equipped with peripherals (like keyboards and mice) that have wireless technology built into them. The leading contender today is called Bluetooth, a radio frequency-based technology that allows devices to communicate with each other without cables. A Bluetooth-enabled device will be equipped with a small microchip containing a radio module capable of transmitting and receiving at around 2.45 Ghz, a frequency that is essentially unused for other purposes. Each microchip will have built into it both software controls and unique identity codes so that the device can be positively identified by other devices, and so that only those devices that have been given permission to communicate can do so.

The adoption of wireless devices like Bluetooth-equipped keyboards (Microsoft received approval for its version from the Federal Communications Commission in mid-August 2002) will give employers another avenue for monitoring and recording the keystrokes of an entire office. Nobody is advertising tools for conducting eavesdropping on Bluetooth devices so far, but the day can't be far off. Recognizing the dangers of interception, Bluetooth developers are working aggressively to develop techniques to minimize unauthorized eavesdropping by corporate spies. But a corporation may well feel no compunction about intercepting the transmissions of its own Bluetooth devices for surveillance purposes and will be in a much better position to do so than some corporate interloper.

## No Legal Protection for Surfing or Game Playing

Do you have any reasonable expectation of privacy in your surfing habits or the Web information stored on your computer? In a word, no. Even if you could credibly argue that you have a reasonable privacy interest in the URLs that you type into your Web browser, that minimal privacy interest is easily trumped by the very real business concerns faced by your employer: productivity, appropriate use of bandwidth, and reduction of potential sources of liability. In fact, the situation is worse than you may think: Not only do you have no privacy interest in your Web surfing habits at work, you have no possessory interest either. If you choose to reveal your interests or hobbies or consumer preferences by using your office computer to access the Internet, that information is increasingly a potential source of revenue for your employer. Admittedly, the vast majority of businesses don't have enough employees to interest potential marketers, but there are certainly a large number that do. For instance, if the Web surfing habits (or attempted habits) of the 7 million people currently monitored by *Websense* could be aggregated (which certainly could be done), that's a reasonable pool of marketing data. The same is true for Websense's larger individual clients, including General Motors (265,000 employees), American Express (84,400), Blue Shield (150,000), IBM (319,876), and Pepsi (37,000).[15]

Do you surf the Web each morning for news about your favorite sports team? Perhaps your employer can make a few cents marketing that information to the NBA or the NFL. Have you been recently e-mailing your brother about your receding hairline? Companies that specialize in hair replacement treatments might be interested in purchasing that information to help target their marketing. The possibilities for matching particular employees with particular marketers are unlimited.

The thought of your employer analyzing your e-mails and Web surfing habits for potentially marketable information may be abhorrent to you. But as we've seen, employees have very few (if any) real privacy rights when it comes to information transmitted across a company-owned computer system. As matters currently stand, employers don't get anything back from personal use of Internet access by employees, apart from decreased productivity and greater potential liability. The sale of such data may be a price that employees have to pay if they choose to reveal their interests at work.

## Data Mining: There's Gold in Them Thar Bits

Web surfing data is not the only source of potentially valuable employee information. One of the more interesting by-products of technology is the phenomenal value that it can add to existing data. It's all well and good to have millions of census forms moldering in a government warehouse, but if they have to be sorted and collated by hand, their value and utility is limited. Even the relatively cumbersome punch card technology helped make the data on those census forms much more useful. Computers, with their vastly faster data handling capabilities, more compact storage, and programmability, are capable of extracting even greater value. With the enormous improvements taking place in computing power, massive amounts of data can be manipulated, sorted, massaged, and viewed from an almost infinite number of angles.

The ability of computers to organize and extract value from large databases has given rise to a new term and a new segment of the software industry: data mining. The key element in data mining is the discovery of relationships between various pieces of data. Using the information contained in its customer database, for instance, an online retailer might quickly be able to determine which items in its inventory are doing well in different areas of the country. With a little more massaging, a company can tailor its e-mail advertisements to its customers based on their recent purchases, both in terms of interest and the amount they typically spend on given types of products.

During the summer of 1999, the online bookstore Amazon.com received some criticism for its enthusiastic implementation of data mining technology. Using a combination of zip codes and domain names, Amazon began compiling specialized bestseller lists, detailing the most popular books in specific communities, businesses, and educational institutions. Amazon called its new feature "purchase circles," and marketed them both as a diversion and as a gift-giving guide. If your brother worked for National Semiconductor, for instance, you might think about giving him a copy of *101 Nights of Grrreat Sex*, which hit the National Semiconductor bestseller list that summer.

The public outcry that followed the introduction of purchase circles gave Amazon some pause, and the company instituted policies (albeit moderately well-hidden ones) that allow customers to block the collection of their purchase information. The company also no longer promotes its purchase circles as aggressively as it first did, although you can still find the top-selling books for various communities, governmental bodies, and organizations. On October 6, 2002, for example, the top five best-selling books among Microsoft employees were:

- *Yookoso! An Invitation to Contemporary Japanese* (student edition plus listening comprehension audio cassette)

- *Trust on Trial: How the Microsoft Case is Reframing the Rules of Competition*

- *Proudly Serving My Corporate Masters: What I Learned in Ten Years as a Microsoft Programmer*

■ *The Person and The Situation*

■ *Communicating and Mobile Systems: The Pi-Calculus*

One industry that has quickly adopted data mining technology is the National Basketball Association. A number of teams in the NBA use an IBM program called *Advanced Scout*, which analyzes the reams of data generated during the league's basketball games. Coaches can download the data, use *Advanced Scout* to organize and assess it, and then run different queries on the data to locate and identify patterns and trends. The information provided by *Advanced Scout* can then be used to make game films more informative and educational for both the coaching staff and players.

Similar technology is making its way into more mainstream companies, where the queries are not so much "who are the best scorers and in what game situations?" as they are "who are our best salespeople and with what types of customers?" Software that allows employers to ask those types of questions, of course, is entirely in keeping with the normal goals of business—figuring out how to make the best use of the assets on hand, so as to maximize profits and minimize costs.

Some of the data mining software that's hitting the market threatens to go beyond the boundaries of normal business analysis. For instance, a Boulder, Colorado software company called Fatline recently released a new program called *FastTracker*. Ostensibly, *FastTracker* is designed to enable management and employees to analyze all of the information on each other's hard drives so that when a new issue arises or specific information is required, it's possible to locate the person in the organization who is most knowledgeable.

An important subsidiary purpose of *FastTracker* is to introduce peer-to-peer pressure into the workplace, by making it possible for employees to see what other employees are doing on the Web or are storing on their hard drives. While a coworker's Web surfing habits might reveal that she has developed an expertise in an important new technology, privacy specialists are concerned that peer-to-peer peering will further eroded employee privacy.

A similar, albeit more tightly controlled product, *AltaVista Enterprise Search*, is offered by former search engine leader AltaVista. Like *FastTracker*, the *AV Enterprise Search* program is designed to scan files located in disparate places on a company network and prepare an index that can assist the company in locating information and resources. AltaVista stresses that its program is structured in such a way that a company's management can limit the resources available to employees. Without such controls, it might be possible for employees to gain access to highly sensitive material typically stored on computers in the human resources department: salary schedules, evaluations, medical records, etc.

As we've seen, businesses are fairly cavalier in how they treat their employees' privacy for their own purposes (security, productivity, etc.), but so far, at least, there are no indications that companies are selling large quantities of employee data for economic gain. Most companies are undoubtedly aware that it would be extremely difficult to attract good candidates if they were discovered making a practice of selling private employee information.

The very real possibility exists, nonetheless, that at some point, the value of such information may prove to be too great a temptation. A number of major corporations are saving costs in their human resources departments by providing employee payroll and work history information to a third-party database. When other employers, banks, and income verification services need information about a particular employee's work history, they call the third-party database rather than the employee's former company. By turning employment information over to the central database, companies are able to shrink the size of their HR departments and reduce their personnel costs.

One of the leaders in this growing field is Talx Inc., which operates a service called The Work Number, which prospective employers can call to verify a job applicant's information (at a charge of ten to thirteen dollars per inquiry). Since 1995, Talx has contracted with companies to obtain data on their employees' employment dates and income; in June 2002, the company said that it had 70 million employment records on file. Taking into account duplicate records, Talx says that its Work Number service has information on roughly 20 percent of the American workforce.

Talx minimizes the potential privacy concerns by stating that the data it collects and redistributes is limited to employment dates and salary. The system does not contain more subjective information like job evaluations or recommendations, although it's certainly not hard to imagine a system that would offer copies of your last three evaluations for an additional fee. The Work Number also contains several security checkpoints to prevent unauthorized access: In order to get access to your employment data, your prospective employer must be a subscriber of The Work Number and must have (surprise!) your Social Security number.

The temptation to peddle employee information will surely rise as data mining software grows more sophisticated and allows employers to draw increasingly detailed portraits of their employees. In this regard, employees may ultimately be hoisted by their own petard. The ability of employers to compile detailed information about their employees—information that might eventually be attractive to third parties—is a direct result of the employees' tendency to use company Internet resources to send e-mail, surf the Web, and engage in online chats.

According to a February 2001 *Forbes* article by Victoria Murphy, the growing use of e-mail and Web surfing by employees, when tracked and analyzed by software like *FastTracker* and *AV Enterprise Search*, is allowing businesses to identify employees with particular skills or experience. For instance, if a printer company is considering adding Wi-Fi capabilities to its machines, a manager could use software from companies like Tacit Knowledge Systems or the London-based Autonomy to find out if there's anyone in his company who's been quietly developing expertise in the new technology.

## End Notes

1. "'Sneaky' software may be watching you," CNN.com (February 19, 2002).

2. The bill would also have required service-oriented government agencies to use people instead of machines to answer telephones before 5:00 P.M. EST.

3. Again, this discussion applies primarily to the 85 percent of the country that uses a member of the Windows operating system family or its predecessor, MS-DOS.

4. The File Allocation Table is arguably the most important collection of data on a hard drive or storage disk. It contains the road map that allows the operating system to correctly read every other file on your disk. That's one of the reasons that viruses that target the File Allocation Table are so dangerous; if the File Allocation Table is destroyed, your hard drive becomes an undifferentiated mass of data that is essentially worthless.

5. There's no question that the surprising durability of computer files has been a hidden blessing for thousands of computer users. During my first week as an associate in a Burlington law firm, I earned serious brownie points by helping an older attorney recover a lengthy brief that he had accidentally deleted. Programmer Peter Norton, whose utility I used to recover the file, built a multimillion dollar software company largely on the strength of his disk editing and file recovery programs.

6. Dana Hawkins, "Who's Watching Now?," *U.S. News & World Report* (September 15, 1997).

7. The immense repetition required to comply with DOD specifications results from the fact that with the appropriate technology and a very high-tech lab, some data can still be recovered from drives or disks that have only been overwritten once or twice. Most experts seem to agree that the data on a drive or disk can only be truly destroyed by destroying the drive or disk itself. Bits are remarkably durable little critters.

8. 480 U.S. 709 (1987).

9. ___F.3d ___(2d Cir. 2001).

10. Kendra Mayfield, "Neither Rain nor Hail nor E-Mail," *Wired.com* (June 7, 2001). The postal service claims that e-mail is not a threat, because many of the messages sent by e-mail (jokes, chain letters, multilevel marketing schemes, and so

on), would not have been sent by regular mail anyway. Nonetheless, current predictions are that first-class mail levels will fall an average of 2.5 percent per year from 2003 to 2008. Id. Clearly worried about the impact that e-mail is having on first-class mail, the postal service has floated various plans to charge for the delivery of secure e-mail. None of these plans has borne fruit, however, as the evolution of e-mail technology has vastly outstripped the postal service's ability to design and implement a viable system.

11. Voice mail raises some interesting questions, but is generally considered to fall under the definition of "wire communications," which makes it subject to antiwiretapping laws.

12. While it is obviously illegal to destroy evidence of possible wrongdoing during litigation, companies are generally not penalized if potentially relevant evidence was destroyed during routine archive maintenance.

13. Ironically, Smyth and Pillsbury agreed to a settlement of Smyth's lawsuit against the company on the same day that the District Court dismissed the suit. The court's order, however, was entered before notice of the settlement was filed with the court.

14. "Nonvolatile" means that the memory retains the information stored in it even after the computer's power is turned off.

15. Figures regarding number of employees drawn from capsule corporate summaries prepared by and displayed on the Hoover's Online website (www.hooveron line.com).

# CHAPTER SEVEN

# Tracking Employees by Cell: The Biological Version

For more than 2,400 years, the relationship between physician and patient has been buttressed by a principle of strict confidentiality. In 400 B.C., the Greek physician Hippocrates developed an Oath of Medical Ethics, and among the tenets he crafted was the following:

> What I may see or hear in the course of the treatment or even outside of the treatment in regard to the life of men, which on no account one must spread abroad, I will keep to myself, holding such things shameful to be spoken about.[1]

In 1847, when the American Medical Association was founded, the new organization chose not to adopt the Hippocratic Oath. Instead, the AMA endorsed a Code of Medical Ethics, which contained a similar but slightly less explicit secrecy provision:

> §2. . . . Secrecy and delicacy . . . should be strictly observed; and the familiar and confidential intercourse to which physicians are admitted in their professional visits, should be used with discretion. . . . The obligation of secrecy extends beyond the period of professional services;—none of the privacies of personal and domestic life, no infirmity of disposition or flaw of character observed during professional

attendance, should ever be divulged by him except when he is impera-
tively required to do so.

The vast majority of medical professionals take the concept of confidentiality very seriously. They recognize that their ability to treat their patients depends on the patients' openness with them and their trust that
potentially embarrassing information will be kept private. Few people would
put up with the rigors of medical school and residency without a genuine
desire to help people, and patient confidentiality is an important tool in
being able to properly diagnose and treat the sick.

However, as we'll see in the first part of this chapter, health care costs
are one of the most challenging issues facing the nation's employers. At the
same time, various technological innovations, ranging from more sensitive
drug tests to DNA testing, are making it easier to assess both the current
fitness and future health of employees. Taken together, these trends make it
all too compelling for insurance companies and employers to peer over a
doctor's shoulder as she is examining her patients.

## The Rapidly Fading Privacy of Employee Health Records

A visit to the doctor's office often involves taking off all your clothes, putting
on a remarkably thin gown, and sitting in a chilly room trying to ignore the
draft of cold air running up your backside. Needless to say, that's not something you want to do in the waiting room, which is why you are usually
directed to a small private exam room where you are seen by just a doctor
and perhaps a nurse. Because of the perceived privacy of the exam room,
you are more likely to reveal to the doctor things that you wouldn't reveal
to anyone else.

Increasingly, however, the doctor and nurse are not the only ones in
the exam room with you. If you rely on a health insurance company to pay
the doctor's bill, a claim representative is present in spirit, checking to make
sure that the doctor's treatment is covered by your health insurance policy
and is not unnecessary or experimental. If your employer pays your health
insurance premiums, then your employer is there as well, quietly watching
as the doctor pokes and prods and inquires about your recent onset of high
blood pressure. All of sudden, that small exam room has gotten crowded.

Why are all those other people there? The chief culprit is the phenomenally high cost of medical care and the corresponding cost of health
insurance. Before paying your medical bills, the insurance company understandably wants some information: What was the treatment for? Is the con-

dition one that your policy covers? How long will the treatment go on? How much will the treatment cost? Are there less costly alternatives?

As much as they sometimes try to pretend otherwise, health insurance companies are for-profit businesses and their main objective, at the end of the day, is to take in more money in premiums that they pay out in claims. In order to accomplish that goal, an insurance company needs to minimize expenses, chiefly by avoiding "unnecessary" procedures, coverage for high-risk individuals, and fraudulent claims.

Patient information—the more, the better—is an insurance company's chief tool for screening potential subscribers and combating fraud. Does your medical history indicate that you have a preexisting condition (a common health insurance exclusion)? Are you seeking treatment for a condition that is not covered by (or excluded from) your policy? Do you have dietary habits or other addictions that may be contributing to your medical condition? Are you requesting reimbursement for an elective or cosmetic procedure? Is the proposed treatment experimental? All these inquiries are of interest to health insurance companies, because they help to determine whether the insurance company is responsible for paying for your treatment.

The information about your physical condition begins to be even more widely disseminated when your employer pays your health insurance premiums. Without question, the single biggest threat to the privacy of employee medical records is the fact that most employers pay some or all of the cost of medical care for their employees, either through the payment of premiums for health insurance or through a program of self-insurance. In either case, the company can require the insurance company to turn over the medical records it collects. In fact, many employers require newly hired employees to sign a blank waiver that allows the employer to collect medical records from any source. And when a company self-insures its employees, it has a powerful incentive to identify employees with potentially expensive medical conditions.

The grim reality is that what was once a way for employers to offer employees a higher level of effective compensation at a lower per-dollar cost (and offer greater peace of mind as well) has become a tremendous drain on the corporate bottom line. Since corporations are in business to maximize profits, it's not particularly surprising that most of them work aggressively to reduce one of their largest and most rapidly rising expenses.

## Health Insurance as a Benefit of Employment

In theory, health insurance is a terrific idea: It allows the cost of providing medical services to be spread across a broad population, with the premiums of the healthy members of the group supporting the cost of providing care to those in need of medical attention. This helps to reduce the risk of potentially ruinous medical costs and makes it possible for more people to receive a higher level of medical care than they might be able to provide for themselves.

The concept of health insurance first appeared in the 1850s. In London, England, the Accidental Death Association was formed to provide sick or injured individuals with insurance against a loss of income; and in Hartford, Connecticut, the Franklin Assurance Company was founded to offer care insurance for a handful of different diseases.[2] In 1929, a group of schoolteachers in Texas negotiated health coverage from the Baylor Hospital in Dallas as part of their compensation package. That program gave rise to what we know today as the Blue Cross plan, which was later joined by the physician-initiated Blue Shield plan.

From an employer's point of view, health insurance was an attractive idea. In the cash-strapped years immediately following World War II, it enabled employers to offer employees a form of compensation that was not subject to federal income taxes or Social Security contributions, which meant that the same amount of money went further. Health insurance proved so popular, in fact, that by the mid-1950s, 77 million people in the United States were covered (roughly half of the country's then 160 million residents). In the race to find and retain good employees, many companies began offering health insurance plans that offered 100 percent coverage with no deductibles. It was, without question, the high-water mark of the employer-provided health insurance system.

Unfortunately, what was once a marvelous idea has been steadily breaking down for years. The cost of insurance premiums is generally determined in one of two ways: community rating or experience rating. Broad-based insurance plans like Blue Cross and Blue Shield typically establish their premiums for a community by looking at the community's overall medical needs and costs, and then everyone in the community pays the same premium. By contrast, private insurance companies that offer health insurance coverage typically base their premiums on an actuarial assessment of the risk of the insured group. For instance, an asbestos removal company would probably pay higher health insurance premiums than a bookseller.

The development of experience rating as a method for calculating health insurance premiums in turn led to the concept of self-insurance. If a company has a large enough number of employees, it can do its own analysis of medical costs and set aside sufficient funds each year to cover its actual costs if doing so is lower than paying health insurance premiums (which, given the enormous popularity of self-insurance, must frequently be the case).

Government policy has also played an important role in the rise of self-insurance by corporations. Although health insurance is a tax-free benefit to employees, the premiums paid to insurance companies are taxed by state revenue agencies. The insurance company typically passes the cost of that tax on to the customer (i.e., employer); companies that self-insure don't have to pay the cost of the tax on premiums. In addition, under the terms of the 1974 Employee Retirement Income Security Act, companies that self-insure are not subject to state insurance regulations that mandate the provision of specific types of health care coverage.

As the level of self-insurance has grown, however, the size of the "community" for establishing premium levels has fallen, making it more difficult for insurers to set affordable premiums. In addition, the companies most likely to self-insure are those that face a lower level of risk with respect to medical costs. As more and more lower-risk groups opt out of the broader health insurance market, private insurers and the Blue Cross/Blue Shield system are left with a pool of higher-risk groups. Add in the perpetually skyrocketing cost of medical care in general and an aging population and it's not surprising that the cost of health insurance has increased so dramatically over the last few years. In fact, the cost of health care insurance rose an estimated 20 percent in 2002 alone, and it's expected to increase an average of another 15 percent in 2003.

The increased cost of health insurance has had a number of deleterious impacts: reduced coverage, outright elimination of coverage, and an increased willingness on the part of some employers to risk wrongful termination suits by culling out employees with expensive and/or long-term medical conditions or, more frighteningly, employees that might someday perhaps develop such long-term conditions. It is particularly unfortunate that these types of financial pressures have arisen at a time when technology is making it increasingly easy to identify individuals who may be prone to long-lasting and expensive medical conditions.

## The Tyranny of the Fit: The Rise in Medical Discrimination

Under the terms of the American with Disabilities Act (ADA), the only time that a medical condition is supposed to be taken into account by your employer is if it in some way impairs your ability to perform your job (or the job for which you are applying). Even if your ability to do your job is affected by your medical condition, your employer is supposed to try to make reasonable accommodations to your condition before concluding that they need to hire someone else.

But as we've seen, your fitness for a particular job is only part of an employer's motivation for keeping tabs on your general medical condition and what you do during your private time. Another motivation, if not the primary motivation, is limiting the cost of providing you and your family with medical care, either through the payment of health insurance premiums or the bills themselves under a self-insurance plan. The analysis is fairly straightforward: Employees with long-term, typically expensive medical conditions raise an employer's costs. Thus, according to a variety of surveys conducted over the last five years, roughly 35 to 40 percent of employers use medical records or health information in one manner or another to make employment decisions.

The timing of those employment decisions can often be horrific. In 2002, the *South Florida Sun-Sentinel* carried a story about a woman named Susan Mabe, an accounts receivable manager for a southern Florida construction consulting firm, who had undergone surgery for cervical cancer. While she was lying in her hospital bed, attached to a morphine drip for post-operative pain, her supervisor called to give her the news that she had been fired. Mabe had never received any negative evaluations or reviews, so the only reason for her firing seemed to be the cost of treating her cancer.[3]

It's not only employees themselves that are at risk, but also employees with family members who have high medical bills. The *Houston Chronicle* has been following the case of Michael Ogg, a former pipefitter for Enpro Systems in Channelview, Texas, whose son Brendan was born three months premature, weighing just one and a half pounds. The infant spent four months in the hospital, a stay that ultimately cost nearly a half million dollars. When he was finally discharged, Brendan was diagnosed with chronic lung problems and has required repeated follow-up visits for his medical problems.

Less than a month after Brendan was sent home, Michael Ogg was laid off from his job. It would have cost him $823 per month to maintain his health insurance. Ogg told the *Chronicle* that he suspected the cost of his son's medical care was the reason for his layoff, particularly since he had just recently received a pay raise and was expecting another one at the time he was let go. His suspicions were confirmed when he ran into his former supervisor, who said that he had been ordered to get rid of Ogg because of the impact of his son's condition on the company's health insurance premiums. The supervisor, who provided an affidavit for the claim that Ogg filed with the Equal Employment Opportunity Commission, also said that two other pipefitters had been laid off to cover up the reason for Ogg's dismissal. Enpro Systems President John Painter categorically denied Ogg's allegations, saying that in the thirty years that the company had been in business, the rights of his employees had never been violated.[4]

A spokesman for the American Cancer Society, contacted by the *Indianapolis Star* regarding a similar story, said that the Society receives several calls each month regarding workers who have lost their jobs shortly after they or someone in their family has been diagnosed with cancer.[5]

Unfortunately, employees who lose their jobs due to their own illness or that of a family member often have little or no legal recourse. The Americans with Disabilities Act, for instance, only applies to businesses with fifteen or more employees. Similarly, the Family Medical Leave Act (FMLA), which guarantees up to twelve weeks of unpaid leave to deal with illness, only applies to businesses with fifty or more employees. If you're fired from a small business that is not covered by either law, it's not clear that you would have any recourse, unless you can demonstrate some other violation of federal or state law (such as discrimination based on a forbidden criteria like age, sex, race, etc.).

## Treadmills for the Rat Race

One of the more positive approaches being adopted by employers in the fight against rising medical costs is a renewed emphasis on employee fitness. A significant percentage of the people in this country work in sedentary office jobs, a fact that contributes to the fact that nearly 60 percent of all Americans are overweight. While the correlations are not absolute, there is evidence that suggests that employees who are obese (i.e., who have a body mass index of twenty-five or higher) have higher rates of absenteeism and higher health costs. According to a report prepared by the former Surgeon General Dr. David Satcher, obesity cost the U.S. economy $117 billion in 2000 and resulted in 39 million missed workdays.

Given the connections between employee weight, general health, productivity, and health costs, employers have a double-vested interest in helping their employees find time to exercise. According to a National Worksite Health Promotion Survey conducted in 1999, roughly half of the companies with more than 750 employees offer a comprehensive employee health promotion program.[6] Coincidentally, a 2002 survey of more than 1,000 corporate managers revealed that the number one perk requested by job seekers is a health club membership.[7]

As beneficial as employer-sponsored fitness programs are for employee health, they are virtually certain to come with a privacy cost. The first level of detail is whether or not you've used the company exercise facility on a particular day. Collecting that type of data is as simple as having a sign-in sheet at the front door; some of the other technologies that were discussed earlier in the book, such as magstripe readers, infrared badges, or even radio frequency IDs, can help a company automatically log your visits to the gym. Another source of usage data is to offer an incentive program that ties reward levels to the number of visits you make to the gym. The Chrysler

Group, for instance, hands out "well bucks" to employees who participate in the company's various fitness programs. The "well bucks" can be redeemed for assorted athletic equipment, giving the company additional information that can contribute to its profile of each employee's general fitness habits.

The information gathered by a company fitness program, of course, can go far beyond simply recording whether you've visited the gym. Many of the programs in place today include routine medical check-ups, which raise a host of medical privacy concerns. Other medically related company programs are less broadly invasive (programs specifically designed to control weight, stress, or help employees quit smoking) but they still have the potential to collect and distribute very private information.

Even the act of exercising itself can be a source of information. One of the hot trends in athletic equipment is the use of monitoring devices that can collect data and then transmit it to a personal computer or personal data assistant. This trend toward interactive athletic equipment is likely to accelerate as Bluetooth technology becomes more widely implemented. Imagine that you have a Bluetooth-equipped heart rate monitor. All you have to do after your morning run is walk into the room where your computer is located; your heart rate monitor automatically recognizes the computer and downloads its data directly to your fitness program. Another device, laced onto your shoe, transmits a step-by-step summary of your run, including detailed pacing information, elevation changes, and even temperature changes.

Some of the interactive devices already on the market are intended to work with websites that will track your progress and provide you with an ongoing fitness assessment and recommendations for workouts. The high-end FitSense FS-1 Pro Speedometer, for instance, can track a wide variety of information for runners and then transmit the information wirelessly to a separate NetLink component, which takes the data and feeds it into a personal computer. The training information is then uploaded to a Web page on the FitSense website.

It would be a relatively simple matter for an employer to offer a similar service to its employees. With an appropriately equipped gym, a company could help its employees establish fitness goals, monitor the overall health of its workforce, set up contests and competitions, and answer the burning questions of our time (for instance, "How much can the average network administrator bench press?").[8]

There's no indication that companies are currently collecting information about exercise habits, but as health insurance costs continue to skyrocket, the temptation for businesses to do so will grow steadily stronger. Lifestyle discrimination (something not covered by the Americans with Disabilities Act or the Civil Rights Act of 1964) is already a problem for smokers and overweight workers, and the extent to which you exercise could easily become a factor in how much you are required to contribute to your health insurance coverage at work (or whether you qualify for it at all).

# Alcohol and Drug Testing

In a twenty-year stretch that began in 1950 with Bing Crosby crooning his way through "White Christmas" and ended with Creedance Clearwater Revival banging out "Bad Moon Rising," the United States saw a virtually unprecedented rise in illicit drug use. According to the 1998 National Household Survey on Drug Abuse, in 1962, about 4 million Americans had tried an illegal drug. By 1998, the number who had done so (not including those who didn't inhale) was just over 78 million people.[9]

## Blame It on Vietnam (or the Sixties)

Much of the growth in drug use occurred in the middle and late 1960s, when a wide variety of social factors encouraged enthusiastic experimentation in sex, drugs, and rock and roll. At the same time, more than 8,000 miles away, over 50,000 Americans were dying in a steamy jungle nation called Vietnam. As a large number of books and movies have made painfully clear, the daily reality of fighting in Vietnam was so fundamentally horrific that virtually any altered reality was preferable.

As a result, the military became the front line in the nation's battle against illegal drug use. As concern grew about the use of drugs (particularly heroin) in Vietnam, the Department of Defense began a preliminary program in 1972 to test soldiers for drug use. For various reasons, that program was not aggressively implemented. The situation changed in 1981, however, when a pilot crashed a jet while landing on the aircraft carrier Nimitz. The crash killed fourteen people, injured forty-eight others, destroyed seven planes, and badly damaged a number of others. After drug testing revealed the compound THC (the active ingredient in marijuana) in a number of the deceased (including the pilot), the DOD's support for random drug testing grew, and by the end of that year, the military had implemented a wide-ranging random drug-testing program. Over the next six years, according to DOD surveys of military personnel, drug use declined dramatically. In 1986, for instance, only 4 percent of those tested were positive for drug use.

Encouraged by its success with the military, the federal government imposed mandatory drug screening requirements for all federal employees in 1986. Eight years later, legislation extended mandatory testing to every industry regulated by the federal government, including nuclear energy, petroleum, aviation, railroad, maritime, and road transportation.

Public sector employees made some efforts to challenge random drug testing programs as an invasion of privacy under the Fourth and Fourteenth Amendments. However, in a pair of 1989 decisions, the U.S. Supreme Court upheld the concept of random drug testing in unusually broad language. The first case, *Skinner* v. *Railway Labor Executive Assn.*, dealt with a challenge to the government's practice of drug testing the entire crew of a train following an accident.[10] The second case, *National Treasury Employees Union* v. *Von Raab*, was brought by a group of U.S. Custom Service employees who objected to the Service's practice of testing any employee who applied for a promotion.[11]

In each case, the Court rejected the challenge. According to the Court, a drug test is in fact a "search" within the meaning of the Fourth Amendment and thus must be "reasonable." However, the Court also concluded that "neither a warrant, nor probable cause, nor, indeed, any measure of individualized suspicion is an indispensable component of reasonableness in every circumstance." Thus, as long as the federal government can demonstrate "special needs," it is entitled to disregard traditional constitutional protections, at least insofar as your urine is concerned.

Even for the federal government, however, the ability to conduct random drug testing is not unlimited. Although this is still an evolving area of the law, it is clear that there must be some legitimate relationship between the drug-testing program in question and the government's claim of "special need." In general, federal courts have upheld drug-testing programs for jobs that involve the following: public safety (i.e., transportation jobs); firearms (i.e., prison guards or police officers); and/or access to top-secret information (i.e., Department of Justice lawyers with high security clearances).

## Urine Trouble: Be Careful Which Bagel You Choose

On October 2, 1982, at about the same time that the military was dramatically expanding its random drug-testing program, President Ronald Reagan announced the War on Drugs. Even the most rosey-eyed public policy nerd would be hard-pressed to declare the twenty-year-old war a victory, or even a significant holding action. Apart from incarcerating an unprecedented number of Americans, the war's most tangible by-product has been cheap and readily available drug-testing technology.

The low cost of drug testing today (a simple do-it-yourself urine testing kit can be purchased today for as little as ten dollars, although laboratory tests typically run forty-five to fifty dollars) is a perfect illustration of the principle that in the absence of well-crafted legislation, high-priced technology is the best protection for employee privacy. Time and again, employers have demonstrated that as the cost of implementing a new surveillance technology drops, the number of businesses adopting the new technology vastly exceeds the number of businesses that actually need it. Call it keeping up with the corporate Joneses, call it an excess of caution in a litigious world, call it impressive salesmanship on the part of security companies, but time and again, a drop in the cost of surveillance technology has been matched by a corresponding drop in workplace privacy.

Given the low cost and ease of use, it's not surprising that the frequency of workplace drug testing has steadily increased; according to the American Civil Liberties Union, in the dozen years from 1987 to 1999, the amount of workplace drug testing in the United States nearly tripled. Larger corporations are particularly enthusiastic drug test users: Nearly 100 percent of Fortune 500 companies conduct preemployment drug tests and/or random drug tests of workers. By contrast, only 3 percent of small businesses do drug testing.

Private employers have powerful motivations for conducting drug testing: According to the National Institute of Drug Abuse, there are approximately 11.7 million active drug users in the United States today, and three-quarters of them are employed. As many as 23 percent of the employed drug users use illegal drugs while on the job. In 2001, the U.S. Department of Labor's Bureau of Labor Statistics estimated a short time ago that workplace drug use costs employers $75 to $100 billion per year in lost employee work time, accidents, health care costs, and workers' compensation claims.[12] Moreover, 65 percent of all workplace accidents are related to drug and alcohol use.[13]

With both the federal government and the private sector increasingly interested in conducting drug testing, a great deal of time and effort has gone into developing quick, easy, and inexpensive drug tests. Although scientists have developed techniques for testing a variety of substances for evidence of drug use—blood, urine, hair, saliva, and sweat—the U.S. Department of Health and Human Services declared in 1988 that urine was the only acceptable sample specimen for federal drug-testing programs. Most private companies have followed suit, in part because they prefer to use labs accredited by HHS, and because the focus on urine as the primary means of testing for drugs has helped to drive down the price of testing urine samples.

The most accurate type of test is a blood test, which shows whether a particular drug is actually present in the bloodstream (by contrast, urine is tested for drug metabolites, the by-products created after your body has absorbed and broken down the drugs). However, blood tests are perceived as invasive (which is quite literally true), and the information they provide, while highly accurate, is limited to a fairly short time frame (usually two to three days, depending on the individual).

Increasingly, companies are considering the use of saliva as a testing medium. Like blood, saliva is useful for showing recent drug use. For instance, if someone smokes a joint on his lunch break, the active compound THC will not show up in his blood until after he leaves for home, and the metabolites will not show up in his urine until much later that evening or the following morning (although they will remain detectable for a number of days). However, THC will be present immediately in his saliva (although it can only be detected there for twenty-four hours or so). Collecting saliva is also less invasive than drawing blood or collecting urine, and nearly as tamperproof. On very short notice, a nurse or lab technician can have you hold a swab between your lower cheek and gum for two minutes, seal the swab in a container, and send the container off to be tested. The cost of a saliva test for drugs is comparable to that of laboratory urine tests—roughly forty-five to fifty-five dollars per test.

Hair can also be used to detect the presence of drugs. From a collection point of view, hair is probably the least invasive means of testing, but it is also the most expensive and time-consuming. Nonetheless, some employers prefer using hair, primarily because of hair's superior ability to reveal drug use—depending on the individual and the amount of drug use, hair can reveal traces of drug use over a period of time as long as three months.

For a variety of reasons, however, urine has become the testing medium of choice. For companies that find even the cost of laboratory testing too high (or the turnaround too slow), an aggressive industry has arisen that produces and markets virtually instantaneous drug-testing kits. In just five minutes—and without the need to send anything to a laboratory—an employer can check to see whether an employee's urine exceeds the standards established by the Substance Abuse & Mental Health Services Administration (SAMHSA) limits for five different drugs: amphetamines, marijuana, cocaine, opiates, and methamphetamines.

One typical system is the QuickScreen Drug Test, produced by AAA Rapid Drug Testing Service in Key Largo, Florida. The kit consists of a collection cup (with a temperature sticker on the outside) and a test card with various panels for testing for different substances. The company claims that its most popular product is a five-panel card that tests for marijuana, cocaine, opiates, PCP, and amphetamines.[14] After the card is inserted in the urine sample, it indicates the presence or absence of drugs within three to five minutes. The cost is just fourteen dollars. With a little bit of searching, the same type of product can be purchased on the Web for just over ten dollars per unit.

The growth in the popularity of urine drug-testing kits has not been slowed very much by serious questions about their accuracy. For example, the Ontario Information and Privacy Commissioners' Office recently concluded that up to 40 percent of drug testing kits on the market produce inaccurate results.

One common error made by the test kits is to identify a common drug for Parkinson's disease—Depronil—as an amphetamine. Another is to mistake ibuprofen for marijuana. Even more disturbing is the potential (albeit remote) tendency of drug-testing kits to finger poppy seed bagel lovers as heroin users. As Cecil Adams, the marvelously sarcastic author of the syndicated column "The Straight Dope," puts it:

> Let's not beat around the bush. The answer to [the] question is yes—
> eating a couple of poppy seed rolls, bagels, etc., can cause you to fail a
> routine drug test. This news will produce one of two reactions, de-
> pending on whether you're a law-abiding citizen or a drug fiend:
>
> 1. Panic (if law-abiding citizen): "I could lose my job by eating
>    breakfast!"
>
> 2. Elation (if drug fiend): "I could keep my job by claiming I ate
>    breakfast!"
>
> So the real corporate drug test is to tell your employees about poppy
> seeds and watch their reactions. The happy ones get the ax.[15]

Other false positives can result from the presence in the urine of over-the-counter medications like Vicks Formula 44-M, Advil, Nyquil, Nuprin, Contac, and Sudafed. Even though no employer would (or at least should) base an employment decision on a single positive result (and 87 percent of all initial positives get reversed in a second test), the impact of even an initial false positive can be enormously destructive.

There are serious questions about the underlying validity of other testing methods as well, including hair analysis. In 1990, the Food and Drug Administration released a statement that read in part: "the consensus of scientific opinion is that hair analysis . . . for the presence of drugs of abuse is unreliable and is not generally recognized by qualified experts as effective."[16]

Using hair to test for drugs also raises concerns about disparate impact. In addition to the fact that women tend to have longer hair than men (and thus can often be monitored for a longer period of time), there are also questions about whether hair color affects the extent to which medication and drugs can be detected. In the summer of 2002, the Boston Police Department (BPD) released figures showing that during three years of testing officer hair samples, forty-five officers tested positive for drugs. Sixteen of the officers were white and twenty-nine were minorities (twenty-six blacks and three Hispanics). The results were challenged by the BPD's association of minority officers and the NAACP, which argued that the color and structure of dark hair absorb and retain drug traces in higher quantities than light hair. They also suggested that dark hair retains drug traces for a longer period of time than light hair.[17]

There is considerable dispute in the scientific community over whether hair color does affect the extent to which drugs can be detected. In the case of the BPD tests, department representatives also stressed that the threshold for declaring a positive result is fairly high, and a retest is required to confirm the initial findings.

## Drug Tests and Their Impact on Employee Privacy

As is frequently the case with difficult social issues, the increase in random employee drug testing has largely occurred without any significant discussion of whether the procedure actually reduces on-the-job drug use, and whether the inherent invasiveness of the tests are justified by their preventative capabilities. These are questions that have not been subjected to any type of rigorous debate.

From an employee's point of view, drug testing raises two separate privacy concerns: personal space privacy (your ability to be free from unwanted observation or invasion) and lifestyle privacy (your ability to engage in activities that do not impinge on your ability to do your job). The primary impact of the collection process is on your personal space privacy, and it can range from mildly inconveniencing to sharply intrusive. The primary impact of the drug test results themselves is on your lifestyle privacy.

Of the three most popular testing methods—urine, hair, and blood—the collection of a hair sample is by far the least immediately invasive of your personal space privacy. A pair of sharp scissors, a quick snip by a nurse, and you're done. But the limited privacy impact of using hair is outweighed by the factors of cost and time discussed above, leaving blood and urine as the more popular choices. The popular perception among both employers and employees is that collecting urine is less of a privacy infringement than drawing blood. On the surface, that's true: Having someone stick a needle in your arm and withdraw a vial of blood is more invasive of your personal space than collecting something your body wants to get rid of anyway.

But the provision of a urine sample is in fact a far greater intrusion of your personal space privacy than having a blood sample drawn. In case you haven't been exposed to an employment drug test, here's a quick rundown of what typically takes place:

- Your employer or prospective employer will ask you to report to a "collection site," which might be a company facility but which is more likely a doctor's office or clinic.

- You will be asked to show a picture ID and fill out a medical history questionnaire. Your signature on the questionnaire will typically allow the testing lab to share the test results and the information on the questionnaire itself with your employer.

- You will be faced with the question of whether to tell the testing facility about medications you are currently taking, because a number of prescription drugs and over-the-counter medications can easily be mistaken for illegal drugs. Of course, that information can and probably will be included in the report that is provided to your employer.

- You will be asked to take off your coat and store any personal belongings in a storage locker, to reduce the chances that you are carrying with you any substance designed to mask the presence of drugs in your urine.

- You will be given a small plastic cup, roughly the size of a juice glass, and directed to enter a bathroom stall or small lavatory. To prevent attempts to dilute your urine sample, many testing facilities shut off the water in the bathroom sink and dye the toilet water blue.

- You'll be given embarrassingly specific instructions on how to properly pee into the cup. This part of the procedure can be difficult for many people and excruciating for some, particularly those that suffer from "shy bladder" syndrome.

- You may be required to produce a urine sample in full view of an observer, whose job it is to make sure that no substitution or alteration of the sample occurs. (Despite the obvious intrusiveness of being asked to urinate on demand in front of another person, courts have been reluctant to uphold employee challenges to random drug testing.)

- The sample will be checked for color and temperature and sealed in a tamper-proof container, and you will be asked to initial the container to verify its proper handling.

- If your initial test is positive for one or more drugs, you'll be asked to take a second, more precise test. If that test is also positive, your test results will be reviewed by a doctor with experience in substance abuse. He will discuss your tests with you and try to determine if anything—including current medication or diet—might have contributed to a false positive.

The rise in the amount of drug testing has led to the development of an entire industry aimed at fooling drug testers. One of the most common techniques is to try to substitute a "negative" or "clean" urine sample during the course of the test. There are dozens, if not hundreds of companies that offer "clean urine" in either liquid or freeze-dried form, along with instructions on how to make the substitution. One typical example is Assured Testing Resources, which offers a complete urine substitution system for thirty-five dollars that is "So small, it fits in the palm of your hand!".

In addition, there are also a bewildering number of companies that offer products designed to mask or temporarily eliminate any evidence of drug use for a period of time, usually ranging from one to five hours. These substances range from pills and gel caps for urine tests to shampoos that will allegedly clean drug toxins from the hair for a short period of time. In addition, there are numerous websites that offer information and advice on beating urine tests. Needless to say, drug-testing technicians emphatically state that it is very hard, if not impossible, to successfully prevent the detection of drug metabolites in urine or hair.

Ironically, as the efforts to defeat or fool urine tests grow more elaborate, the level of scrutiny and intrusive observation will continue to increase. In the summer of 2002, for instance, while complying with a court-ordered drug test, a Texas college student was caught wearing a fake penis attached to a heat-controlled sample of synthetic urine. Known as "The Whizzinator," the device comes in five different skin colors and costs $150. The supervising probation chief admitted that he and his drug-testing technicians might have to pay closer attention to people while they take the test.

Not surprisingly, a handful of states—including New Jersey, Pennsylvania, Texas, and Missouri—make it illegal to use a device like the Whizzinator to fake a drug test. In May 2002, a man named Donald Milligan Jr. was charged in Cuyahoga County, Missouri, with "possession of a forging instrumentality," i.e., the Whizzinator. Milligan was caught, reports said, because the probation officer "was trained to observe the sights and sounds of urination."

The impact of a urine test on personal space privacy is obviously real, but at least it is of limited duration. The impact of drug or alcohol testing on lifestyle privacy in general is far more pervasive and long lasting. In theory, the point of alcohol and drug testing is to assess an individual's fitness to do his job. For most jobs, drunkenness or drug use on the job raises serious productivity concerns; for a small but significant percentage of jobs, it's potentially lethal. No rational person would defend the right of a school bus driver, for instance, to do his job while stoned. If an employer has any reasonable suspicion that someone is working while under the influence of drugs or alcohol, then requiring some type of test is a perfectly reasonable safety measure.

But it's far less clear that someone who got drunk or smoked marijuana on Friday night is incapable of performing his job on Monday morning, and the connection between an employee's casual drug use two months earlier and his ability to do his work on a particular day is even more tenuous. Employers seek this information, however, because they believe that it tells them something about the safety or security risk that their employees might pose on the job.

When it comes to lifestyle privacy, a blood test is the least invasive form of testing, because drugs generally pass through the blood stream in two to three days. Urine tests are somewhat more invasive, because the drug metabolites that show up in urine can linger for as long as a couple of weeks, depending on your weight and your level of drug use. But neither type of testing compares to the invasion of lifestyle privacy that results from testing a sample of hair: It's not uncommon for drug metabolites to remain in hair for two to three months, sometimes longer.

The other privacy issue raised by drug-testing programs is the potential for employers to test for medical conditions completely unrelated to drug or alcohol use. In theory, employers can't use random drug tests to check for other medical conditions, but it shouldn't come as a huge shock that it happens. In 1988, the Washington, D.C. Police Department collected urine samples from female officers for drug-testing purposes and then surreptitiously tested the same samples to determine if the officers were pregnant. And as we'll see, with the improvements in DNA testing technology, a single drop of blood or urine, regardless of the purpose for which it was originally collected, offers employers the potential to gather unprecedented amounts of private medical information about their employees.

## When Employment Bias Is More than Skin Deep

Employment discrimination has (and continues to be) a long-standing problem in this country. Until recently, bias has been based on visible characteristics—skin color, gender, age, and disability. Although it took an unconscionably long time to do so, legislation was eventually adopted to make it illegal to discriminate against employees and potential employees on the basis of superficial criteria. Increasingly, however, the grounds for employment bias only show up in a medical laboratory.

One of the most egregious examples occurred nearly ten years ago, when workers at the Lawrence Berkeley National Laboratory at the University of California–Berkeley made a deeply disturbing discovery: For years, their blood had routinely been tested for evidence of syphilis, sickle cell anemia, and pregnancy.[18]

The testing came to light in 1994, when an employee named Marya

Norman-Bloodsaw requested a copy of her medical records and noticed the code "RPR." Norman-Bloodsaw recognized the letters as the code for a syphilis test, but knew that she had not requested or authorized such a test, nor had she authorized other tests run on her blood. Nonetheless, as part of her required medical exam, her blood had been tested not only for syphilis but also for pregnancy and sickle cell anemia. Not only was she never notified that the tests were being conducted, she was not given any of the results.

Norman-Bloodsaw told some of her fellow employees about the secret testing and encouraged them to request copies of their own medical records. As the records were received, it became clear that the Lawrence Berkeley Lab had been conducting secret tests on employees' blood for at least thirty years. Even more disturbing was the clear implication that the testing was directed primarily toward African-American and Latino employees. For example, while all new hires at the Laboratory were tested for syphilis, only African-American and Latino employees were retested during subsequent exams (the only white males who were retested were those married to African-American women). Similarly, the only other regular blood screening that was done was for sickle cell anemia, which is a condition primarily associated with African Americans.

With the help of San Francisco's Legal Aid Society, employees filed a class action lawsuit against the Laboratory, arguing that the tests were a violation of their civil rights and an invasion of privacy. The Laboratory defended its testing program by arguing that it was conducted under the auspices of the U.S. Department of Energy and that by consenting to a comprehensive medical exam, each employee had effectively agreed to have such tests done. The Laboratory was successful in persuading U.S. District Court Judge Vaughn Walker to dismiss the lawsuit, but Judge Walker's decision was overturned by the Ninth Circuit U.S. Court of Appeals, which ruled that performing tests without the knowledge or consent of employees is unconstitutional.

Left unanswered was the question of whether the Department of Energy was secretly conducting a long-range study of disease patterns in minority communities. Contractors for DOE are given a guidebook for conducting medical testing, in which the DOE states that employee medical records are "considered valuable epidemiological research records." For many employees, the secret nature of the testing called to mind the notorious Tuskegee medical experiments, in which African-American men were infected with syphilis and then left untreated to track the course of the disease. Various other surreptitious government testing programs have also come to light recently, including one where scientists at the University of California–Berkeley secretly injected plutonium into state prisoners and mental patients to test human biology.

# A New Twist in Employment Law: the Loss of DNA Privacy

It is difficult to imagine anything more personal and private than our DNA, the genetic code that is at the root of our physical development and appearance. In the last few years, scientists have made fantastic strides in their ability to decipher the human genetic code. They are using this knowledge to better understand the origins of different diseases, and in some cases, to identify people who face an increased risk of developing certain diseases.

As scientists blaze their way through the jungle of genetic information, marking new discoveries and potentially valuable avenues for exploration, health insurance companies and employers are close on their heels. Many physical conditions that have a genetic origin—Alzheimer's, sickle cell anemia, even obesity—are extremely expensive to treat. As we've seen, insurance companies don't want to cover individuals with long-term illnesses, since they need to pay out more to settle claims, and employers prefer not to hire or keep such workers, since their claims drive up the employer's insurance premiums or self-insurance costs. As the sophistication of genetic testing improves and researchers grow more confident about the relationship between certain genes and specific medical conditions, the threat of genetic bias will steadily increase.

## The Human Genome Project

The first linking of genetics and work occurred in 1938, when geneticist J.B.S. Haldane discovered that not all workers exposed to the same conditions contracted the same diseases. Based on his observations, Haldane recommended that people with a history of or predisposition to bronchitis not be allowed to enter the pottery industry.[19] By the 1960s, scientists had more formal evidence for the theory that certain genetic traits could make individuals extremely susceptible to workplace diseases.

Despite the theoretical advances, the level of genetic testing in the workplace has remained quite low, in large part due to the cost, the uncertainty of the results, and the strong disapproval of such tests among workers. Congress's Office of Technology Assessment found that only 1.6 percent of the nation's 500 largest industrial companies did any kind of genetic testing in 1983, and 5 percent in 1989. A decade later, in 1999, an American Management Association survey initially indicated that 5.7 percent of its 10,000 members conducted genetic testing. When the AMA did follow-up interviews with human resource departments, however, it became clear that the definition of "genetic testing" was not well understood—many respondents had included any test that required blood, while others had included any test for disease. When the correct definition was applied, the AMA concluded that only one percent of its members had true genetic testing programs. However, as many as 14 percent of AMA members include genetic testing as part of a preemployment medical exam in order to determine susceptibility to workplace conditions.

The traditional impediments to genetic testing—cost and the utility of the results—are vanishing quickly. There are already relatively inexpensive tests for a genetic predisposition to Huntington's disease, alcoholism, and various types of cancer. In addition, a massive research project is rapidly expanding our understanding of the connection between our genes and disease. As that pool of knowledge increases, employers will be increasingly tempted to draw a connection between your genetic make-up and your likely cost to the organization in health insurance premiums and medical costs.

The primary engine driving the advances in genetic testing is the Human Genome Project (HGP), a thirteen-year-old collaboration between the U.S. Department of Energy and the National Institutes of Health. Begun in 1990, the HGP is an organized effort to discover and map each of the 30,000 to 35,000 human genes contained in our DNA. Even more ambitiously, the HGP hopes to correctly identify the sequence of the more than 3 *billion* chemical base pairs that make up those genes and ultimately determine their function.

As the HGP works toward those two goals, it is also developing tools for storing the data, creating and improving the tools for genetic analysis, and establishing protocols and licensing procedures to transfer genetic information and technology to the private sector. Perhaps most importantly, the HGP is actively evaluating the ethical, legal, and social issues (ELSI) that arise out of genetic research.[20]

Thanks in large part to advances in computer technology, the mapping of the human genome has gone much faster than anticipated. A rough draft of the map was completed in June 2001, and scientists expect to have a polished version completed in 2003, two years ahead of the planned fifteen-year completion date.

One of the expected benefits of the HGP will be to help researchers identify which of our genes are responsible for different medical conditions and diseases. Already, scientists are able to test for a wide range of genetically-based illnesses, including:

- Amyotrophic lateral sclerosis (ALS, or Lou Gehrig's disease)

- Alzheimer's disease

- Inherited breast and ovarian cancer

■ Cystic fibrosis

■ Huntington's disease

■ Polycystic (adult) kidney disease

■ Sickle cell disease[21]

Most recently, Drs. Stephen B. Liggett and Lynne E. Wagoner of the University of Cincinnati published a paper in the *New England Journal of Medicine* announcing their discovery that people who inherit variants of two specific genes are ten times more likely to develop congestive heart failure.[22] While the discovery offers hope for dealing with one of the nation's most expensive medical problems—more people are hospitalized for congestive heart failure each year than all cancers combined—it also underscores the potential scope of genetic testing.

The same phenomenal advances in computer technology that are aiding in the identification of the human genome are also making genetic testing both inexpensive and deceptively easy to do. Already, a variety of companies are marketing devices that can be used in a doctor's office to test for specific genetic abnormalities, most of which report their results in just a few minutes.

These devices use a new tool called a biochip to break apart a DNA chain and look for predetermined genetic combinations. One variation, called a microarray, is manufactured by etching a complex series of walls, grooves, and pillars into a small piece of glass. A tiny electrical current pushes a prepared sample of DNA through the etched channels in the microarray. Once the DNA has been pushed as far as it can through the tiny maze, the chip is placed in an analyzer to see if the maze has trapped any of the DNA fragments being sought.

Another biochip variant, known as a DNA array, is a combination of circuitry and genetic material, in which specific DNA fragments are embedded in the glass chip as it is being manufactured. As with the microarray, a DNA sample is pushed across the chip using a weak electrical field. If any of the DNA in the sample matches the DNA embedded in the chip, the sample DNA will bond to it. Once the sample has moved through the entire array, the biochip analyzer can determine if any of the embedded DNA fragments have captured material from the sample.

Despite the reality that the tests can't yet accomplish what some employers hope that they can, companies are becoming increasingly enthusiastic about the possibility of testing their employees' genes for signs that they might develop an expensive illness or be susceptible to diseases resulting from the work environment. More often than not, the presence of a genetic marker in your DNA is merely an indication of a predisposition toward a particular disease, not a guarantee that you will contract it. Nonetheless, genetic discrimination has the potential to be a major social problem in the near future.

Despite the still murkily understood connection between genes and disease, at least one company has already turned to genetic testing in an effort to cut down on both medical costs and worker compensation claims. The secret testing came to light when a railroad worker's union filed a lawsuit against the Burlington Northern Santa Fe (BNSF) railroad in February 2001, alleging that the company was secretly conducting genetic testing on its employees' blood.

BNSF's testing program was discovered when Gary Avery, a track laborer for the railroad, returned to work after successful surgery to relieve a carpal tunnel condition. Avery received a letter from BNSF instructing him to have seven vials of blood drawn for a blood test. Avery showed the letter to his wife Janice, a registered nurse, who immediately questioned why so much blood was being drawn. When she called BNSF, she was told that the blood was being drawn for a "genetic test."

According to the union's lawsuit, BNSF was attempting to show that its employees who developed carpal tunnel syndrome were genetically predisposed to do so. Typically, an employer is required to pay worker compensation claims for injuries that occur on the job; BNSF hoped to argue that it was not liable for carpal tunnel claims because the workers who developed the condition would have done so regardless of where they were working. In addition to the union lawsuits, BNSF was sued by the Equal Employment Opportunity Commission under the Americans with Disabilities Act, which argued that simply gathering genetic material from employees constitutes a violation of the ADA. On May 9, 2002, the parties reached a mediated settlement in which BNSF agreed to pay thirty-six workers a total of $2.2 million for conducting the secret testing. While not admitting any wrongdoing under the ADA, BNSF also agreed to discontinue the practice in the future.

BNSF's effort to find a genetic basis for carpal tunnel syndrome illustrates the uninformed hype that surrounds genetic testing. In fact, medical experts believe that there is not any genetic predisposition for a condition like carpal tunnel syndrome, which is brought on by excessive repetitive motion. While the genetic testing by BNSF is the only case to come to light so far, it is highly unlikely that BNSF will be the last company to attempt to use genetic information to weed out employees at risk for expensive physical conditions.

Public concern over the invasiveness of genetic testing is amply reflected in the speed with which many state legislatures have acted to protect genetic privacy. As of February 2001, thirty-seven of the fifty states had adopted legislation to outlaw genetic discrimination by insurance companies, and thirty-one now forbid genetic discrimination in employment.

The federal government has also begun to look at this issue, although so far it has limited its protection to federal employees. On February 8, 2000, President Clinton signed Executive Order 13145 (appropriately enough, the first to be issued in the twenty-first century), which bars discrimination in federal employment based on genetic information:

> It is the policy of the Government of the United States to provide equal employment opportunity in Federal employment for all qualified persons and to prohibit discrimination against employees based on protected genetic information, or information about a request for or the receipt of genetic services. This policy of equal opportunity applies to every aspect of Federal employment.[23]

President Clinton's action was spurred in part by reports of secret blood testing at the Lawrence Berkeley Laboratory. Health and privacy activists hoped that the news (and in particular, its racial overtones) would spur Congressional action, but various bills introduced to ban genetic discrimination by private employers have failed to gain much traction.

The bills have languished in part because of the limited attention given to domestic issues following the terrorist attacks, but also because the bills are strenuously opposed by the insurance industry and other business groups. Insurance companies in particular are concerned about the potential for Congress to limit the industry's ability to use a person's medical records, including her genetic predispositions, to establish her insurance premiums—or to decide whether to cover her at all.

## The Vial Future of Employment?

As anyone with an interest in modern criminal procedures is aware, the use of DNA to identify criminals (and in many cases, to free wrongfully convicted individuals) is a burgeoning area. All fifty states have passed laws to require blood sampling and DNA identification of certain classes of felons, and in 1992, the Federal Bureau of Investigation established the Combined DNA Index System (CODIS) to help states match DNA from crime scenes to other crime scenes or individuals with DNA on file in the system.

Currently unexplored is the potential for cooperation between employers and law enforcement. Fingerprints are already required from applicants for certain types of jobs. It seems a relatively minor leap to expand the statute to require job applicants to get a clean bill of health, so to speak, from CODIS before starting work.

One area, at least, where genetics will take much longer to have any particular impact is in the day-to-day identification of employees. While DNA profiles are proving to be a powerful tool in criminal investigations, the process of doing a complete genetic profile is currently much too time-consuming and expensive for DNA testing to serve as a biometric identifier for workplace security. Compared with the effort required to determine if you have a particular genetic anomaly, the process of parsing your genetic code to the level of detail required to distinguish you from someone else is far more complicated, intricate, and time-consuming.

Given the speed with which technology advances, however, it is not hard to imagine a future in which in order to get to your desk at certain high-security facilities, your DNA profile will have to match the DNA profile stored in the facility's central database. The first steps in this direction have been taken by a Phoenix, Arizona, company called SecureCard Technologies, which manufactures the Gene Card™, which the company describes as "the first DNA identification card in the world." The digitally printed card contains a smart chip, a full-color photo, various identifying information, a scan of the employee's right thumbprint, and a profile of the employee's DNA. Right now, it takes two to three weeks to create a Gene Card™ for a new employee, and the DNA profile is of limited utility, since there's no available device to check his DNA profile in the lobby of his office and compare it to the information on the card.

As genetic testing equipment becomes more efficient, it's not difficult to imagine a day when a popular biometric security device will painlessly remove a few cells from the tip of your finger, extract the DNA, analyze it, and compare the results to a DNA profile established when you were hired. Two factors might slow the adoption of DNA verification equipment. One is that DNA is not actually the most distinctive biometric identifier; for example, identical twins have identical DNA but different irises. The other is that it has the greatest privacy implications, given the amount of information a sample of DNA can reveal about each of us. Nonetheless, given the popular belief in DNA as the ultimate identifier of who we are, there is little doubt that its role as a security tool is likely to expand.

# End Notes

1. Translation from the Greek by Ludwig Edelstein *From The Hippocratic Oath: Text, Translation, and Interpretation*, by Ludwig Edelstein (Baltimore: Johns Hopkins Press, 1943).

2. In time, so many insurance companies established their headquarters in Hartford that it became known as the "Insurance Capital of the World."

3. Nancy McVicar, "Salt in the Wound," *South Florida Sun-Sentinel* (October 5, 2002).

4. L.M. Sixel, "Sick infant caught in middle of discrimination dispute," *Houston Chronicle* (August 30, 2002).

5. Gregory Weaver, "Dad loses job—and insurance," *Indianapolis Star* (August 4, 2002).

6. Alexandra R. Moses, "From yoga to walks, employers are finding ways to encourage good health," *Boston Globe* (April 22, 2002).

7. L.M. Sixel, "Sweating in Fat City," *Houston Chronicle* (April 12, 2002).

8. Of course, any network administrator worth his salt is going to have the ability to pump up and massage the data.

9. "Drug Use in the U.S.," Narcknowledge (2002). Available online at www.narc knowledge.com/druguse.html.

10. ___U.S. ___, 109 S. Ct. 1402 (1989).

11. ___U.S. ___, 109 S. Ct. 1384 (1989).

12. Judith A. Swartley, "Testing for Drugs," *Plumbing & Mechanical* (October 2002).

13. Les Rosen, "Intro to Drug Screening . . .", *HR Forum* (August 1999).

14. Customers can also purchase testing panels for methamphetamine, barbiturates, benzodiazepines, and methadone.

15. Cecil Adams, "Will poppy-seed bagels cause you to fail a drug test?", Straight Dope website (April 3, 1998). Available online at www.straightdope.com/classics/a5_116.html.

16. FDA Compliance Policy Guide #7124.06, released on June 13, 1990.

17. Francie Latour, "Drug test for Hub officers stirs bias fear," *Boston Globe* (June 22, 2002).

18. Dana Hawkins, "A Bloody Mess at One Federal Lab," *U.S. News and World Report* (June 23, 1997).

19. Roger Jansson, Ph.D., et al., "Genetic Testing in the Workplace: Implications for Public Policy," Institute for Public Health Genetics, University of Washington (September 30, 2000).

20. Human Genome Project Information, "What's New," available online at www.ornl.gov/hgmis/project/about.html. The Human Genome Project has an extremely thorough and well-organized website.

21. Human Genome Project Information, "Gene Testing," available online at www.ornl.gov/hgmis/medicine/genetest.html.

22. Gina Kolata, "Two Genes Linked to Congestive Heart Failure," *The New York Times* (October 10, 2002).

23. Executive Order 13145.

# CHAPTER EIGHT

# Convenience and the Death of Privacy

There is a persistent tension between "privacy"—our innate desire to control the information that is known about us—and "convenience"—our equally innate desire for day-to-day life to be a little easier. As we'll see in more detail below, the credit card is the perfect embodiment of that tension: It is much easier to pay for things by signing a small slip of paper than to carry around large amounts of cash or write out checks at each store. But in exchange for the convenience it offers, the credit card extracts a payment in personal privacy. Each time you use your credit card, your bank knows a little bit more about your spending habits, your dietary preferences, and your movements.

The trading of privacy for convenience has become so commonplace that we often don't even think about it. Rather than clip coupons, we use a grocer's savings card to get automatic deductions at the cash register—but at the same time, a record of our specific purchases is steadily being compiled.[1] On the Internet, we accept "cookies" from websites so that we don't have to reenter our user ID and password each time we enter a site like nytimes.com—but those same cookies help websites track which pages we look at and the sites we visit afterwards.

Companies make the exchange of privacy for convenience more palatable by offering the carrot of improved service. It's an old idea, of course: Five-star hotels thrive in part because of the detailed (and highly personal) notes that they keep of their repeat customers. The invasion of the guest's privacy is more than compensated by the hotel's ability to provide individualized service, to make the guest feel truly welcome. And we all enjoy feeling welcome, even if it's just a bunch of barflies yelling "Norm!" when we walk through the door.

The sacrificing of personal privacy for convenience occurs in the workplace as well, but the exchange is less voluntary. If you are expected to use a company car, phone, or credit card, those items will reveal information about you regardless of whether you want it revealed. In fact, many employers actively seek out the information that can be collected from company vehicles or credit cards. Anytime you go out on the road, whether it's in a dusty van with the company logo plastered on the side or on the Concorde, an inherent tension arises between the freedom of being outside the office and your responsibility to your employer. At a bare minimum, there's the question of productivity: Are you spending your time wisely? Until recently, employers had relatively few means of monitoring your productivity outside of the workplace. Essentially, the employer's assessment was limited to results: Did you finish your route? How do your sales figures compare to other employees? Do customers complain about you?

To varying degrees, employers were willing to give their employees some latitude in how they did their work outside of the office so long as the work actually got done. But as our culture and legal system have changed over the last century, more serious questions have arisen: Are you being loyal? Are you doing something that will reflect badly on the corporation or cause it to be sued? The answers to those types of questions depends in large part, obviously, on what you were doing and when you were doing it.

## The Problems of Detour and Frolic

With the invention of the automobile, the amount of work that a business could conduct and the area in which it could be conducted both expanded tremendously. But with the increased economic opportunity came an increase in the potential for liability and an increased difficulty in monitoring employee conduct outside of the office. Like the nervous parents of a teenage driver, employers are concerned about what their employees are doing when they're out of sight, and they are using increasingly sophisticated tools to monitor where employees go and what they're doing when they're out of sight.[2]

It's not completely unreasonable, of course, for your employer to want some idea of what you are doing outside of the office during the workday. You are, after all, being paid to do a job, not to spend the afternoon shopping. Increasingly, however, the tools employers are using to gather legitimate information about how you're doing your job are also being used to track how you spend your personal time. Technology doesn't make a distinction between work time and personal time; that distinction needs to be made by the people using the technology. Unfortunately, the tendency of employers is to err on the side of collecting more information and not less.

Like so many of the changes in our society, employer surveillance is driven in large part by fear of litigation. Within company walls, harassment or hostile work environment lawsuits cause the most problems; outside the walls, one of the leading types of lawsuits that businesses face are personal injury claims resulting from employee negligence.

If employees were solely responsible for their own actions, the need for surveillance would be greatly reduced (although employers would still be concerned that their employees might be doing something that would reflect badly on the company—a company van parked at a local strip club is bound to cause some comment). But over the centuries, the doctrine of *respondeat superior*—which provides that an employer is liable for the negligence of an employee—has become an integral part of our legal system.

The theory behind the doctrine is that employers have the ability to control the actions of their employees, through both training and company policy, and therefore are liable for the injuries that their employees cause within the scope of their duties. The practical motivation is that the employer generally has greater resources (or can afford more insurance) and is therefore in a better position to compensate an injured party.

The classic example is the pizza delivery person who causes an accident while speeding to deliver a pizza within the company's advertised half-hour time limit. Since the employee is acting within the scope of her employment, the pizza company would almost certainly be liable for the damages resulting from the employee's negligence.[3]

A more difficult issue arises when an employee causes an injury while doing something that is not clearly within the scope of his employment. For instance, if a package delivery person stops to visit his son at his daycare and then sideswipes a parked car as he's leaving, the question is whether or not the employer should be held liable for the employee's negligence.

The answer depends in large part on whether the employee's visit to his son is considered a "detour" or a "frolic." Over the years, the courts have developed a distinction between cases involving a minor deviation from the employee's routine (a detour) and a major departure from it (a frolic). If the daycare center is on a fairly direct line between two package delivery stops, the employee's visit to his son is likely to be considered a detour, and the employer would likely be on the hook. On the other hand, if the daycare center is forty-five minutes off the delivery route, the visit is more likely to be considered a frolic.

Obviously, it can be difficult to determine whether a midday visit to a daycare center is a frolic or a detour. Recently, courts have tried to make it easier for juries to reach a decision by instructing them that in order for an employer to be liable, the employee's conduct must have been "foreseeable." It's no defense that the employee's actions were intentionally harmful or even criminal; if the actions were in furtherance of the employer's business interest, then the employer can still be liable. For instance, if a bouncer injures someone while forcibly ejecting him from a nightclub, his employer may well be liable. By contrast, if a hotel masseur sexually assaults a hotel guest during her massage, is that in furtherance of the hotel's business interests? At least one court has concluded that it is not.[4]

A major goal of employee surveillance outside of the workplace, then, is to keep detours and frolicking to a minimum. Time and again, employers report that when employees know that their vehicles are equipped with Global Positioning System (GPS) tracking devices, they're more focused and less likely to take detours, long lunches, or afternoon naps.

But there's a subtle trap lurking for employers in the use of the impressive new surveillance technologies discussed in the remainder of this chapter. On the one hand, surveillance tools like GPS and smart credit cards will certainly make it easier for businesses to prevent or stop inappropriate or negligent behavior. At the same time, however, it will enable employers to compile extensive information about their employees' work habits, activities, and so forth. Since one of the important distinctions between a "detour" and a "frolic" is the foreseeability of an employee's actions, then an argument can be made that the more information an employer has about its employees' activities, then the greater the scope of "foreseeable" activity and the less likely an employer will be able to argue that a particular employee was in fact frolicking.

## Digital Footprints

Even before the Industrial Revolution and the wave of invention that followed, employers had some basic tools for tracking what their employees were doing during the course of a day: Delivery records, customer receipts, travel logs, expense reports, and other types of business records could be used by an employer to analyze the effectiveness and efficiency of their employees.

As various technological innovations became commonplace, the information companies have been able to collect regarding employee behavior has grown steadily more comprehensive and detailed. In most cases, information gathering is incidental to the main purpose of the technology: For example, the point of a company credit card is to facilitate business travel and purchases, not to generate information about what employees are doing outside of the office. Yet the use of a credit card does generate that kind of information, providing employers with a powerful tool for learning more about the people who work for them.

## Credit Cards Get Steadily Smarter

In truth, the amount of information that can be generated by a small plastic rectangle—the now-ubiquitous credit card—is stunning. Thanks to the marvels of the modern telecommunications system and increasingly powerful computers, and depending on your usage habits, a credit card can compile a nearly step-by-step record of your daily activities.

The first credit cards were issued during the 1920s. For instance, General Petroleum Company issued a card in 1924 that allowed employees to charge gasoline and the cost of auto repairs. After the bugs were worked out of the system, GPC expanded its charge card program to established customers and then to the general public.

Despite the Great Depression in the 1930s, the popularity of charge cards continued to grow. American Telephone & Telegraph instituted the "Bell System Credit Card," and a number of airlines and railroads created similar programs. The only thing that slowed the growth of the charge card industry was World War II: In the summer of 1941, in an effort to curb war economy inflation, the U.S. government issued "Regulation W," which severely limited the issuance of consumer credit (including charge cards) and the maximum time allowed for the repayment of loans.

Following the end of the war, consumer consumption began steadily increasing. In 1952, "Regulation W" was repealed and, to the horror of those who survived the Depression, credit became a increasingly popular means of financing purchases. To meet the increased demand for consumer credit, companies began issuing general-purpose credit cards, which were not limited to a single business but could be used at a variety of establishments.

The first such card was offered by Diners Club, Inc. in 1950; American Express made its appearance in 1958. The primary competition for these credit card companies was the cards issued by individual banks. Bank cards had one significant advantage: revolving credit. Banks quickly discovered that consumers were willing to spend more if they did not have to pay the entire amount each month, and that banks could earn significant amounts of money by charging interest on the outstanding balance. In 1965, California's Bank of America entered into licensing agreements with banks in a variety of other states and created the national BankAmericard system, which would be rechristened "Visa" in 1977; in 1967, four other Californian banks formed a coalition to offer the MasterCharge card, which became MasterCard in 1979.

The fundamental requirement for a successful credit card system is accurate record keeping. When you make a purchase using a credit card, you voluntarily set in motion a large flow of information. In order for a merchant to receive payment for the goods or service you've charged, the merchant must correctly record your name, the item or service being purchased and its cost, any applicable taxes, the name of the merchant, the location of the purchase, and the date.

The impact of credit cards on employee privacy depends in large part on who's paying the bills. If the credit card is in your name, your employer has no legal right to access your spending records. Even if you use your personal credit card for business-related expenses, your employer will only know about those activities if you turn in the charges for reimbursement. But if the credit card bills are paid by your employer, then it should come as no surprise that your employer can and probably does review how you're using the card. You might be under the impression that if the bill for your corporate card is sent directly to you and you pay it out of your own pocket, your purchases are free from inspection. Far from it. A copy of your charges is also typically provided to the organization that requested the card. The logical conclusion is that if there are things that you don't want your employer to know about your personal spending habits (what you've bought, where you ate lunch, your midday assignation at a local motel), the best solution is to leave the corporate charge card in your pocket.

Increasingly, however, that may be difficult. As we saw in Chapter 3, there's a steady trend—led by the Department of Defense—to issue smart cards to employees. The primary purpose of smart cards is to provide a more secure identification of the bearer, but the steadily increasing capabilities of the cards offer a host of other possibilities, including charging meals at the company cafeteria and buying snacks at a vending machine. Already, a number of colleges and universities use cards that combine identification and payment systems. The Smart Card Alliance, in fact, reports that one in seventeen college students is currently carrying a smart card. Depending on their institution's system, students can use the card to enter school facilities, buy food, purchase school supplies and books, do laundry, pay library fines, make copies, receive scholarship and grant funds, and even make tuition payments.[5]

At first, a smart card ID that doubles as a payment card (also known as combo cards) will be limited to the facility or organization that issued it. Right now, for instance, you can use a combo card to buy a meal at a company cafeteria, but you can't use most combo cards to purchase lunch at a local restaurant. But the desire for convenience (and the need to cut down on multiple cards) will eventually merge smart IDs with general payment systems like Visa and MasterCard. And if the use of smart cards is to make micropurchases (the morning newspaper, a cup of coffee, etc.), employers issuing combo cards will have access to yet another level of detail about what their employees do during the course of the day.

At least one government agency has already experimented with a smart card that combines both identification and financial services. In 1999, the General Services Administration (GSA) issued a combo card to 450 of its employees at its Willow Wood, Virginia, facility. One side of the card was a traditional Citibank Visa card, which the GSA employees could use for various financial services under Citibank's contract with GSA. On the other side of the card was a smart chip running the Java Card operating system developed by IBM. The smart card functions as a key to the GSA building, regulates network access by comparing a stored fingerprint to the data gathered by a keyboard fingerprint reader, and contains a digital signature that card carriers can use to sign their e-mails. The GSA smart card program is just one of at least fifty-five smart card pilot programs that the GSA/Office of Electronic Government is tracking at the federal level.[6]

## E-ZPass and MetroCards

One way to significantly cut down on the size of the paper trail that you leave during the day is to avoid credit cards altogether and pay cash. Increasingly, however, other types of convenient payment systems are being developed that threaten to expand the tracking capabilities of both employers and marketers.

For nearly a decade, drivers in the New York area have been using an electronic toll collection (ETC) system called E-ZPass. The system consists of a small radio transponder or tag that is attached to the windshield of an automobile and a receiver that can read a number emitted by the transponder as it goes by. The system can process E-Zpass-equipped vehicles nearly four times faster than coin-paying vehicles. In October 2001, *The New York Times* reported that there were six million E-ZPass tags in use in the Northeast.[7]

There are a variety of other ETC systems in use across the country, and the main concern for state and federal highway administrators is what can be done to make the systems compatible. Ultimately, the goal is to resolve the technical issues so that people can drive from one end of the country to the other without having to fish for change.

Convenient? Unquestionably. The problem, as we've seen from the start of this chapter, is that convenience is paid for in the coin of privacy. When your ETC tag is read by a receiver, it creates a data record marking the specific location of your car at a certain date and time. The pool of potential data entries is likely to grow steadily in the months and years to come. McDonald's, for instance, is field-testing the use of the E-ZPass technology for its drive-up windows, and ETC companies are exploring numerous auto-related applications, including gas stations and parking garages.

It's not only cars that can be tracked through the use of ETC tags or their equivalent. Urban metro systems have been using ETC cards for years. Unlike auto transponders, however, mass transportation ETC cards are still fairly anonymous; for instance, if I go into the Washington or New York metro system and use cash to buy a MetroCard, there's no electronic record to link me to that particular card. Even though the MetroCard system tracks the fact that a particular card was used at a particular station at a particular time, the card is one of hundreds of thousands of anonymous cards purchased each day. (Of course, if I'm arrested with the card on me, or if the police successfully search a trash barrel and lift my fingerprints from a discarded card, then all bets are off.)

For the time being, even the privacy cost of having a transponder in your car is fairly low. The companies that operate ETC systems are adamant that they do not market information about the travel habits of drivers. The problem, however, is that there is no impediment to their doing so at some point in the future.

While aggregate ETC usage information is interesting to highway and metro administrators, to city planners, and to the providers of emergency services, data about the specific habits of individuals is of intense interest to retailers. The problem with most advertising methods is that they are overly broad; only a small percentage of the people who see a newspaper ad, for instance, are actually interested in what the ad offers. The Holy Grail of advertising is the perfectly targeted ad: the ideal pitch to a specific person with a particular interest. There's a widespread consensus that the travel data collected by systems like ETC brings advertisers closer to that goal. As the amount and accuracy of the information collected continues to grow, its value will steadily rise, and companies will be increasingly tempted to add another revenue stream by licensing or selling it to advertisers.[8]

Moreover, regardless of how loudly ETC companies trumpet their privacy policies, they are relatively meaningless in the face of a prosecutorial subpoena. In the spring of 2001, the E-ZPass records of a defendant in a murder trial in Poughkeepsie, New York, were subpoenaed to show that the defendant had time to meet with a coconspirator at a highway rest stop. The defendant's E-ZPass data showed that he took nearly an hour to travel nineteen miles, which the prosecutor successfully argued was more than sufficient time to hold a meeting along the way.

Earlier this summer, a thirty-five-year-old former Transit Authority employee was convicted of murder based in part on information collected by the MetroCard system. Charles Stewart, who worked as a subway motor-man for eleven years, was given an employee identification card that doubled as a MetroCard. He denied murdering his ex-girlfriend, Angelique Williams, but MetroCard records showed that Stewart boarded a bus heading toward Williams's home just before the murder and returned to his house from the murder scene shortly afterwards. According to prosecutors, it was the first time that MetroCard data had been used in a homicide prosecution. It is highly unlikely to be the last time.

As with credit cards, the person other than yourself who can easily request tag data is the person paying for the tag. If your company is paying for an ETC tag on the automobile you drive, there is nothing to prevent the company from asking for the location of the tolls paid with the tag and the times the tolls were paid. With relatively little effort, a company can compile fairly detailed information about an employee's daily driving habits, up to and including the employee's average speed between toll booths.

An employer's access to such information raises interesting privacy questions. Is it appropriate for an employer to map out exactly when an employee went through a particular toll booth? Is the employer entitled to know how fast its employees drive? Should your boss be able to check which train or bus you take to work? As a practical matter, if your employer is paying for your E-Zpass or MetroCard, there is little you can do to limit your employer's access to that type of information.

## Roam, Sweet Roam

The convenience and versatility of the cellular phone has made it one of the most rapidly and widely adopted technologies in history. According to wireless industry analyst EMC, the world's one *billionth* cellular subscriber signed up for service in the first week of April 2002. The growth from 500 million subscribers to one billion was particularly impressive: It took just twenty-five months, with subscribers joining at the average rate of 450 people per *minute*. EMC predicts that the number of cellular subscribers will double to 2 billion by 2005.

The appeal of cellular phones is easy to appreciate: You want to meet your friends for a movie, but they're not home. You call their cellular number and discover that they're just two blocks away—you can even meet for a beer before the movie starts. Or perhaps your car breaks down on the highway. There's no need to hunt for a working public phone—just call AAA from your cell. The possibilities are endless. Around the world, people are using their cellular phones to find each other in crowded places, play games, pay for sodas, watch videos, check sports scores, and so on.

## Cell Phones and Who You Call

In one sense, the information that a cellular phone can provide about you is the same as that provided by any other type of phone—a monthly bill that contains a list of telephone numbers you've called. But because cellular phone users in the United States pay for cellular air time regardless of whether they place the call or receive it, cellular phone bills also record the phone numbers of the telephone calls (cellular or otherwise) that were made to you.

As with credit cards, if you pay your own cellular phone charges, your employer will have access to that information only if you submit a request for reimbursement. But large numbers of businesses provide cell phones for their employees, which means that a copy of the bill (or the bill itself) for those phones is available to the employer, who then has the opportunity to review it.

In the not-too-distant future, your cellular phone bill may not only list the people with whom you spoke, but also pinpoint your specific location at various times. In Europe, for instance, cell phones are routinely used to make small purchases at vending machines, restaurant jukeboxes, and even car washes. In order for a vending machine to accept payments from a phone, the machine is assigned its own unique phone number; to obtain a soda, for instance, you dial the number of the vending machine, and a voice menu instructs you to press "one" for Coke, "two" for root beer, "three" for orange soda, etc. The cost of the soda is automatically added to your phone bill. That small transaction, while undoubtedly more convenient in many ways than trying to find correct change, is a potential treasure trove of information about your purchasing habits and your movements. As the pool of data steadily grows, the phone company's interest in offering that data to marketers will also grow. Moreover, if you use a company cell phone to make vending machine purchases, your employer knows what you've been buying, and with relatively little effort, can determine where you were when you made each purchase.

So far, the use of cell phones as payment devices (a trend known generally as "m-commerce") has not made much headway in the United States, but three of the largest cellular companies—Ericsson, Motorola, and Nokia—have been working on an open, standardized system for secure mobile electronic transactions. In addition to payments at vending machines, the companies also envision using cellular phones at cash registers, toll booths, or parking meters.

In addition, communication giant Sprint has announced a collaboration with eOne Global LP, an affiliate of First Data Corp., to create a national mobile payment system. Sprint hopes that cell phone users can be persuaded to store credit card and other banking information in their phone. When they're ready to make a purchase, they can transmit the data to the store's cash register, which can then transmit the information to the credit card computer for authorization. Presumably, users will also have the option to charge smaller purchases directly to their phone bill.

If successful, m-commerce initiatives will have the effect of turning each cellular phone into an ETC (electronic toll collection) device or credit card. How much purchasing behavior and location data is collected from each phone, of course, will depend on the extent to which you trade the convenience of cellular payment for the loss of privacy.

The monthly phone bill is only one potential source of information about how you are using your company cell phone. Most cell phones on the market today are equipped with the ability to store dozens or even hundreds of names and phone numbers. In situations where employers are concerned that an employee is stealing information or trade secrets, a cell phone can be a valuable source of information regarding the employee's contacts. The same is true for corporate litigation: Attorneys and private detectives now include cell phones and personal data assistants (PDAs) like Palm Pilots in their search for potential evidence.

The value of cell phones as potential sources of evidence will only increase as they are configured to work with or merged with personal data assistants. Devices like the Handspring Treo, the T-Mobile Pocket PC Phone, and the Kyocera Palm OS Smartphone combine the features of a phone with PDA operating systems like Palm OS or Windows CE. Again, the combination is undoubtedly convenient: You can look up a phone number in the PDA address book, tap a button, and have the device automatically dial the number. But if your employer has adopted a policy stating that it will periodically search any such employer-provided devices, the convenience of using the device must be balanced by the realization that any information you enter can be viewed by your employer.

## Cell Phones and Where You Are

The chief benefit of the cellular phone—its portability—relies on a worldwide system of transmission towers, each located in a separate coverage "cell" (hence the name "cellular"). When you dial a call on a cellular phone, the call is broadcast from the phone to the nearest transmission towers. The call is then rebroadcast through the other towers in the network until it reaches the receiving phone, either by being rebroadcast to another cellular phone or by being connected to a landline.

Geography has always been a critical component of the cellular phone system, for reasons of both billing and call completion. In the United States, the cellular phone system began as a series of regional systems and initially, callers were only able to make cellular calls in the region in which they obtained their phone. But consumers quickly demonstrated an interest in being able to use their phones while traveling outside of their home region. To accommodate them, the cellular phone companies worked out agreements that allow cellular phone users to make calls anywhere near a transmission tower, regardless of which cellular company built it. In the process, the phone companies came up with the concept of "roaming," a term used to describe a cellular phone traveling outside of its home subscription area. Calls made while roaming generally cost more than calls made in the home area, largely because each cellular network that carries the call needs to be compensated for doing so.

It is the technical requirements of actually completing cellular calls that raise the most profound privacy concerns. In order for a telephone call to reach your cellular phone, the cellular phone system has to know where your phone is at any given time. When your phone is turned on, it periodically emits a brief signal that is picked up by one or more cellular towers. The system then knows to which tower a call should be routed so that your phone can receive the transmission.

If the only value of the locating signal were to receive phone calls, there would be few privacy issues raised by cellular phone use. To complete a call, the only thing the network needs to know is the location of the tower closest to you. Although cellular coverage cells vary dramatically in size, even the smaller ones in urban areas are large enough that it would be difficult to locate a particular caller.

But sometimes the location of the call is critically important. For instance, when 911 calls are made from land lines, the equipment used by emergency services is configured to provide the address from which the call was made. That's obviously not possible with cellular phones, and it has become a real problem for emergency personnel. In 2000, according to the National Emergency Number Association, fully one-third of all 911 calls were made from cellular phones. If the person making the call does not know where he is, it can be next to impossible for emergency personnel to find the caller in time to provide care.

Recognizing the problem, particularly as reports began surfacing of cellular callers who died because emergency personnel could not find them, Congress passed the Wireless Communications & Public Safety Act, which President Clinton signed into law on October 24, 1999. Pursuant to the provisions of that law, the Federal Communications Commission adopted a regulation requiring that either cell phones or cellular networks be equipped with technology that will enable the location of a cell phone to be detected within 300 feet. The initiative, known as E-911 (for "enhanced 911") was originally scheduled to be fully implemented by 2004, but due to complaints from cellular networks, various technological difficulties, and equipment delays, the deadline has been pushed to 2005.

Cellular networks and phone manufacturers are taking two different approaches to meeting the FCC's location requirement. One approach—triangulation—takes advantage of the fact that the locating signal emitted by each phone is usually picked up by more than one cellular tower. By measuring the strength of the locating signal from the phone, the phone's distance from each tower can be determined, and using those distances, its physical location can be determined.

Other companies plan to comply with the FCC requirement by using Global Positioning System technology (which is discussed in more detail later in this chapter). These companies are putting a GPS chip into their cellular handsets that will alert emergency personnel to the caller's location.

Not surprisingly, law enforcement is very interested in the growing capabilities of the cellular network to track the physical location of individual callers. In 1994, Congress passed the Communications Assistance for Law Enforcement Act (CALEA), which provides that the telecommunications industry must modify its equipment to enable the Federal Bureau of Investigations to continue its ability to monitor (i.e., wiretap) communications as new technologies are introduced. In August 1999, after a fruitless year of negotiations between the FBI and the telecommunications industry over how exactly to implement CALEA, the Federal Communications Commission stepped in and passed a number of regulations aimed at breaking the logjam. One new regulation requires that the telecommunications industry provide law enforcement with the "cell site at the beginning and termination of a mobile call," provided that an officer or FBI agent has obtained a warrant from a court before requesting the information.[9]

The fact that your cellular phone can show roughly where you are at any given time is disconcerting enough. More disturbing is the capability of such information to be tracked over a period of time, yielding a detailed history of your movements and habits. Law enforcement's interest in such information is unquestionably real: Five years ago, in Switzerland, the *Sonntags Zeitung* newspaper reported that authorities were able to recover the location of any mobile phone call made during the preceding six months. At roughly the same time, a London prosecutor cited the importance of cell phone records in tracking the movements of a drug dealer and convicting him.[10] Late last year, in Palo Alto, California, a man named Kenneth Fitzhugh was convicted of murdering his wife Kristine after a Verizon wireless engineer testified that signals received by the Verizon system from Fitzhugh's cell phone showed that it would have been impossible for him to have been far from the murder scene—his home—at the time of the murder.

For the time being, at least, the tracking capabilities of the cellular phone system apply to the phones themselves and not people (much like the infrared badge technology discussed earlier). But in large part because of the information that they can contain, PDAs and PDA-equipped cell phones are becoming an increasingly popular target for thieves. One recent survey concluded that at least one out of ten lost or stolen PDAs can give access to the owner's bank account. PDAs also offer fruitful possibilities for people engaged in corporate espionage or industrial spying. In order to protect such information and minimize the chances of misuse, various companies are working to incorporate biometric technology into cell phones and other portable devices.

A British company, Domain Dynamics, announced in 1999 that it had developed voice-recognition technology that could be incorporated into cell phones in order to prevent unauthorized calls. The more common approach, however, is the one being pursued by Veridicom, one of a handful of companies that is developing a fingerprint identification chip that can be incorporated into cell phones, PDAs, laptops, and other equipment. Veridicom, based in Santa Clara, California, is a joint venture between U.S. Venture Partners and Lucent Technologies, which developed the sensor on which the chip is based. The company's solid-state silicon sensors currently retail for fifty dollars each, and prices are expected to continue to fall; most analysts envision widespread implementation of fingerprint biometrics in mobile devices when per-unit prices drop into the ten to fifteen dollar range.

Obviously, one consequence of the incorporation of biometric security into wireless devices is that it will irrefutably tie you to the device. If your fingerprint or voice print is required to make a phone call on a cellular phone, then it will be extremely difficult to deny that you made the call, or that you were not in a particular location at a certain time.

The law enforcement uses of cellular phone tracking will garner the most attention and are most likely to wind up as a plot device on *CSI* or *Law and Order*. However, it's the commercial potential of such tracking information that poses the greatest threat to personal and workplace privacy. While the legislation signed by President Clinton in 1999 contained a provision that prohibited cellular phone tracking information from being released without the customer's permission, such permission has generally been easy to obtain from consumers directly (largely by offering discounts or some type of service in exchange) or through their employers, who can make such permission a condition of receiving a company cell phone.

# GPS: The "Pointy-Haired Boss" in the Sky

A stock comic character is the conspiracy nut in the aluminum foil hat who's convinced that the government has secretly planted electronic tracking devices in everyone's head. Played to bug-eyed perfection by Mel Gibson in *Conspiracy Theory* and with somewhat more aplomb by Jeff Goldbloom in *Independence Day*, these characters are convinced that when the black helicopters of the New World Government swoop over the hills, the tracking devices will make it impossible to hide.

Apocalyptic images aside, even the biggest nuts have a kernel of truth. In fact, we're well on our way to a time when each of us carries a real-time tracking device: a cellular phone or other wireless device equipped with a GPS chip.

Unlike the erratic information provided to employers (and others) by credit card and cellular phone records, GPS technology is capable of providing a constant stream of data about an employee's location. It's not a perfect record of what you have been doing, of course, but if your employer knows where you have been during the course of a day, then it's possible to make some reasonable guesses about what you have been doing.

## Brought to You by the Same Folks Who First Funded the Internet

The devices that enable accurate tracking of your movements are small, square satellite receivers that can be incorporated into virtually any size device, ranging from a cellular phone to an automobile. The receivers listen for radio signals transmitted by twenty-four satellites that constantly orbit the earth at a distance of 12,600 miles. Known collectively as the Global Positioning System, each of the seventeen-foot wide, one-ton satellites orbits the earth twice each day, and at any time, a receiver can hear as many as eight signals at once. Using those signals, a GPS receiver can provide you with highly accurate information regarding your location, your speed, your altitude, and the local time anywhere in the world.

The skyrocketing popularity of the GPS is due to the radio signal constantly emitted by each satellite. The signal contains two pieces of constantly updated information: the satellite's precise orbital location and a hyper-accurate time stamp.[11] A GPS receiver is designed to listen to the signals from the satellites. By comparing the time information in a satellite data stream to its own internal clock, the GPS receiver can calculate how far it is from the satellite transmitting the signal.

As long as the GPS receiver can hear the signal transmitted by at least three satellites, the receiver can calculate its location on earth using a process called triangulation. If the GPS receiver can hear the signal from a fourth satellite, then the receiver can also determine its altitude. Unlike FM radio or broadcast television, the GPS only functions when the receiver can "see" the satellites in orbit; thus, GPS only works outdoors, and it functions better in rural areas than in cities.

Like many of the electronic conveniences we take for granted, the GPS was originally a Defense Department project. (The military still operates the GPS system and controls the broadcast of the satellites' signals.) With the development of the atomic clock, the military realized that the superaccurate timepieces could be used to help establish locations and aid navigation on earth. In 1964, a Polaris submarine became the first vehicle on earth to establish its location by using a satellite signal.

In the early 1970s, the Defense Department began implementing the Navstar GPS, and by 1978, Rockwell International had launched ten prototype satellites. A decade later, the first of twenty-four new GPS satellites was launched, and the last one was put in orbit on June 26, 1993. As was the case with the Internet, which was originally built by the Defense Advanced Research Projects Agency (DARPA), civilian access to the GPS was originally barred. However, the companies building GPS equipment (including, not surprisingly, Rockwell) saw the commercial possibilities of the new location technology and began pressuring the Pentagon to open up the system to public use.

In an effort to limit the risk of the system being used by criminals, terrorists, and opposing armies, the Defense Department developed a two-signal system known as "selective availability." One data stream transmitted by each satellite contained the satellite's correct time and location, and one contained intentional errors. Only authorized personnel could purchase receivers capable of receiving the unadulterated signal, which allowed location calculations to within ten yards. By contrast, GPS receivers intended for civilian use could only receive the flawed signal, which meant that their accuracy was limited to a radius of about one hundred yards.[12]

Both the Pentagon and the Clinton administration continued to receive pressure from GPS manufacturers, mapping companies, and other commercial ventures to free up the GPS by eliminating selective availability, and on May 1, 2000, President Clinton announced that he was discontinuing it. Civilian GPS devices immediately became ten times more accurate, and analysts predicted that the GPS industry would double in size, from $8 billion per year in 2000 to $16 billion in 2003.[13] That estimate proved to be conservative. The terrorist attacks on the United States on September 11, 2001, have greatly increased interest in GPS technology, and some analysts now predict that the burgeoning industry may see annual revenues as high as $34 to $41 billion by 2006.[14]

For both technical and business reasons, GPS systems have concentrated first on vehicles. The Washington, D.C.-based Strategis Group estimates that by the end of 2005, as many as 17 million light trucks and cars in the United States will be equipped with devices that combine GPS and wireless technology (known collectively as "telematics").[15] Cambridge-based Forrester Research goes further, estimating that by 2006, fully 80 percent of all new vehicles will be equipped with telematics devices.[16]

## Where Have You Been and What Have You Been Doing?

Even before President Clinton ordered the unscrambling of the GPS, the ability to track vehicles was attracting enthusiastic attention from the private sector. Operating even a small fleet of vehicles is expensive, and employers are anxious to know that the vehicles are being used as efficiently as possible. Moreover, the threat of a big personal injury lawsuit is always lurking in the back of an employer's mind. Given the havoc that employees can wreak with or to company vehicles, employers are particularly interested in tracking where their employees have taken their vehicles during the course of the day and how they're using them.[17] Long-range trucking companies have shown the greatest interest in GPS tracking data, since the potential for lost productivity, detouring, and outright frolicking grows dramatically when an employee's workplace is 3,000 miles wide. As early as 1997, some major trucking companies were using GPS and onboard computers to track the movement of individual trucks, monitor repair schedules, and provide assistance in case of emergencies.

Over the last few years, the increased affordability and power of the GPS system has made it possible for even modest-sized businesses to track their vehicles—and their employees' movements—with amazing precision. Employers are hailing the reams of incredibly specific information that can be gathered: a log of the times a vehicle spent moving and parked; a detailed map of the vehicle's route; highly accurate mileage tallies (without the need for employee recording); the speed of a vehicle during the course of the day; increased security (some systems can record and report on the times and locations that cargo doors were opened); and the ability to provide lost drivers with accurate instructions.

A typical system is the Time Manager GPS System offered by Formetco, Inc., a Duluth, Georgia, outdoor media marketing company. The system consists of a GPS-equipped monitoring unit that is installed in a vehicle. The unit contains a memory module that records a variety of data; on a periodic basis, the memory module is swapped for a new module, and the data in the old module is downloaded into a personal computer and displayed in the Time Manager software. In a typical configuration, the Time Manager shows the number of the vehicle for which the data was recorded, the date on which each trip took place, the start and end time of each trip, the amount of time the vehicle spent moving, its maximum speed during each trip segment, the amount of time the vehicle spent idling in traffic, and the amount of time spent at each stop. The system can also be set up to monitor and record door openings, tailgate openings, boomlift operations, and more.

As one of Formetco's customers put it, "[i]t gives us peace of mind knowing where our vehicles have been and how they are being utilized." Greg Yarborough, the director of operations for Tib's Electrical Services Co., a Decatur, Georgia, electrical contracting firm, went on to add:

> The GPS has helped us identify poor practices such as leaving trucks idling unnecessarily and speeding. I believe that technicians are more conscious about using their driving time wisely and eliminating unnecessary stops . . . .
>
> The GPS system also keeps the technicians from taking excessive lunch breaks, taking the long way around, or just killing time riding around. We are able to check payroll to match times that the technicians are physically on the job site and the time they said they were on the job . . . .[18]

Private employers, of course, are not the only potential market for GPS systems like Time Manager. Some school systems use GPS tracking technology to make sure that none of their drivers are using the school busses to conduct personal business, like grocery shopping or errands, and in some cases, to let parents know that their children are skipping school. If a child purposely misses the bus and then claims that it never showed up, a school system can call up the GPS information for the bus in question and show the precise time that it arrived at the bus stop. Other municipalities have outfitted sanitation trucks and public works vehicles with GPS systems to monitor the effectiveness of routes and the efficiency of their employees. In Chicago, the city's snow plows are equipped with GPS systems, which enable supervisors to track plowing progress, reroute trucks to areas that need more attention, and generally oversee the process of snow removal.

Not surprisingly, if you work for a company or government agency that uses a GPS-equipped vehicle, you have relatively little control over whether your employer collects location information and what it does with that information. The most benign use of the information generated by a GPS system is simply to confirm that you've done the work you were supposed to do during the day. Less reasonable uses of the information spring to mind, however: What if you stop at Planned Parenthood on your lunch break and your supervisor wants to know if you're pregnant? Or what if your employer decides to lay you off because you stop at McDonald's for lunch two days out of three and there's concern that the cost of providing you health insurance and medical care will be increased by your weight? If you're an at-will employee, it can be very difficult to determine the reason you were terminated and even harder to show that the termination was in violation of federal or state law.

Employers unquestionably find it valuable to know where their vehicles have been during the course of a day. But increasingly, they are demonstrating a willingness to purchase and install GPS systems that are capable of giving them real-time information about where their employees are located. The ability of your boss to know where your vehicle is at any given moment is the result of the merger between two technologies: GPS and wireless communications.

## OnStar™ Knows Where the Bat Cave Is

In one amusing television commercial, a dark figure swoops down out of the sky, lands lightly on the ground, and leaps into his black, jet-propelled vehicle. He notices a new set of buttons on the dashboard, including one with a light blue background, the word "On," and a small star over the "n." His butler, Alfred, gravely informs him that he's equipped the vehicle with new features to provide roadside assistance, emergency help, and directions. As the sleek, lethal-looking car roars out of the cave, the masked driver presses the "OnStar" button and a courteous voice asks, "How can I help you, Batman?"

Apparently, Alfred did not realize that he had given away the location of Batman's secret cave. In order for OnStar™ to be able to provide its services (which currently include such location-sensitive features as emergency services, stolen vehicle tracking, route support, and ride assistance), it needs to be able to locate your vehicle. It does so through a combination of a satellite and wireless technology: A GPS receiver keeps track of where the vehicle is at any given time, and the information is periodically transmitted to OnStar™ by an onboard wireless phone that uses the nation's cellular system.

The OnStar™ system, which is currently installed in 1.5 million cars on the road today, is a standard feature on various makes and models of mid- and high-end vehicles, including Acura, Buick, Cadillac, and Saab. At the request of its customers or in limited circumstances, of the police, OnStar™ can identify the location of any one of those cars. At present, the company does not keep any historical information about where each car has traveled, but there is certainly no technological impediment to doing so.

What customers get when they fork over $16.95 each month to On-Star™ for its Safety & Security program is just that—the comfort of knowing that if something goes wrong, the location information generated by the OnStar™ system can help provide assistance. As *Wired* magazine reported in December 2001, the OnStar™ system has some obvious benefits for law enforcement as well: When the OnStar™-equipped car of Akram Jaber was carjacked on Chicago's South Side in late September 2001, he called 911 to report the crime and then called OnStar™. A company operator called the OnStar™ unit in Jaber's vehicle, retrieved GPS information on a minute-by-minute basis, and relayed the car's location to police. The police intercepted and captured the carjackers within minutes of the commission of the crime.[19]

As GPS technology becomes more common, a wide variety of other services will be introduced. For instance, the car manufacturer Ford and the telecommunications company Qualcomm have formed a joint venture called Wingcast, which will offer a new service to purchasers of 2003 Fords and Nissans. Called GeoSensing, the system will automatically notify the car's owner by e-mail and/or phone if the vehicle is taken outside of a specific predefined area. Mercedes also offers a similar system, TeleAid, for its vehicles.

With the convenience of more accurate information about location and movement, however, comes matching concerns of invasions of privacy. The cost of developing and implementing telematics systems like OnStar™ or Wingcast is extremely expensive, and the companies that run them are obviously interested in finding ways to defray the cost. The information generated by a telematics system about your driving habits is potentially quite valuable, and the temptation to tap into a new revenue stream by making that information available to marketers is only going to grow.

The premise is the same as with grocery store cards—that consumers are willing to give up a certain amount of privacy in exchange for some benefit, in this case the ability to quickly request assistance if something goes wrong. Currently, OnStar™, TeleAid, and Wingcast require customers to "opt-in" to receive advertisements and special offers, which means that they will not receive unwanted advertisements from every Starbucks on their way to work. In time, however, it is likely that companies that offer telematics services will either simply market usage data or require customers to opt-in when they sign up.

Not all uses of telematics systems are going to be as benign (albeit annoying) as marketing. In the summer of 2001, James Turner, a New Haven, Connecticut, resident, sued Acme Rent-a-Car for invading his privacy. The previous fall, Turner had rented a car from Acme for a business trip down to Virginia. When Turner used his ATM card after returning the car, he was stunned to discover that Acme had withdrawn $450 from his account. What Turner had apparently overlooked was a clause in the rental contract that stated that the Acme vehicles are equipped with GPS technology, and that each time the car exceeded the company's maximum speed threshold (seventy-nine miles per hour), he would be assessed a surcharge of $150. Acme—which uses a telematics system called AirIQ—was able to show Turner on a map the three different locations where his speed exceeded seventy-nine miles per hour.

Outraged by the company's actions, Turner filed suit in small claims court in New Haven; the court deferred its decision until it obtained a ruling from the Connecticut Department of Consumer Protection about whether Acme's actions constituted an unfair business practice.[20] In January 2002, Connecticut State Attorney General Richard Blumenthal filed a complaint against Acme, claiming that the company had no justification for its arbitrary fine of $150 per infraction. The Department of Consumer Protection agreed with the attorney general and ordered Acme to refund Turner's money, along with the twenty-seven other people the rental company had previously fined.

## Nowhere to Hide: the Marriage of GPS and Personal Wireless Devices

Conceptually, it is a relatively small leap from providing location-based services to drivers to providing those same types of services to pedestrians. First, however, it was necessary to reduce the size of the GPS receiver to the point where it could comfortably be incorporated into portable devices. Thanks in large part to the impetus provided by the FCC's E-911 mandate, the functions of a GPS receiver have now been squeezed onto a microchip that can be incorporated into a wide array of consumer electronic devices.

For example, Applied Digital Solutions (which we met earlier as the developer of the RFID VeriChip) is the marketer of a product called Digital Angel, a combination watch and pager that uses GPS technology to provide location data about the wearer. The Digital Angel costs $400 per unit, plus a minimum of twenty-five dollars per month for the tracking service. In just three months, Applied Digital has signed up over 1,300 users.

A Westport, Connecticut, company, Pomals (an acronym standing for "peace of mind at light speed") is planning to introduce a hard plastic sleeve that slips over a person's cell phone, Blackberry device, or wireless PDA. Equipped with a GPS chip, the Pomals device will use the main device's wireless connectivity to constantly send location information to a map website. Subscribers to the Pomals service can log onto the website, enter a personal identification number for the GPS device, and instantly see a map showing the device's physical location. Pomals hopes to bring GPS-equipped device sleeves to market for less than $100, and charge five dollars per month for the online mapping service. It plans to release its products by the second quarter of 2003.[21]

But Pomals may rapidly be overtaken by developments in the wireless industry that will eliminate the need for an external, GPS-equipped sleeve. Location-based services have enormous economic potential: The research firm Allied Business Intelligence estimates that services that push information to cell phone users will generate more than $40 billion in annual revenues by 2006.[22] With those types of figures being tossed around, there is a tremendous incentive for cellular and electronics companies to hop on the bandwagon by incorporating GPS technologies into their handsets, Blackberries, PDAs, and so forth.

Europe and Asia are well ahead of the United States in the adoption of cellular systems, and location-specific applications are already being introduced in both regions. One example is Finder, a service introduced by the Swedish telecommunications firm Cellpoint Systems. Relying on the European technology Global System for Mobile Communications, Finder enables a cellular phone user to set up a "mobile buddy list." Once a friend's name is on your list, you can use your cellular phone to find out her current location. Your phone queries the network for the location of your friend's phone and then displays a text message, giving your friend's location in reference to a nearby landmark and distance from you. In the summer of 2002, Cellpoint announced a partnership with the Icelandic company Trackwell, which focuses on developing location-based applications. One such application is My Child Tracker, a system that allows parents to enter a password, click on a child's cell phone number, and view a map showing the location of the phone (and presumably, the child).

## Defensive Measures

Remarkably enough, there are times when you might not want to be found, or when you'd just as soon not receive a sales pitch or coupon to the latest Hollywood blockbuster as you walk past a movie theater. With most wireless devices on the market today, there is one simple, straightforward way to prevent tracking: Simply turn the wireless devices off. A cell phone that is not turned on doesn't send out its brief, "Hi, I'm over here," signal to the cellular network. The same is true for wireless PDAs and laptops: No juice means no signal. In addition, some programs like AT&T's "Find Friends" come equipped with an "invisible" mode, which allows you to take advantage of location-oriented information services without letting others know where you are.

But the trend in wireless devices is clearly toward "always on, always connected" (AOAC). In the week following the 9/11 attacks, *Wired* magazine reported that the addition of GPS chips to cellular phones would enable cellular phone companies to locate those phones even when they are turned off.[23] Bluetooth technology will take this further, since it is purposely designed to facilitate the concept that "the data I want always finds me."[24] Each Bluetooth-enabled device will be equipped with a small radio that will listen for queries from other Bluetooth-enabled devices.

Not surprisingly, not everyone is sold on the idea of AOAC. Some people are deeply concerned about the privacy implications of carrying wireless devices that always report their location to central networks, whether they are cellular systems or office network systems. Privacy Gear, a recently founded Brooklyn company, is offering small pouches made of a fabric called Cloaktec, which is designed to prevent wireless devices from sending or receiving signals. The mobileCloak (twenty-four dollars) and the larger mCloak r5 (thirty-four dollars) are designed to hold a variety of wireless devices, from cellular phones to toll payment devices like EZ-Pass.

For employees, the main question will be the consequences of using something like the mobileCloak—or even of turning off their GPS-equipped mobile device—to hide from their boss. If a constant stream of location data is the norm in your workplace, then information gaps are going to be suspicious. Sometimes, the absence of data can be just as problematic as reams of it.

# End Notes

1. As we'll see later on, it's one thing for a consumer to agree to allow a grocer to track purchases in exchange for discounts. It's another thing altogether for the grocer to turn around and then market your purchasing profile to a third party. At the very least, the question arises as to whether you've been adequately compensated for the further use of your information.

2. Not surprisingly, many of the surveillance tools and techniques that we'll discuss in this chapter were or are marketed to parents as well. There's a natural symmetry between the two markets.

3. The pizza company would argue—as Domino's repeatedly did—that it was not within the job description of its pizza delivery people to drive faster than the speed limit. However, juries routinely found that drivers were in fact urged to do whatever was necessary to meet the company's promised thirty-minute delivery time.

4. *Stern* v. *Ritz Carlton Chicago*, No. 1–97–2148, slip op. (Ill. Ct. Appeals Sixth Div. 1998).

5. By focusing on colleges and universities, the manufacturers of smart cards are following a trail blazed by the personal computer industry. In the early and mid-1980s, many if not most educational institutions had programs that let students

purchase computers through the school. Students grew increasingly comfortable with personal computers, and carried that experience with them into the workforce when they graduated. Similarly, today's graduates will be increasingly comfortable with the use of smart cards as cashless payment devices.

6. "SmartData," U.S. General Services Administration, n.d. Available online at egov .gov/scripts/sc_viewer.asp.

7. Jeffrey Selingo, "It's the Cars, Not the Tires, that Squeal," *The New York Times* (October 25, 2001).

8. The tempting value of customer information was amply demonstrated in the summer of 2000, when the Web retailer Toysmart went belly-up and tried to sell its customer list to raise funds for its creditors. The Federal Trade Commission sued Toysmart, and the company settled the suit by agreeing to abide by the terms of its privacy policy.

9. "FCC Adopts CALEA Technical Standards," Federal Communications Commission press release (August 27, 1999). Available online at www.askcalea.net/pdf/fccrelease3.pdf. The Amercian Civil Liberties Union, the Electronic Frontier Foundation, and an assortment of other Internet privacy groups have sued the FCC over its regulations.

10. Peter Wayner, "Technology that tracks cell phones draws fire," *The New York Times* (February 23, 1998).

11. Every GPS satellite contains a cesium-based atomic clock that keeps stunningly precise time (accurate to roughly one second each 100,000 years).

12. The Defense Department also retains the capability in times of national emergency to introduce even more serious errors into the civilian satellite signal, reducing their accuracy to a circle with a radius of about 300 yards.

13. "Clinton Unscrambles GPS Signal," Reuters (May 1, 2000). Downloaded on May 4, 2000, from www.wired.com/news/print/0,1294,36021,00.html.

14. "Terrorism Attacks Accelerate Interest in GPS Applications," *SpaceDaily* (December 11, 2000).

15. For comparison, approximately ten to fifteen million new vehicles are sold in the United States each year. Lou Hirsh, "Satellite Radio: Will Drivers Tune In?," *OSOpinion.com* (January 3, 2002).

16. Geoff Keighly, "Moving violations," *Boston Globe* (March 18, 2002).

17. Nighttime use is also an issue. While an employee's unauthorized after-hours use of a company vehicle is not likely to be within the scope of his employment, the employer is still likely to be sued if the employee causes injury. Even a successful defense can still be painfully expensive.

18. "GPS Testimonials," Formetco, Inc., n.d. Available online at www.formetco.com/links/testimonials.htm.

19. Adam L. Penenberg, "The Surveillance Society," *Wired* (December 2001).

20. Robert Lemos, "Car spy pushes privacy limit," *ZDNN* (June 20, 2001).

21. Elisa Batista, "A Kiddie GPS for the Masses?" *Wired.com* (October 12, 2002).

22. Hiawatha Bray, "Something to watch over you," *Boston Globe* (January 22, 2001).

23. Elisa Baptista, "E911 Wouldn't Help at WTC," *Wired.com* (September 20, 2001).

24. "Introduction," "Enabling Always On, Always Connected (AOAC) Computing with Bluetooth Technology," Intel Corporation, *Intel Technology Journal* (2d Quarter 2000).

# CHAPTER NINE

# Breaching the Castle Walls

At the beginning of this book, we saw how the privacy rights that we enjoy today were an outgrowth of property ownership—"A man's home is his castle," and all that. When it comes to the government and private property, the walls still stand reasonably strong—the Supreme Court ruled last year, for instance, that law enforcement can't use infrared devices to look for the heat sources used by marijuana growers—but in the constant privacy battle between employees and employers, the moat has been drained and the walls are being scaled.[1]

Paradoxically, the tension arises in large part from the fact that in some ways, employees today have far more power and influence than they've ever had before. The Internet is a tremendous leveler: It gives employees access to virtually unlimited amounts of information, the ability to search for new jobs and opportunities, and the ability to exchange news and opinions with other like-minded individuals both inside and outside the workplace.

At the same time, the computer revolution has also given employees startling new capabilities to harm their employers. With a few keystrokes, an employee can effectively wipe out years of intellectual property; with a single Web posting, an employee can cause a company's stock to plummet. Logically enough, companies are reacting to the real or perceived threat by intensifying their surveillance efforts. The paradox, of course, is that the same technology that makes individuals so potentially powerful also allows employers to invade their privacy in previously unimaginable ways.

In addition, property interests are giving employers grounds on which to challenge how employees behave even when they're not on company property. Because corporate reputation and brand identity fall within the broad definition of "property rights," businesses are taking aggressive steps to make employees take down offending websites, stop posting critical messages on the World Wide Web, and discover the identities of employee critics despite the clear efforts of the employees to remain anonymous. If current legal trends continue, it's unclear that employees will be left with any safe harbors of privacy.

# Are You Ever off Duty?

There are two main trends that are driving employer interest in the off-duty activities of their employees: the ready availability of surveillance tools that make little distinction between work time and play time, and the potential impact of employee conduct that is outside of the employee's job description. The fundamental issue at stake is the protection of property, and over the last few years, the lengths to which employers can go to protect their property interests have been steadily increasing.

## Coffee Breaks, Lunch Hours, and After Hours

The first and most obvious place that the tension between on-duty and off-duty activities arises is in connection with so-called personal time for employees during the work day. Most businesses give employees coffee and lunch breaks (in fact, such breaks are usually mandated by state and federal law). In addition, it's increasingly common for employees to remain at their desks after normal working hours.

Many employees who are scrupulous about not doing recreational Web surfing while they're working see no problem with doing a little shopping or checking sports scores during break time. And many if not most businesses recognize that some leeway is necessary to help maintain positive morale. Most employers don't object if employees make a limited number of personal calls during the day, particularly when they're on a break, and many have no objection if their employees do some recreational Web surfing or Solitaire-playing during their lunch hour. In some work environments, network game playing is even seen as a valuable team-building exercise, particularly among salaried employees who don't earn overtime when they're required to stay past normal work hours.

The problem is that if an employee is using company equipment on company property, an employer may still face liability issues, even if the employee is on a break. For instance, if an employee uses the company e-mail system to send out a racially or sexually offensive e-mail, the fact that he did so while on a coffee break or lunch hour is unlikely to relieve the employer of liability for permitting or failing to prevent a hostile work environment.

The practical issue for employees is that an employer who monitors Web activity is unlikely to stop doing so simply because it's lunch time or the clock has struck five. Put another way, if your employer does not want you visiting Playboy.com at 10:00 A.M., it almost certainly does not want you to do so at 5:05 P.M. either.

The debate over whether an employer is relieved of liability because an employee is off-duty has proven particularly important in sexual harassment cases. As a general rule, a court will look at whether the coercive or unwelcome behavior is based on the harasser's authority at work, and not whether the behavior actually occurred on company property or company time. If those elements are missing—if the alleged harassment occurs between co-workers with similar positions in the company and takes place, for instance, in the harasser's apartment—then it's exceedingly unlikely that the employer would be liable for sexual harassment.

However, a recent decision against Delta Air Lines illustrates how the boundaries of employer liability keep expanding. In March 1998, Delta flight attendants Penny Ferris and Michael Young worked a flight from New York City to Rome, Italy. During the layover in Rome, the flight crew stayed at the Savoy Hotel in a block of hotel rooms reserved by Delta. On the evening of March 17, Young invited Ferris to his room for a glass of wine. After about half a glass, Ferris felt faint and tried to return to her room, but was physically unable to do so. She lost consciousness and, while she was incapacitated, Young raped her. Ferris did not immediately report the assault to Delta officials or employees, but did so approximately two weeks later. Eventually, she identified Young as her assailant, and after an extensive internal investigation, Delta notified Young on November 5 that he was slated for termination. He chose instead to resign.

In July 1999, Ferris filed suit against both Young and Delta, claiming among other things that Delta was liable for sexual harassment. A year later, the U.S. District Court in New York City granted Delta summary judgment on the sexual harassment claim, saying that Young had no supervisory authority over Ferris and that the attack did not occur in a "work environment." Late last year, however, the Second Circuit Court of Appeals reversed the lower court decision and held that Ferris could pursue her claim against Delta for sexual harassment.

The court first concluded that a jury could find that the hotel rooms used by the flight crew constituted a "work environment." It also held that although Young had no supervisory authority over Ferris, a jury could still find that Delta was negligent in permitting harassment to continue despite knowledge of Young's proclivity to rape. Specifically, the court found that there was evidence that Delta had knowledge of at least three incidents in which Young attacked or harassed female flight attendants. "The more egregious the abuse and the more serious the threat of which the employer has notice," the Second Circuit Court of Appeals said, "the more the employer will be required under a standard of reasonable care to take steps for the protection of likely future victims."

The circumstances of *Ferris* are obviously somewhat unique, given the distance of the Delta employees from home and the role the company played in providing them with a place to stay. However, it does underscore the amount of supervision (and thus surveillance) that companies feel they must exercise when they arrange trips for employees to conferences, seminars, sales meetings, and so forth. Each could lead to the type of virtual "workplace" that tripped up Delta.

## Romantic Entanglements

Sexual harassment and rape are obviously at the extreme end of employee interaction. Far more common in the workplace are romantic relationships that, at least in the beginning, are undertaken with mutual consent. A variety of studies conducted over twelve years have consistently found that between 75 percent and 85 percent of all employees have either been exposed to or involved in a workplace romance.[2]

Companies are clearly worried about the consequences of office courtship; in 1998, a workplace romance survey conducted by the Society for Human Resource Management (SHRM) found that 81 percent of human resources professionals and 76 percent of company executives agreed that workplace romances were dangerous because they could lead to conflict within the workplace.[3] Surprisingly, nearly three-quarters of all human resource professionals reported that their organization did not have a written policy regarding workplace wooing. Of the organizations that have a written policy regarding office romance, only 7 percent banned them outright; the majority either permit romances, or state that they are "permitted but discouraged."

Companies are interested in preventing or monitoring workplace romances for a variety of reasons. Some companies worry that office relationships will raise the issue of favoritism, particularly if one of the participants is in a supervisory or management position. The SHRM study found that 28 percent of human resource professionals felt that favoritism does occur as a result of a romantic relationship in the workplace.

Productivity is another concern. The same study found that 24 percent of human resource professionals felt that the coworkers involved in a romance are less productive, and 11 percent felt that an office romance reduces the productivity of other coworkers. Sixteen percent also felt that office romances reduced employee morale.

An additional headache is the public displays of affection that often accompany a new romance. Many companies that do not have policies regarding office romances do have formal or unwritten policies that discourage physical displays of affection between coworkers. Part of the concern is to keep other employees from feeling uncomfortable. But the main concern is that by allowing public displays of affection to occur without restriction, the company would be implicitly condoning unwanted physical advances that might lead in turn to a sexual harassment or hostile work environment claim.

Without question, however, the most serious risk regarding workplace romance is the potential for the romance to play a starring role in one of the more than 15,000 sexual harassment claims filed each year, either because the attention was actually unwanted in the first place, or because the relationship turned sour, bitter, and antagonistic. In an effort to head off these types of problems, many employers forbid workplace relationships and sometimes go to great lengths in order to make sure that they're not occurring.

One of the more infamous antifraternization policies was the one adopted by the superstore giant Wal-Mart, which used to require that employees get the permission of their supervisors in order to date each other. The policy was challenged in New York by two employees who were fired for dating, on the theory that the policy was in violation of the state's 1993 Legal Activities Law, which protects an employee's right to engage in various recreational activities. Remarkably enough, a New York appellate division court ruled that dating is not a "recreational activity," at least within the meaning of the New York statute.[4]

If a company adopts a policy regarding certain activities, then the question becomes what steps it will take to enforce it. A workplace romance policy such as Wal-Mart's creates a situation in which the company feels entitled to ask exceedingly personal questions about their employees' off-duty behavior. In 1996, for instance, Joe and Tiffany Peters met while working at a Wal-Mart in Dodge City, Kansas. Joe Peters informed his boss that he wanted to date Tiffany and was told that under the terms of Wal-Mart's policy, either Tiffany or Joe had to request a transfer or resign. Tiffany gave the company her two week's notice.

In an interview with Dana Hawkins, a reporter with *U.S. News & World Report*, Tiffany Peters said that her last day on the job was traumatic. She told Hawkins that two Wal-Mart district managers questioned her aggressively for two hours about the specific details of her emotional and sexual relationship with Joe. Daphne Davis, a spokesperson for Wal-Mart, contested Tiffany's account, saying that whatever questions were asked by the district managers were necessary to make sure that Wal-Mart's policy had not been violated by the couple.[5]

As a practical matter, there's no question that workplace romances are very common and will continue to occur. And not all of the consequences of workplace romance are necessarily negative: there is some evidence that coworkers who are dating spend more time at work, have higher motivation, fewer sick days, and less turnover.[6] However, most employers would probably agree that the risks of workplace romance outweigh the potential benefits. The chief consequence for employees is that a workplace romance offers an employer an excuse to probe the intimate details of their employees' personal lives. As a general rule, the less of an impact a relationship has on your work and conduct in the workplace, the less of an excuse your employer will have to start asking personal questions.

## The Expanding Definition of Company Property

In an era when the comic strip *Dilbert*—which doesn't even pick on a particular corporation, just corporations in general—is banned in a growing number of cubicle farms, it should come as no surprise that employers are willing to go to great lengths to prevent their employees from saying nasty things about them, regardless of whether or not the comments were made when the employee was on company property or engaged in company business.

Until recently, the damage that you could do by badmouthing your employer was relatively limited. If you work in a small town, you might be able to start a whispering campaign that has the potential of damaging your employer's reputation or business prospects. But you probably would be unable to mount a campaign widespread enough to effectively attack or undermine even a midsize business.

In this respect, at least, the World Wide Web has dramatically altered the balance of power between employers and employees. You don't even have to own a computer to be able to spread damaging words about your company across the nation; all you have to do is stop off at your local library on your lunch hour, log onto a message board, and post a message to a newsgroup. For example, a few well-chosen words about a publicly traded company can dramatically affect a company's stock price. And that's just the beginning. The Web offers an almost limitless number of possibilities for mischief, from ginned-up Web pages with phony news stories to entire websites devoted to savaging a company's reputation. And in the course of a chat room conversation, you could accidentally (or intentionally) reveal valuable intellectual property secrets to a competitor.

Needless to say, the tools that technology has made available to employees raise some interesting questions: Is a corporation entitled to know the identity of people who use anonymous accounts to post critical comments about the corporation or management to Internet message boards? Can a corporation monitor Internet chat rooms or Internet relay chat (IRC) channels and use information gathered there to discipline employees? In other words, how far can a business go in protecting what it perceives to be its property interests?

## Trespass: It's Not Just for Real Property Any More

In the eyes of the law, corporations are people, with nearly all of the same rights and responsibilities. The analogy only goes so far, of course: When a corporation breaks the law, as Arthur Andersen did in 2001 when it shredded Enron documents in an attempt to frustrate a Securities and Exchange Commission probe, it can't be thrown in jail—real live company executives are needed for that.[7]

Nonetheless, a corporation's status as a person under the law gives it the ability to enforce the same rights that an individual can enforce, including those dealing with real property. Typically, the right that owners of real property are keenest on enforcing is the one against trespass, i.e., the ability to determine who can and cannot come onto their property. If you own property in a rural area and you're dead set against people in bright orange clothing trying to thin out the deer herd each year, you can post your land and forbid hunters from trespassing on your property. If a corporation doesn't want you on its property, it is entitled (assuming that it's not illegally discriminating) to have its security personnel use all reasonable force to keep you out.

It used to be that easy to keep people off a company's computer system. For the first two decades or so of the computer revolution, you couldn't trespass on a company's computer system without trespassing on the company's property at the same time—there was simply no way to get access to the computer without having physical access to the machine itself.

But a series of inventions—networking, the modem, the Internet, and e-mail—have created new ways for people to gain access to a computer system. The result is that there is now a new type of property for companies to protect: the virtual space existing within the corporate computers. Obviously, a limited amount of public access to a corporate computer system is an asset: The value of e-mail, for instance, lies in the fact that it can be sent to and received from any other Internet-connected computer in the world.

The downside, of course, is that just as in the physical world, unfettered access exposes a company to the risk that its assets and resources will be damaged or destroyed. As businesses grow increasingly aware of the potential harm that can be caused by unauthorized access, they are spending large amounts of money on firewalls and gateways in an effort to protect their networks.

Companies are also increasingly interested in filtering or blocking e-mail based on its content. Much of the effort is aimed at blocking the ubiquitous spam; most companies don't see much value in multilevel marketing schemes and ads for adult websites, and few employees would disagree. And logically enough, companies are also interested in blocking e-mails that could create liability or reveal trade secrets.

But does ownership of a network over which e-mail travels give a business an unfettered right to filter or block an e-mail message because it disapproves of its political or ideological content? One ongoing case that directly raises that question involves Kourosh Kenneth Hamidi, a former engineer for Intel Corporation. Hamidi is also the principal spokesman of Former and Current Employees of Intel (FACE-Intel), a nonprofit organization that exists to give current and former Intel employees an opportunity to air their grievances about the company's working conditions.[8] According to the *Sacramento Bee*, Hamidi was fired in 1995 after a long disagreement with Intel management over workers' compensation.[9]

In his capacity as FACE-Intel spokesman, Hamidi sent e-mails to large numbers of Intel employees describing Intel's allegedly "abusive and discriminatory employment practices." Court documents indicate that Hamidi sent six mass mailings, reaching between 8,000 and 35,000 Intel employees each time. Intel unsuccessfully tried to block Hamidi's e-mails and subsequently filed suit against him, alleging nuisance and trespass to chattels ("chattels" is defined as "tangible movable property").

In November 1998, Sacramento Superior Court Judge John R. Lewis ruled that Hamidi had committed trespass to chattels (the nuisance claim was dropped) and ordered him to stop sending unsolicited e-mails to Intel employees over Intel's network. The injunction was upheld by the California Court of Appeals, which found that Hamidi's e-mails harmed Intel through a loss of productivity, based on the time spent by employees reading the FACE-Intel mailings and the time spent by Intel technical support personnel in trying to block them.

The lawsuit filed by Intel against Hamidi illustrates the difficulty of applying age-old legal doctrines to the brave new world of cyberspace. Under principles of common law, there are two different kinds of trespass: trespass to real property, and trespass to chattels. As we saw in Chapter 1, the protection of real property is one of the fundamental goals of our legal system; when someone enters onto someone else's property without permission, it's considered a threat to public order. As a result, a property owner can sue for trespass to real property even when there has been no harm at all to the property itself. In contrast, if someone sues for trespass to chattels, he must demonstrate that there has been some actual harm to the moveable property, or that he has been deprived of its use for a period of time.

Since no one can credibly argue that a computer network is "real property" in the same sense that an acre of land is, Intel based its suit on a claim that Hamidi committed trespass to its chattels, i.e., its computer system. In his brief to the California Supreme Court, Hamidi argued strenuously that the transmission of his e-mails through the Intel system did not cause any harm to the Intel computer system, nor did they deprive Intel of its use:

> It is undisputed that Mr. Hamidi's e-mails caused no physical harm or disruption to Intel's computer equipment, nor was Intel dispossessed, even temporarily, of its computer equipment by reason of receipt of Mr. Hamidi's e-mails. . . . But the Court of Appeal ruled that the "loss of productivity" that Intel suffered as a result of the time spent by technical personnel attempting to block Mr. Hamidi's messages, or as a result of time that Intel employees spent reading the messages, constituted sufficient injury for purposes of trespass to chattel. . . . In other words, the court created a trespass to chattel doctrine that completely ignores the physical status of the chattel itself.
>
> In doing so, the court reversed age-old legal authority. Its decision is flatly inconsistent with every decision by the California courts to consider the trespass to chattel doctrine, which requires the owner to prove either physical harm to his property, or that he has been dispossessed of his property for a period of time.[10]

Apart from corporate criticism, the other major e-mail trespass conflict between employers and employees involves union activities. Union leaders have discovered that e-mail offers a fast, convenient, and inexpensive means of communicating with large numbers of employees at once. Not surprisingly, employers frequently object to a union's use of the corporate e-mail system. Some argue that it cuts into workplace productivity, since the union e-mails are inevitably read at work. Others argue that to the extent that union e-mails are unwanted by the business, they constitute a trespass of the company's property.

A typical situation occurred in the summer of 1997, when the Florida Professional Association tried to form a union among the engineers at the Pratt & Whitney plant in Palm Beach, Florida. Two officers of the nascent union, Kenneth Coolidge and Brian Waldron, sent out organizing e-mails to each of the company's 2,000 engineers over the company e-mail system. Coolidge and Waldron said that they were able to send out ten mailings before Pratt & Whitney officials found out; both men were then suspended by the company for using the company e-mail system for "personal business."[11] Two years later, the union (which did successfully form) and Pratt & Whitney reached a settlement in which the union agreed to drop an unfair labor practice complaint and the company agreed to allow limited use of the Pratt & Whitney e-mail system for union-related e-mails.

To date there has been no specific ruling by the National Labor Relations Board about whether e-mail is protected under the terms of the National Labor Relations Act, although that appears to be the direction in which the Board is moving. In the absence of a statutory pronouncement by Congress, the question will be whether e-mail use by unions is considered to be more analogous to "one-on-one solicitation," which is permitted anywhere on company property as long as it takes place during a work break, or the "distribution of literature," which companies are entitled to regulate more closely.

## Employers Lurking on the Web

Regardless of whether a business is entitled to block particular e-mails that enter its computer system, it shouldn't come as a terrible shock that the company is at least aware of what's being said. As we've seen repeatedly throughout this book, companies have powerful reasons to be aware of what's traveling across their computer network.

The next level of inquiry is the extent to which employers should monitor what employees say about them when the messages don't necessarily travel across the company network. You can use a home or public computer to post messages about your employer in Usenet newsgroups, on website message boards and chat rooms, and on IRC channels. With relatively little difficulty, you could set up an entire website devoted to criticizing your company, without coming anywhere near your employer's computer system. But that may not offer you much greater protection; because of the potential impact on their business interests, companies take an active interest in what's being said about them, regardless of the source.

Of course, Internet newsgroups, message boards, chat rooms, and websites are generally public forums; anyone, including the management of your company, can visit them. In fact, monitoring relevant news groups, message boards, and websites is a good way for a company to learn about consumer and shareholder concerns.

Tension arises chiefly when a corporation reads something it doesn't like, particularly when the comment or information has been (or the corporation thinks it has been) posted by an employee. The conflict that arises at such times is between a corporation's right to defend itself and an employee's right to exercise her right to free speech under the First Amendment.

As a practical matter, employees are at a tremendous disadvantage in resolving that type of conflict. It's unequivocally clear that employees have very limited constitutional rights while on company property. Outside of the workplace, employees have a slightly greater level of protection, at least if they get sued in one of the nineteen states that has passed a so-called anti-SLAPP (Strategic Lawsuits Against Public Participation) statute.[12] However, employees have relatively little protection if their employer decides to terminate them because the company's management disliked what the employee was saying online. While there are fairly solid federal and state protections against various types of discrimination, there's really nothing that extends the protections of the First Amendment to the workplace.

Of course, even if the First Amendment or SLAPP statutes protected statements by employees, they wouldn't protect statements intended to manipulate the price of a publicly traded stock. Calhoun Consulting Group (CCG), a Waltham, Massachusetts, company that advises other businesses on stock fraud, routinely reviews postings made to investment websites. In one typical case, CCG came across postings by an engineer at 3M Corporation to Silicon Investor, a popular stock bulletin board, in which the engineer boasted about 3M's new products and bargain stock price. While there was no indication that the engineer was making the postings for his own benefit, such disclosures could nonetheless expose the company to sanctions by the Securities and Exchange Commission.[13]

Even if a corporation is not directly liable for the actions of its employees, apparent manipulation of the company's stock price can have a devastating effect on the company and its reputation. Take the case of Gary Dale Hoke, a midlevel engineer for PairGain Technologies, Inc., an Irvine, California-based telecommunications equipment company. With only a few hours work, Hoke was able to significantly affect the price of PairGain's stock. Although Hoke did not benefit from his manipulation, it would have been a fairly simple matter for him to try to do so. Of equal if not greater interest is the daunting rapidity with which Hoke was identified and arrested. It's an object lesson not merely in how seriously both companies and law enforcement take these types of activities, but also in the tremendous investigatory tools that are now available.

On the morning of April 7, 1999, visitors to the Yahoo! finance bulletin board regarding PairGain saw a posting from someone purporting to be Stacey Lawson of Knoxville, Tennessee. The message stated that PairGain was about to be purchased for roughly $1.35 billion by the Israeli company ECI Telecom, Ltd. The message also contained a link to an article on

Bloomberg L.P.'s news site, which purported to have an announcement about the sale. In reality, the Bloomberg "article" was a phony page created by Hoke.

Following the Yahoo! posting, the price of PairGain's stock rose from $8½ to $11, an increase of more than 30 percent. When PairGain issued a statement that afternoon that the report of a buyout was false, the price of the company's stock fell back to $9. In the process, some investors lost thousands of dollars.

That same afternoon, the U.S. Attorney's Office in Los Angeles and the Los Angeles branch of the FBI began an investigation. An inquiry by the Securities and Exchange Commission revealed no unusual trading activity either before or after the hoax, so the investigation focused on the Web activity. The messages posted to the Yahoo! finance board and other stock discussion sites were clearly fake, so they offered little potential evidence. However, the fake Bloomberg site was hosted by a free website hosting company called Angelfire, which provided the FBI with some useful information.

Specifically, Angelfire gave the FBI the IP (Internet protocol) addresses of the computer used to post the fake Bloomberg article onto the Angelfire system. The FBI then compared those IP addresses to a public directory of IP addresses and learned that some were associated with computers at PairGain and some were associated with an Internet service provider called Mindspring. The IP addresses and access times were presented to Mindspring, which matched them up with activity on a Mindspring account by someone with the user name "ghoke." As it turned out, Mindspring also maintained something called "radius logs" (similar to consumer caller ID), which tracks the phone numbers used to call into the service. The calls made by user "ghoke" were made from a telephone owned by one Gary Hoke, a PairGain employee at the company's Raleigh, North Carolina, branch.

Armed with that information, the FBI was able to obtain a search warrant for Hoke's home and during the search, seized a laptop that contained portions of the fake Bloomberg website. Hoke was arrested by the FBI just one week after posting the fraudulent messages, and he pleaded guilty to two counts of securities fraud on June 21, 1999. Two months later, on August 30, Hoke was sentenced to five months of home detention and five years' probation. He was also ordered to pay $93,000 in restitution to investors who lost money due to the fraudulent report.

Proving once again that timing is everything, the impact of Hoke's hoax was heightened by the fact that when he posted his fake messages on the Yahoo! finance bulletin board, the PairGain headquarters in California was still closed. In addition, April 7, 1999, was an Israeli holiday, so there was no way to verify the posting with ECI Telecom. Not wanting to be left out of a possible stock surge, a number of investors plunged ahead and bought PairGain stock before the company opened for business on the West Coast and refuted the buyout announcement.

Bulletin boards and newsgroups are obviously a potential source of concern, but companies are also paying close attention to online chat rooms and IRC channels. The chief danger for businesses is that conversations in those forums take place in real time, which increases the likelihood of inappropriate disclosures and makes it more difficult to prevent them from occurring.

While it's not difficult to understand why companies want to monitor employee Web postings, the methods they use can be troubling. For instance, companies often hire people to secretly monitor chat rooms and newsgroups (a phenomenon known on the Web as lurking), or instruct trusted employees to pose as consumers or disaffected employees in an effort to draw out unguarded comments by other employees.[14]

This practice backfired recently for Hawaiian Airlines, which was in a disagreement with the union representing its pilots. Robert Konop, a Hawaiian Airlines pilot, set up a website so that he and his fellow pilots could exchange information and freely criticize airline management. To protect the identity of message posters, Konop password-protected his website.

Frustrated by his inability to view Konop's site, a Hawaiian Airlines vice president persuaded two airline pilots to let him use their passwords. In the lawsuit that Konop later filed against the company, he claimed that the vice president had disclosed the contents of his site to a rival faction within the pilot's union (one that was allegedly more sympathetic to management), and that he had threatened to sue Konop personally for defamation. Konop also argued that by viewing his site without permission, the airline violated the federal Wiretap Act and the Stored Communication Act.

In a decision handed down at the end of this summer, the U.S. Court of Appeals held that Hawaiian Airlines did not violate the Wiretap Act because the law only covers "interceptions" that occur at the same time that a transmission takes place. Since the vice president was looking at stored data, his actions did not constitute an "interception."

By contrast, the court found that the airline may have violated the Stored Communication Act, which forbids unauthorized access to stored material. Hawaiian Airlines argued that since it had the permission of a password holder, its viewing of the site was authorized. However, the court ruled that it was unclear whether the pilots who turned over their passwords were actually "users" of Konop's site.

More significantly, the court ruled that Konop's website constituted "union activity" under the terms of the Railway Labor Act (which also covers airlines), and that by viewing the password-protected site, the Hawaiian Airlines executive was engaged in unlawful surveillance.

## The Struggle for Anonymity

Given the potential for retaliation by an angry employer, it's not particularly surprisingly that employees will go to great lengths to remain anonymous when they post critical comments online. The simplest method is to sign up with one of the many e-mail services that permit anonymous registrations, like Yahoo!, America Online, or Hotmail.

Another technique is to use an anonymous remailer to post messages. An anonymous remailer is a service that receives e-mail messages, strips away identifying information about the sender, substitutes an anonymous term or code, and then forwards the message on to its destination. To the frustration of law enforcement, corporations, and despotic regimes around the world, a well-constructed anonymous remailer is effectively a one-way door: Once a message passes through the remailer, there is no way for anyone, including the remailer itself, to tell where the message originated.[15]

Legitimate concern over the myriad illicit uses of online anonymity (libelous statements, sexual harassment, stalking, fraud, child pornography, etc.) has encouraged lawmakers to draft legislation that would outlaw the use of anonymous remailers. The Georgia state legislature, for example, made it illegal to send out computer transmissions that "falsely identify" the sender, but the law was declared unconstitutional by a U.S. District Court in 1997. However, many of the antispam laws that have been passed or are currently under consideration around the country include provisions that make it illegal to use software designed to falsify "electronic mail transmission information." Whether those provisions are constitutional is still an undecided question.[16]

Because of the potential damage to a business's reputation, interests, or stock price, employers are becoming increasingly aggressive in their efforts to uncover the true identities of the people who are posting critical messages. While an employer's ability to track down the source of messages posted to Internet bulletin boards through anonymous remailers is fairly limited, that's not true for messages posted by employees using "anonymous" e-mail accounts. Internet e-mail services have shown little desire to get in the middle of a potentially protracted and certainly expensive battle over user privacy. Currently, the practice at Yahoo!, for instance, is to notify a user if a request for his identity has been made; if the user does not respond, then Yahoo! turns over the information.

Appropriately enough, one of the first cases to test the strength of online anonymity involved Raytheon, which manufactures an electronic surveillance program called *SilentRunner*. Raytheon's monitoring program allows network administrators to track everything that passes over a corporate network without notice to the network's users.

In February 1999, Raytheon filed a lawsuit, *Raytheon* v. *John Does 1–21*, in which it sought $25,000 each from twenty-one "John Does," anonymous individuals that Raytheon claimed had made disparaging comments about the company on Yahoo! message boards. Raytheon also claimed that the John Does were employees who were leaking proprietary information online in violation of company policy.

Having filed a lawsuit, Raytheon was entitled to subpoena Yahoo! for the names of the individuals as part of its discovery process. As soon as Yahoo! handed over the names of the message posters, Raytheon dropped the lawsuit. Not long afterwards, four Raytheon employees (including a vice president of the company) resigned. The remainder of the employees entered what Raytheon coyly described as "corporate counseling."[17]

Employees and other individuals who want to remain anonymous online took a great deal of comfort from a ruling last year by a U.S. District Court in Los Angeles in the case of *Global Telemedia International* v. *Docs*. The telecommunications firm, upset by critical comments posted to Internet message boards and chat rooms, filed a libel action to recover damages not only from the individual message posters, but from the online services themselves. In addition, Global Telemedia served subpoenas aimed at uncovering the identity of the message posters.

In a decision issued on February 23, 2001, Judge David O. Carter dismissed the lawsuit, ruling that the messages and chat room conversations were statements of opinion and not fact. In order for a statement to be libelous, the court noted, it must reasonably appear to a listener to be a statement of fact and not opinion. To support his conclusion that no reasonable reader could have interpreted the online statements as fact, Judge Carter quoted a representative passage from the Raging Bull website:

> This company has put it up your arse again this week with no filing no nothin (sic) no chance to buy it off shore on international exchanges . . . stupid flippin puss I got info comin at you that will make you puke about this stock and then you can thank me.

The court made its opinion of the postings clear:

> To put it mildly, these postings, as well as the others presented to the Court, lack the formality and polish typically found in documents in which a reader would expect to find facts. It is unlikely, for example, that a corporation would express the view that investors should "up the volume for some of that 2 dollar love." . . . Nor would the SEC ever state that GTMI is "steering the sinking ship but don't worry they are headed for the calmer waters of the Caribbean where your money

will be safe from federal authorities." . . . the general tone and context [and content and style] of these messages strongly suggest that they are the opinions of the posters.[18]

Despite the potentially valuable support of the *Global Telemedia* decision, lawsuits against John Doe continue to be a tremendously active area of the law. In general, the primary purpose of these lawsuits remains an effort to identify the senders, not to recover monetary damages. However, in at least one instance, a company succeeded in obtaining a monetary verdict: In 1998, a Texas conglomerate called American Eco won an $8.3 million verdict against one "John Doe" for comments that he had posted anonymously. There's no word on the success of American Eco's efforts to collect on its judgment.

## Living in Glass Houses

As we saw in Chapter 6, the nation's courts are generally in agreement that employers, as the owners and operators of internal e-mail systems, are entitled to set rules and regulations for their use and to examine the contents of employee e-mails. Now courts and legislatures are being asked how far this authority extends. If an employee purchases a home computer from his employer, does that give the employer an ongoing right to inspect the computer's hard drive? What if the employer pays for or reimburses the employee for the cost of Internet access? How far can an employer go in monitoring the off-duty behavior of its employees? Is there a difference between off-duty behavior that is public and that which is purely private?

The issue that employees must face is that the scope of company property and business interests continues to steadily expand; as it does, it irresistibly compresses employees' personal privacy space.

### Telecommuters Beware

A significant part of the problem is the fact that the nature of our work day has changed—our hours are longer and for significant numbers of people, an increasing amount of work is done from home. Currently, an estimated 20 million employees and independent contractors work from home at least one day a month, and thanks to the tremendous growth of the Internet, that number is rising steadily. In addition, millions more employees use their home computers to connect to their office networks at night or on the weekend.[19]

Telecommuting offers some significant advantages for both employers and employees, particularly in car-clogged regions of the country like Los

Angeles, Atlanta, New York, Seattle, and San Francisco. But with respect to the relationship between employer and employee, it creates some ambiguity about the boundaries between home and office, particularly when the employer supplies some or all of the equipment used to telecommute. This brings the fundamental conflict between the employer's property interests and the employee's privacy interests squarely into the employee's home.

Like most employees, you might be under the impression that you can avoid the worst of the workplace surveillance by working at home. To a limited degree, that's probably true. So far, at least, your employer cannot legally sneak into your home and install a surveillance camera or microphone, and there's little likelihood that your company would go to the trouble of making you wear an infrared badge system to see just how much time you spend in front of the TV. Beyond that, however, the surveillance possibilities in the home office are just as serious and just as pervasive as those found in the most anonymous cubicle farm.

Once again, we have the computer to thank for helping to turn our homes into glass houses. With the right software, your employer can watch what you're doing in the privacy of your home as easily as if you were sitting at a desk in the middle of the company lobby. More significantly, connecting your home computer to the office network raises the possibility that all of the files on your computer could be examined by your employer without your knowledge. Doing so without your permission would be illegal, of course, but the potential exists nonetheless.

From the employer's perspective, there are some minor differences between a computer on your desk in the workplace and a computer in your home office. If you decide to use the latest *Playboy* centerfold as the wallpaper for your home office computer, there's little likelihood that a coworker or client will see it. But the other potential problems of employee computer use, from poor productivity to harassing e-mails to outright sabotage, can be accomplished as easily from a home computer as from a computer down the hall from the CEO's office. As a result, telecommuting employees are increasingly subject to the same types of surveillance as their hard-wired coworkers, and in fact, surveillance programs such as SmartSuite and Win-WhatWhere are being or have been written to monitor the activity of remote computers.

For all intents and purposes, bringing a company computer into your home is the equivalent of giving your employer a key to the front door. In theory, if your company has no policy in place regarding the use of the computer it provides you for use in your home office, a court might reasonably conclude that you still have a fairly strong expectation of privacy in your home and its contents, including the company computer. But if your employer can demonstrate a reasonably strong business interest in conducting an investigation into your use of the computer, it is likely to be allowed to do so.

And realistically, most businesses that provide their employees with computers with which they can do work at home make sure that they have a detailed usage policy governing how the computer can be used and reserving the company's right to inspect it.

Even if you do not connect your computer to the office network, your employer may still try to see what's on your hard drive. While a group of Northwest Airlines employees were engaged in contract negotiations in 2000, Northwest—suspecting that some employees were conducting an illegal sickout—obtained a subpoena to copy the entire contents of their home computer hard drives. After the contract dispute was settled, the legal battle over the hard drives was dismissed, so there was no ruling on the legality of Northwest's investigation.[20] The mere issuance of the subpoena, however, sent shock waves through the offices of both labor and employment lawyers.

In some cases, of course, employees create their own problems. Take, for instance, the example of Ronald F. Thiemann, a former dean for the Harvard Divinity School. Thiemann had a Harvard-owned computer in his home, and in October 1998, he asked a university information technician to transfer large numbers of files from his hard drive to a new drive. When the technician realized that included in the files were thousands of pornographic images, he reported that fact to Divinity School administrators. Although Thiemann was relieved of his deanship, he remains on the Divinity School faculty.[21]

## Can You Actually Be a Naked Employee?

One surefire way of encouraging your employer to monitor your off-duty activities is to perform them in public. A strong argument can be made that if your off-duty activity, regardless of how public, does not impact on your employer's business, you should not be penalized. However, businesses are generally given considerable latitude in determining what type of behavior is unacceptable.

For instance, the cover of the August 1994 edition of *Playboy* featured the headline "NYPD Nude: One of New York's Finest Steps Out of Uniform," over a photograph of Officer Carol Shaya in a partially unbuttoned New York City police officer's uniform (complete with a nonstandard issue Playboy Bunny key chain on her utility belt). Police Commissioner William Bratton was not amused; he fired Shaya, saying that she had put the department's reputation up for sale.[22] Shaya was not the only New York City police officer to pose this type of problem for the department: In late 1995, patrolman Edward Mallia resigned rather than face disciplinary charges for his nude appearance in *Playgirl*.

For both Shaya and Mallia, the primary problem lay in the fact that the NYPD has policies that prohibit certain types of off-duty conduct, including posing nude. Shaya compounded her difficulties by posing in her NYPD uniform. By comparison, LAPD patrol officer Ginger Harrison avoided disciplinary action when she posed nude in 2001 for *Playboy* in part by leaving her LAPD uniform at home, and in part by reading the LAPD personnel rules carefully to see if posing nude was forbidden. As she told Warner Brothers' *Extra*, "We learned from [Shaya's] experience. We didn't use anything of mine. Everything was rentals or props."[23] Despite Harrison's decision to leave her uniform at home, the Department still referred the matter to the city attorney to determine whether she had broken any department rules.[24]

Companies have shown a particular interest in policing the involvement of their employees in sexually explicit websites. The aggressiveness with which some employers pursue and punish people who run potentially objectionable websites raises some serious questions about personal freedom and free speech.

Perhaps the best-known example is the case of George and Tracy Miller, two Arizona critical care nurses who worked at Scottsdale Healthcare. In the summer of 1999, the hospital learned that the Millers were operating a sexually explicit website in which they marketed images of Tracy posing nude; subscribers to the site received access to more explicit materials, including still images and video clips of the couple having sex. The Millers told reporters that they had set up their site to raise money for their children's college education.

The site was live for about two months before hospital officials learned about it. George Miller said that he didn't know how word began circulating at Scottsdale Healthcare, but he blamed the couple's firing on the fact that coworkers began logging onto the site from workplace computers. As the hospital began investigating the sudden surge of interest in the website touchable.com, administrators realized that its stars were hospital employees.

To the Millers, the hospital's reaction was an unjustified intrusion into their personal life. "Does a big corporation have . . . the right to dictate what you can do on your off time if it in no way interferes with your job?," Miller asked during a MSNBC interview. "I maintain that they do not." The news wasn't all bad for the Millers—the publicity from their dismissal from the hospital doubled the number of their subscribers—but they both made it clear that they were interested in continuing their career as nurses.[25]

The problem for the Millers is that the law in such situations generally favors employers. The Millers were at-will employees, which means that the hospital was legally entitled to fire them for any nondiscriminatory reason.

Although neither Tracy nor George used anything on the website that came from or identified Scottsdale Healthcare, they were still subject to discipline because they had signed an employee policy that specifically stated they could be disciplined for "immoral or indecent conduct while on or off duty." The determination of what constitutes immoral or indecent conduct, of course, is at the discretion of the employer.

The Millers' case attracted the attention of the Arizona branch of the American Civil Liberties Union, which questioned whether the principle of at-will termination was giving employers too much power to pry into the private lives of their employees. As Eleanor Eisenberg, the head of the Arizona ACLU, put it: "[Employers are] making decisions based on information obtained about what people do when they're not at work—particularly when what they do when they're not at work does not affect their job performance."[26]

It's one thing for an employee to be disciplined for posing nude on a website; it's another altogether for an employee to be punished because a family member does something the company considers inappropriate. In North Port, Florida, last year, police officer Daniel Lake was given a three-day suspension for conduct unbecoming an officer after his wife posted sexually explicit photos of herself on the Web. Lake told department investigators that his wife had put the photos online as a surprise for him, and that he was unaware that she had done so. In an interview with the *Miami Sun-Herald*, North Port City Commissioner Tom Williamson dismissed any privacy concerns: "What happened to this family, even if it was in their own home, makes us a mockery."[27]

## Recreational Activities and Lifestyle Choices

Most of us don't have the opportunity to pose nude in a national magazine or on the inclination to set up a nude website. Nonetheless, we make choices every day about how to live our lives: which foods we eat, which sports we play, whether we drink or smoke, and so on. It would seem safe to assume that such activities are beyond the reach of even the most inquisitive employer, but increasingly, that's simply not true. We are steadily approaching the time when nothing is irrelevant to an employer's protection of its business interests.

Occasionally, businesses do have a legitimate interest in their employees' off-duty recreational activities. It's not uncommon for employees with specialized skills to have clauses in their employment contracts that forbid them from engaging in risky activities or require them to adhere to a particular diet. Professional athletes are the most common example: If you're being paid millions of dollars to throw a leather-wrapped ball sixty feet and six inches past a batter bent on driving it out of the park, the ball club is going to be more than a little irritated if you break your leg waterskiing during the All Star break. Likewise, if your job is to thread your way through a herd of 300-pound linebackers intent on your near-dismemberment, your employer is going to be irritated if your off-season diet consists largely of Ben & Jerry's ice cream, chips, and beer. To a lesser degree, the same is true for models, actors, violinists, surgeons, and people in certain other professions.

Similarly, if you engage in an off-duty activity that is directly contrary to your employer's businesses interests, the fact that you're doing so on your own time is not likely to placate your boss. It is reasonable for a company to be concerned about such activity and even to take steps to prevent it. For example, most people would agree that a company should be able to forbid its employees from moonlighting for a competitor. However, it's less clear that a business should be allowed to forbid moonlighting altogether. Similarly, if an employee routinely shows up at work drunk, it is completely reasonable for an employer to discipline or even fire that employee. But it seems unreasonable that an employer should be permitted to discipline or dismiss an employee if a supervisor sees the individual getting drunk at a bar on Friday night, but the employee shows up clean and sober on Monday morning.

If the full extent of the relationship between you and your employer was a salary in exchange for specified work, the ability of your employer to monitor your recreational activities or lifestyle choices would be sharply curtailed. The only relevant questions would be whether you were capable of performing your job on a given day, and whether any off-duty activities were directly in conflict with your employer's business interests.

But for most employees, the relationship with their employer is more complicated. As was discussed earlier, an employer's main motivation for monitoring its employees' recreational activities is the incredibly high cost of health insurance. Employers argue that risky recreational activities or destructive lifestyle choices do affect their business, regardless of whether an employee shows up ready and able to work on Monday morning, by making it more expensive to provide the medical coverage necessary to attract good employees. That's why employers often try to screen out employees who have high-risk lifestyles or engage in high-risk recreational activities; if they do hire them, they frequently charge such employees a premium for their health insurance.

Employees have some limited protection for high-risk activities at the state level: A number of states have passed legislation banning discrimination against smokers, and a few states—notably California, Colorado, and North Dakota—have passed laws that are broadly designed to protect employees from discrimination when they engage in legal activities while off duty. However, state coverage is spotty and federal protection for off-duty activities and lifestyle choices is effectively nonexistent.

The gargantuan Health Insurance Portability and Accountability Act (HIPAA) of 1996 includes a provision designed to protect individuals who engage in high-risk recreational activities from health insurance discrimination. According to the legislative language of HIPAA, the law:

> . . . is intended to ensure, among other things, that individuals are not excluded from health care coverage due to their participation in activities such as motorcycling, snowmobiling, all-terrain vehicle riding, horseback riding, skiing and other similar activities.[28]

The inclusion of that language was the result of the lobbying efforts of a broad coalition of recreational groups, ranging from the American Horse Council to the American Motorcycle Association.

Three government agencies—the Internal Revenue Service, the Pension and Welfare Benefits Administration, and the Health Care Financing Administration—were responsible for developing regulations to implement Congress's intent regarding nondiscrimination. However, when the proposed Interim Final Rules for Nondiscrimination in Health Coverage in the Group Market were released in January 2001, recreational organizations were dismayed to realize that the regulations omitted the protections intended by Congress.

In an odd paradox, the so-called Interim Final Rules (which took effect on May 9, 2001) included language that makes it illegal for health insurance companies to deny health insurance coverage in general to individuals who engage in risky recreational activities. However, the same rules also provide that insurance companies may refuse to provide coverage for injuries that arise out of those recreational activities.

In the grand scheme of things, of course, the amount of discrimination experienced by horseback riders, skiers, and other outdoor enthusiasts is far less than the discrimination faced by people with other potentially health-threatening lifestyles. According to the American Civil Liberties Union, the two groups most frequently targeted during preemployment screening and on the job are smokers and those who are overweight. According to a 1988 survey by the Administrative Management Society, roughly 6 percent of all employers refuse to hire people who smoke, even if they only do so off-duty.[29] Given the aggressive antismoking campaigns of the last few years and the rise in the costs of treating smoking-related illnesses, that figure is almost certainly higher today.

A case in point is that of a woman named Arlene Kurtz, who was turned down for a clerk-typist job with the City of North Miami because she could not sign an affidavit stating that she had not smoked during the previous year. Kurtz filed a lawsuit seeking to have North Miami's 1990 regulation requiring such affidavits declared unconstitutional. A Florida trial court agreed with her, but the Florida Supreme Court reversed the decision, holding that the City's regulation "does not intrude into an aspect of Kurtz's life in which she has a legitimate expectation of privacy":

> In today's society, smokers are constantly required to reveal whether they smoke. When individuals are seated in a restaurant, they are asked whether they want a table in a smoking or nonsmoking section. When individuals rent hotel or motel rooms, they are asked if they smoke so that management may ensure that certain rooms remain free from the smell of smoke odors . . . . Further, employers generally provide smoke-free areas for nonsmokers, and employees are often prohibited from smoking in certain areas. Given that individuals must reveal whether they smoke in almost every aspect of life in today's society, we conclude that individuals have no reasonable expectation of privacy in the disclosure of that information when applying for a government job . . . however, we emphasize that our holding is limited to the narrow issue presented. Notably, we are not addressing the issue of whether an applicant, once hired, could be compelled by a government agency to stop smoking. Equally as important neither are we holding today that a governmental entity can ask any type of information it chooses of prospective job applicants.[30]

In addition, the court found that the City of North Miami had presented evidence of a compelling interest: the reduction of health care costs through the gradual elimination of smokers from its workforce. Among the evidence presented by the City was the fact that it self-insures; that people who have not smoked for a full year are unlikely to start again; and that smokers cost the City up to $4,611 more per year in health care costs than employees who didn't smoke.[31] Kurtz asked the U.S. Supreme Court to review the Florida Supreme Court's decision, but the Court refused to do so.

Figures for the level of discrimination experienced by overweight people are harder to establish, since few companies will openly commit themselves to a policy of discrimination against a particular group of people. (Companies are likely to be even more circumspect today, given studies suggesting that genetics may play a role in obesity, which conceivably could bring obesity under the terms of the Americans with Disabilities Act.) Nonetheless, the National Association for the Advancement of Fat Acceptance believes that anecdotal evidence shows the level of discrimination against overweight employees to be even higher than that experienced by smokers.

There's no question that as a nation, we should exercise more and weigh less. But if businesses are allowed to choose employees based on the employers' concerns over which employees may cost it more in health care, then it's difficult to see what logical limitations there will be on the ability of an employer to monitor the off-duty behavior of its employees. Every choice that we make, to one degree or another, impacts on our health. The question is whether accepting health care as a benefit of employment requires in turn a complete abdication of our personal privacy rights.

## End Notes

1. *Kyllo* v. *United States*, ____U.S. ____(June 11, 2001).

2. Charmine E. J. Härtel, "Vantage 2000: Romance in the Workplace and I/O Across the World," University of Queensland, Australia, January 1998).

3. "SHRM Survey Finds Office Romances Are Often Frowned upon by Employers," Press Release, Society for Human Resource Management (January 28, 1998).

4. New York v. *Wal-Mart Stores, Inc.*, 621 N.Y.S.2d (N.Y. App. Div. 1995).

5. Dana Hawkins, "Who's Watching Now?," *U.S. News & World Report* (September 15, 1997).

6. Art Bell, Ph.D., "Romance at Work," McLaren School of Business, University of San Francisco, n.d. Available online at www.usfca.edu/fac-staff/bell/article16.html.

7. The corporation was given five years' probation, however, and fined $500,000 for its obstruction of justice.

8. Opening Brief on the Merits, *Intel Corp.* v. *Hamidi*, Cal. Supreme Ct. No. S103781, May 16, 2002.

9. Claire Cooper, "High court to hear Intel e-mail case," *Sacramento Bee* (March 28, 2002).

10. Opening Brief on the Merits, *Intel Corp.* v. *Hamidi*, Cal. Supreme Ct. No. S103781, May 16, 2002 (citations omitted). A decision by the California Supreme Court is expected some time in 2003.

11. Noam S. Cohen, "Corporations Try to Bar Use of E-Mail by Unions," *The New York Times* (August 23, 1999).

12. Under the terms of a SLAPP statute, a defendant (usually an individual employee) can compel the plaintiff (usually a corporation) to demonstrate that it is likely to prevail on the merits of its defamation claim before the suit can go forward. The statute is intended to reduce the ability of well-heeled corporations from intimidating Web posters with the threat of an expensive lawsuit.

13. Joann Muller, "Trouble on the Internet . . .", *Boston Globe* (October 23, 1998).

14. Law enforcement uses the same techniques. Officers and federal agents are trained to lurk in sexually-oriented chat rooms, pretending to be young children, and to track down users who solicit them for sex.

15. Employees should keep in mind that as a practical matter, there is little chance of remaining anonymous if they use their employer's computer and network to post messages, even if they use an anonymous e-mail account or remailer. Using a variety of software, an employer can easily record the content of messages long before they are dispatched to the anonymous remailer.

16. Pamela Mendels, "The Two Faces of Online Anonymity," *The New York Times* (July 21, 1999).

17. Tom Kirchofer, "Raytheon Drops Internet Chat Suit," *Yahoo! News* (May 21, 1999).

18. Order Granting Defendants' Special Motion to Strike, *Global Telemedia International, Inc.* v. *Doe 1 et al.*, 132 F. Supp. 2d 1261 (C.D. Calif. February 23, 2001) (citations omitted).

19. "Electronic Monitoring in the Workplace," Workrights.org, n.d.

20. Dolores Kong, "Big Brother may be watching you," *Boston Globe* (October 22, 2000).

21. James Bandler, "Office porn cases raise issues of privacy, protection," *Boston Globe* (June 24, 1999).

22. As a Playboy Cover Girl, Shaya was paid $100,000 for her pictorial.

23. "Cop Poses in Playboy," *Extra* (May 30, 2001).

24. Ironically, Los Angeles is getting a police chief with experience in this area; William Bratton was just appointed to head the department.

25. Mike Brunker, "Cyberporn nurse: 'I feel like Larry Flynt'," MSNBC (July 16, 1999).

26. Luke Reiter, "Arizona nurses' porn site led to their dismissal," ZDNet (July 19, 1999).

27. "Police officer suspended over wife's Internet porn pics," *Ananova.com* (March 9, 2001).

28. "Federal Agencies Propose Adverse Rules on Health Insurance Coverage for Riders," Press Release, American Horse Council (March 26, 2001).

29. "Lifestyle Discrimination," American Civil Liberties Union, 1998. Available online at www.aclu.org/issues/worker/legkit5.html.

30. *City of North Miami, Florida* v. *Kurtz*, 653 So.2d 1025 (Fla. Sup. Ct., April, 1995), cert. denied.

31. Ibid.

# CHAPTER TEN

# In Defense of Employee Privacy Rights

Thanks largely to the phenomenal advances in technology that have occurred in the last twenty years, the time has come for a well-focused national debate on the proper boundaries of employee privacy. Over the last half-century, Congress has made occasional efforts to address the issue of employee privacy, but comprehensive legislation has generally been strenuously opposed by a coalition of business interests. At the same time, labor organizations have not paid particularly close attention to privacy as a workplace issue, given the difficult and more high-profile struggles required to protect jobs, wages, and worker safety. The combination of these factors has created a situation in which employee privacy in the workplace is virtually nonexistent.

The most perturbing development is the growing erasure of any distinction between work and home. The challenge that we face today is not so much how to protect privacy in the workplace—that can best be described as a cultural Maginot line that has long since been circumvented—but how to protect the personal and household privacy of people who are also workers.

As we saw in Chapter 1, there are powerful forces that encourage businesses to peer through the windows of our lives. Any effective effort to shore up employee privacy has to take into consideration the enormous economic and judicial challenges that are facing employers these days.

In fact, the employee privacy situation today strongly resembles that at the end of the nineteenth century, when businesses regularly hired labor spies to investigate not only employees' on-the-job behavior, but also their private lives. While we no longer live in company towns, where our employer is both boss and landlord, the result is effectively the same—an intrusive examination of how we live our lives, with potentially serious economic consequences if our employers do not approve. And thanks to the technological advances that have occurred, the intrusiveness of the inquiry that employers today can command far exceeds anything that Andrew Carnegie, Franklin Gowen, or Henry Frick could have imagined.

The issue is how we as a society should view employee privacy in the workplace. It is not enough simply to pay lip service to principles of individual freedom and human dignity when those principles are largely ignored by employers. While some states have addressed various aspects of this problem, the result has been a hodgepodge of laws that frustrates employer and employee alike. If we are serious about balancing employee privacy with the more invasive aspects of our economic system—and we should be— then the time has come for Congress to establish limits on employer voyeurism.

# Existing Limits on Preemployment Inquiries

Congress has demonstrated that it can act when a national labor issue presents itself in sufficiently pressing terms. Over the last seventy years or so, beginning with the Fair Labor Standards Act in 1938, Congress has passed a variety of laws addressing the hiring and retention of employees. While some of Congress's actions have themselves spurred invasions of employee privacy (most notably Social Security and tax withholding), an opportunity still exists for Congress to establish clear and unequivocal boundaries on the types of inquiries and surveillance that employers can conduct on their employees. The time has unquestionably come for it to do so.

## The Fair Labor Standards Act

Ironically, given the issues being raised by video cameras in the workplace, it was a camera that helped spur the first major piece of federal labor legislation. The old saw is that a picture is worth 1,000 words, but not all pictures are created equal: Some are essentially mute, and others speak volumes. Few photos were as articulate and loquacious as the ones taken by Lewis Hine, who served as a photographer for the National Child Labor Committee from 1908 to 1912. Over the course of those five years, Hine traveled around the country, using his camera to document the often appalling violations and abuses in child labor.[1]

Despite the public outrage inspired by Hine's provocative work, it took nearly another generation for Congress to catch up with public opinion. Finally, at the height of the Great Depression, Congress passed the Fair Labor Standards Act (FLSA). The FLSA is an enormously complicated piece of legislation—made more so by the fact that it attracts amendments and revision the way a ship attracts barnacles—but its main provisions still stand:

- A forty-hour work week

- A federal minimum wage

- Rules and requirements for overtime

- Restrictions on child labor

While the FLSA has relatively little to do with employee privacy or workplace surveillance directly, it is nonetheless an important example of the sweeping action that Congress is capable of taking when necessary. It also helps to underscore the importance of the political environment. The FLSA was in part intended to improve employment in a depressed economy by making it more expensive to pay existing employees for overtime than to hire new employees at regular wages. It was a bill partially intended to reduce the unemployment rate at a time when the nation's workforce desperately needed the help.

By contrast, any effort to limit employee surveillance today must deal with the political reality that in the wake of 9/11 leans toward more surveillance, not less. Between the USA Patriot Act and the Homeland Security Act, the federal government is on the verge of having unprecedented surveillance authority, and it is a reasonable bet that they will be looking to employers for help.

One surveillance issue that does arise in conjunction with the FLSA is the challenge of accounting for the time that telecommuting employees spend working. How much time someone works is obviously an important issue under the FLSA, and it doesn't matter whether the work is performed in an office or in the home. Given the potential legal exposure for underpaying its employees, the FLSA gives employers an incentive to require the installation of computer monitoring software on home PCs, with all of its attendant privacy concerns.

## The Civil Rights Act of 1964

Given the range of topics that it covers, the Fair Labor Standards Act is probably the single most important piece of federal legislation for American employees. But in terms of sheer social impact, the FLSA pales beside Title

VII of the Civil Rights Act of 1964, which strove to eliminate most of the insidious discrimination occurring in the workplace.

Under the provisions of Title VII, any employer with more than fifteen employees may not discriminate on the basis of race, skin color, gender, religious beliefs, or national origin. The legislation covers every aspect of employment: advertisements for employment, the hiring process, promotions or dismissals, pay raises, performance reviews, and benefits. To help enforce the provisions of the law, Title VII also established the Equal Employment Opportunity Commission (EEOC).

An immediate impact of Title VII was to alter or eliminate many of the questions that employers were in the habit of asking prospective employees during job interviews (i.e., "What religion do you practice?" "Do you believe in God?" etc.) Currently, a major employment battleground is the area of personality testing; as we saw in Chapter 2, many so-called "personality" tests are really efforts to ask the types of questions that are forbidden by Title VII.

In terms of employee surveillance, one of the more important amendments to the Civil Rights Act was the 1978 Pregnancy Discrimination Act. Employers are frequently concerned about pregnancy in the workplace because a pregnant woman raises difficult issues regarding exposure to various substances that could potentially harm the fetus and/or the mother. Even a healthy pregnancy is an enormously expensive event that can boost a firm's health insurance costs, and the costs skyrocket if the baby is premature or has health complications. The Pregnancy Discrimination Act was Congress's effort to limit employer practices like undisclosed blood tests to determine pregnancy.

Thanks to a combination of events, a major—albeit unintended—consequence of the Civil Rights Act has been to increase the level of workplace surveillance. In 1986, the United States Supreme Court ruled for the first time in *Meritor Savings Bank* v. *Vinson* that sexual harassment is a form of discrimination banned by the Act.[2] That decision put the onus on employers to police their workplace to eliminate discriminatory behavior. That responsibility would be difficult enough, given the enormous numbers of sexually explicit magazines, calendars, t-shirts, greeting cards, etc. that are available today, but the widespread adoption of the personal computer in the mid-1980s (just as the hostile work environment doctrine was being formulated) and the introduction of the World Wide Web a decade later have made it immeasurably more difficult.

## The Fair Credit Reporting Act

Over the course of just fifteen years, beginning with the widespread commercial introduction of computers in the mid-1950s, credit reporting developed into a secret, unregulated industry capable of wreaking havoc in people's lives with a single uncorrected error. It was an industry that made no pretense of offering due process—credit reporting firms were not liable for the consequences of their errors and there was no clear mechanism for fixing mistakes.

In 1970, Congress passed the Fair Credit Reporting Act (FCRA), which for the first time began to reign in the worst excesses of the credit reporting bureaus. Under the terms of the FCRA, consumers had a right to know what was in their credit files and to demand that any errors be corrected.

As is often the case, mere passage of FCRA was insufficient to correct all of the problems targeted by the law. In 1977, Administrative Law Judge Theodor von Brand criticized the way that one firm, Equifax, handled data, finding that "Some [of the company's employees] resorted to shortcutting techniques with the result that inaccurate reports were produced."[3] Virtually every other credit reporting bureau has been the subject of similar criticism, although recent changes to the FRCA do offer consumers some slightly greater protection from erroneous information in their credit reports. As of September 30, 1997, the credit bureaus are liable up to $250 for each mistake they make.

Amendments to the FRCA since its initial adoption appear to favor employees. An employer is now required to get your written permission to look at the substance of your credit report. Nor is an employer permitted to bury the consent in the fine print of a job application or employment contract: Under the FCRA, you must give separate and unequivocal consent before your employer (or a detective hired by your employee) can view your complete credit information. Of course, as one employment lawyer has pointed out, "If you refuse to give approval to the employer's wandering eyes, you will leave the impression that you have something to hide—and that will likely kill your chances for getting or keeping the job."[4]

In the category of cold comfort, if a prospective employer does reject your job application based in part on the contents of your credit report, the company must inform you of the name and address of the credit bureau from which it obtained the report.

## The Employee Polygraph Protection Act

Congress has also passed at least one law specifically designed to protect employee privacy: the 1988 Employee Polygraph Protection Act (EPPA). The law applies to every company in the United States that conducts interstate commerce, which means every company that does business with or communicates with someone in another state via telephone or U.S. mail.

Under the terms of the EPPA, a company is not permitted:

■ To require, request, suggest, or cause any employee or job applicant to submit to a lie detector test

■ To use, accept, refer to, or inquire about the results of any lie detector test conducted on an employee or job applicant

■ To dismiss, discipline, discriminate against, or even threaten to take action against any employee or job applicant who refuses to take a lie detector test

Employers are permitted to use a polygraph test to evaluate employees being hired for jobs in security or drug handling. They may also use a polygraph test to assist in the investigation of a specific theft or crime. But your boss can't just stroll into your cubicle and begin strapping the wires onto you. The EPPA requires that you be given written notice that you are a suspect at least forty-eight hours beforehand (which gives you just enough time to rent *Meet the Parents* for polygraph test-taking tips).

If your employer does require you to take a polygraph test, the EPPA also imposes some limitations on how the test can be administered. Before the test begins, your employer is required to read to you a statement of relevant information, and must ask you to sign the statement. The statement must include the following information:

■ The list of topics about which your employer cannot ask, including questions regarding your religious beliefs, your sexual preference, racial issues, your involvement in the lawful activities of a labor organization, and your political affiliations

■ Notice of your right to refuse to take the polygraph test

■ Notice that you cannot be required to take a polygraph test as a condition of employment

■ An explanation of how the employer will use the test results

■ An explanation of your legal rights if the polygraph test is not given in the manner required by the EPPA

## The Americans with Disabilities Act

Another form of workplace discrimination was banned by Congress in 1990, when it passed the Americans with Disabilities Act (ADA). The law, widely criticized for the breadth and ambiguity of its language, is intended to prohibit employers from taking certain actions, including:

■ Discriminating on the basis of physical or mental disability

■ Quizzing job applicants about their past or current medical conditions

- Requiring job applicants to take a medical exam prior to being offered a job

- Creating or maintaining a workplace that interferes with the movement of people with a physical handicap

On first impression, the ADA appears to be a strong tool for employees: It does regulate, to a certain degree, the use of medical examinations during the application process. However, while employers can't ask general questions about your health or medical history during a job interview, there is no restriction on the ability of an employer to ask you medically-related questions that pertain to your job. For instance, if you're applying for a driving job, your prospective employer is entitled to inquire about your vision. If you're applying for a job stocking shelves, the interviewer can ask whether you are strong enough to lift and move boxes for six or eight hours a day.

Not unlike workers' compensation laws, the ADA provides nominal protection and benefits to workers, but at the same time it encourages employers to hire private detectives and conduct secret surveillance of employees not only in the workplace but off-duty as well. The law applies to someone who "has a physical or mental impairment that substantially limits a major life activity; has a record of impairment; or is regarded as having an impairment."[5]

Many employers see a claim of limitation of a "major life activity" as grounds for conducting a thorough investigation of the employee. Such an investigation would be straightforward enough in cases where someone has lost a limb, but it can be much trickier, for instance, when dealing with mental disability claims. It can be difficult to assess whether the benefits available under the ADA outweigh the loss of privacy required to exercise them.

# Specific Legal Limits on Workplace Surveillance

Legal limits on workplace surveillance fall into the categories of constitutional protections and specific laws.

## Constitutional Protections

If you're concerned about the privacy of your conversations at work, you're marginally better off if your employer is a government agency or department (see the discussion in Chapter 6 on the legality of searches). At least in theory, a government is barred by the Fourth Amendment (either directly, in the case of the federal government, or indirectly, in the case of state and local governments) from conducting unreasonable search and seizures against its employees. Since the Fourth Amendment does not apply to private employers, they are under no such constitutional constraints, although they may be subject to state constitutional and statutory limitations.

For some years now, civil libertarians have worried that the Rehnquist Court was intent on gutting the Fourth Amendment in an effort to reduce the possibility that obviously guilty defendants would walk free due to a search-and-seizure technicality. Those fears were allayed to some degree by the Court's recent ruling in *Kyllo v. United States*, in which the Court held that police could not use thermal imaging technology to "see" inside a house to determine whether someone was using heat lamps to grow marijuana.[6]

Nonetheless, when it comes to places of employment, the Fourth Amendment is not much of a shield. The lead case in this area is *O'Connor v. Ortega*, which dealt with a university hospital physician who sued the hospital and assorted individuals after they conducted a search of his desk and file cabinets while he was out of the office.[7] Hospital management justified the search on the grounds that they were looking for evidence to support or refute a claim of wrongdoing against the physician.

The Supreme Court's decision was split, but a majority of the justices agreed on a few general principles. First, the Court declared that public employees can in fact have an expectation of privacy at their workplace. However, the Court also said that determining whether a search of a government employee's workspace is reasonable depends on the context of the search. In addition, the employee's legitimate expectation of privacy must be balanced against the government's interest in supervision, control, and the smooth operation of the workplace.

The Court concluded that it would seriously disrupt the operation of the workplace if a government employer was required to get a search warrant every time it wanted to enter employee workspace for a work-related purpose. Likewise, the Court held that imposing the traditional "probable cause" standard for this type of workplace search would also be inherently unreasonable.

The *Ortega* decision helped lead to the somewhat ironic situation that in terms of workplace searches and seizures, an employer's best course of action is to make it clear to employees from the outset that they have little or no right to privacy in the workplace. In *Schowengerdt v. General Dynamics Corp.*, a later decision that relied on *Ortega*, the U.S. Court of Appeals for the Ninth Circuit held that the privacy rights of an employee at a secret weapons facility were not violated when the employer searched his office, desk, and credenza.[8] Specifically, the court found that the employer had clearly warned employees that due to the sensitive nature of the work being done at the facility, both scheduled and random searches would be conducted. As a result, the Ninth Circuit said the employee had no reasonable expectation of privacy.

Similarly, when a police officer who was suspected of misconduct challenged the reasonableness of a search of his desk, a state-owned vehicle, and a locked briefcase, the U.S. Court of Appeals held that the police department was entitled to weigh the interests of the public when deciding whether to conduct the search.[9] The court concluded that there was little question that the searches of the office and the vehicle were justified. While an officer has a greater expectation of privacy in a locked briefcase than in his department-issued patrol car, the court nonetheless agreed that under the circumstances, opening the briefcase was reasonable.

Not every privacy case brought by a disgruntled public employee has resulted in a ruling in favor of her employer, but the majority have. However, the difficulty that public employees have in protecting their privacy in the workplace, despite the nominal aid of the Fourth Amendment, helps to underscore how tenuous privacy is in the private workplace.

## The National Labor Relations Act

As we saw in Chapter 2, the struggle to unionize has been one of the more violent and confrontational themes in our nation's history. Particularly in the tumultuous years at the end of the nineteenth century, the battles between employers and employees were so frequent and so pitched as to nearly constitute a second civil war.

Unions hit their high-water mark over a twelve-year period beginning in 1935, when the National Labor Relations Act (NLRA) was passed, and 1946, when membership in unions hit its highest level of 30 percent of all workers. Since that time, union membership has fallen to less than 15 percent of the workforce, and business organizations have steadily chipped away at the provisions of the NLRA and other proemployee statutes.

Nonetheless, most of the core provisions of the NLRA remain intact, and one of the issues they directly address is the issue of surveillance of employees. Specifically, the Act bars employers from spying on employees engaged in union activity. Forbidden types of spying include eavesdropping on employee conversations; taping, filming, or photographing employees; tapping phones; and/or monitoring attendance at union functions. It is important to note that the NLRA does not require evidence that an employer actually engaged in surveillance of union activities; it is sufficient to show that the employer created the impression that such surveillance was taking place, and that the impression of surveillance intimidated employees from engaging in union activity.

In addition to establishing standards of conduct for employers, the National Labor Relations Act also established the National Labor Relations Board (NLRB) to serve, among other things, as the arbiter of employer/employee disputes over surveillance of union activities. In determining whether a particular type of surveillance is permitted, the NLRB looks at two main factors: the purpose of the surveillance and the locations being observed. If the employer can articulate a legitimate purpose for the surveillance and the location of the surveillance was not chosen in an effort to discourage union participation, then the NLRB will generally permit it.

Not surprisingly, video surveillance has been a particularly contentious issue for the NLRB. In 1994, unionized employees at a Colgate-Palmolive facility in Indiana discovered hidden cameras in an exercise room and company bathrooms. The company removed the cameras, but asserted that it had a right to conduct hidden surveillance without prior agreement by the union. The union disagreed and asked the NLRB to rule that the use of surveillance cameras was subject to mandatory bargaining between the company and the union. The Board ruled that the use of hidden surveillance cameras was a mandatory subject of collective bargaining because "installation of surveillance cameras is both germane to the working environment and outside the scope of managerial decisions lying at the core of entrepreneurial control."[10]

In reaching its decision, the NLRB apparently disregarded an earlier decision in which it accepted a ruling by an administrative law judge that bathroom surveillance was acceptable without union consent. In that case, however, the specific conduct that the company was trying to prevent (tampering with fire alarms) was occurring in the company washrooms. As a result, the administrative law judge concluded that the hidden surveillance was justified.

Overall, hidden surveillance has not been well-received by the Board. Just last year, the NLRB held that even where a union failed to object to hidden surveillance cameras, an employer was still required to bargain over the issue if the union objected to their use at some later date.[11]

Monitoring of employee e-mail is also subject to NLRB scrutiny if union activity is an issue. For example, an employer that permits its employees to use the company e-mail system for personal messages cannot then ban union-related e-mails.[12]

## The Electronic Communications Privacy Act

Belatedly recognizing the fact that technology was making it possible for employers to routinely monitor employee phone conversations and other types of communication, Congress passed the Electronic Communications

Privacy Act (ECPA) in 1986. The ECPA is an amendment to the earlier Omnibus Crime Control and Safe Streets Act of 1968, which established basic standards for wiretapping by federal agents. By the mid-1980s, however, it was clear that courts were struggling to apply the wiretap law to new technology. Ironically, the same thing is now happening to the ECPA.

The basic principle of the law is straightforward: It is unlawful (with certain exceptions) to "intercept" any wire, oral, or electronic communication or to access any stored wire or electronic communication. One major problem is that when the ECPA was adopted, e mail systems were not yet common, particularly in the private sector. In the sixteen years since the ECPA was adopted, of course, e-mail has become a phenomenally popular and common means of communication.

While the law offers greater electronic privacy for most people (since it extended the prohibition against interception from telephone conversations to e-mail and other forms of electronic communication), it can be viewed as a step backward for employees. As a general rule, federal law prohibits eavesdropping or the recording of a conversation unless at least one party to the conversation has given her consent (or the eavesdropping was previously approved by court order). However, the ECPA contains a number of exceptions that weaken the application of that principle in the workplace.

The primary problem is that the ECPA allows a "systems provider" to access electronic communications like e-mail without liability. There is a broad consensus that the provision covers commercial providers like America Online and Yahoo!, but there is some debate over whether it covers so-called employer-providers, i.e., a company that creates and maintains its own internal e-mail system. By and large, however, most legal analysts assume that a business that provides an internal e-mail system is a "systems provider" within the meaning of the statute, and therefore is free to examine e-mail on its system.

As we saw in Chapter 6, surveillance of voice communications is a little trickier for employers, since relatively few companies are providers of telephone systems within the meaning of the statute. However, under the ECPA, businesses can rely on at least two other exceptions to conduct surveillance of employee phone calls.

First, the ECPA contains a provision that allows an employer to monitor conversations in the "ordinary course of business," so long as the company uses equipment typically furnished by a telephone company in connection with phone service. This is the reason you often hear the phrase "This call may be monitored for quality assurance." Second, if an employee has given his consent (either actual or implied), then the employer may also monitor telephone conversations. Your employer can create implied consent for telephone call monitoring through the simple expedient of informing you that your conversations will be monitored and by describing the manner in which such monitoring will take place.

In either case, your employer is required to stop monitoring as soon as she determines that a phone call is personal and not job-related; however, that determination can take a few minutes, which is often all the time an employee spends on a personal call.

As is so often the case, the pace of technology has outstripped Congress. The ECPA was virtually out-of-date when it was passed, and the technological innovations of the last sixteen years have exacerbated the problem. When the law was passed, for instance, the World Wide Web was still a gleam in the eye of Timothy Berners-Lee; communication tools like ICQ, Internet relay chat, and AOL Messenger were still years in the future; and completely unforeseen were technologies like Internet telephony and the rapidly approaching video conferencing.

Clearly, in passing the ECPA, Congress intended to permit the providers of an e-mail system to engage in surveillance to protect their rights and property interests. Frankly, it's unrealistic to expect a pronouncement any time soon from Washington that businesses cannot monitor their employees' e-mail or other forms of online communication—there are too many sound reasons for doing so. But at the very least, Congress could require businesses to tell employees what they're doing and how they're doing it, and prohibit businesses from making any use of nonwork-related information it might obtain.

## The Health Insurance Portability and Accountability Act

It is difficult to think of any proposed legislation over the last decade that inspired as much venom and sheer ill-will as the Clinton national health care plan. From the beginning of 1993, when President Clinton appointed his wife, First Lady (and now Senator) Hillary Clinton to head the health care task force, to the bill's ultimate rejection by Congress in late 1994, the debate marked one of the recent low points in political discourse.

Out of the ashes of the Clinton proposal came the Health Insurance Portability and Accountability Act (HIPAA), a more modest health care reform championed by Senators Edward Kennedy (Massachusetts) and Nancy Kassebaum (Kansas). Passed in 1996, the bill is designed to make it easier for employees to change jobs without losing their medical insurance. In addition, HIPAA also sets new standards for the handling of personal health information (PHI), which is defined under the law as:

- Information that relates to the physical or mental health of a person (such as the individual's medical history or particular condition)

- Provision of health care to the individual (including insurance processes such as an individual's insurance case management)

- The payment of health care (including claim payments and coordination of benefits)

Under the terms of the HIPAA, the Secretary of Health and Human Services was authorized to enact standards to insure the privacy of individually identifiable health information if Congress did not pass comprehensive health care legislation by August 21, 1999. For various reasons, Congress did not meet its own deadline, so HHS Secretary Tommy G. Thompson ordered his Department to prepare the necessary standards. A proposed Rule was issued on November 3, 1999, and comments were solicited from the public. The response was enthusiastic: HHS reported that it received over 52,000 comments on the proposed Rule. After reviewing the comments and taking them into consideration, on December 28, 2000, HHS issued "Standards for Privacy of Individually Identifiable Health Information ('Privacy Rule')."

The Privacy Rule is a enormously complex regulation. Nonetheless, absent an extension from HHS, businesses that routinely receive or handle personal health information will be required to comply with HIPAA's privacy provisions by April 14, 2003. As with other types of federal business statutes, small businesses (those with fewer than fifty employees) are exempt. In addition, if a business establishes procedures that help it avoid the receipt of personal health information, then the business is not required to comply with HIPAA's regulations.

HIPAA stipulates that businesses must take the following steps (among others):

- Create the position of chief privacy officer (CPO) to establish procedures for the handling of PHI, and to provide appropriate training to personnel who handle PHI.

- Document all privacy procedures, communications, and plan actions and maintain records for six years.

- Upon request, provide an accounting of all uses and disclosures of information to a member (including the individual or entity receiving the information, a description of the information, and the reason for the use and disclosure).

- Implement new written contracts with claims administrators, utilization review providers, and other business associates assuring they comply with the privacy rules.

- Write a detailed policy notice to employees, in plain English, outlining the plan's practices on privacy of health information.

- Decide whether to require consent forms from employees on specific employer functions.

- Separate health plan administration and PHI from other company functions, to protect the employer from a lawsuit claiming, for example, an employee was fired because her claims were costing the company medical plan too much money.

- Establish a clear, written procedure for addressing complaints and grievances.

- Amend plan documents to include a list of permitted and required uses and disclosures of protected health information with examples, including payment and processing of claims.

- Tell plan participants they may access their PHI, amend the information, receive an accounting of their PHI disclosures, and advise them of the process to address complaints.[13]

It's still unclear exactly how businesses will respond. There is considerable concern that the complexity of the regulations and a slow economy will make it very difficult for organizations and businesses to successfully meet the April 2003 deadline. Among other consequences, the regulations are driving the growth of a new software business sector—companies specializing in software for the handling of electronic medical records—because those types of systems can be tied into user authentication devices, including biometrics. Such devices would make it possible for a hospital, for instance, to maintain a log of everyone who accessed a particular patient's file.

## Good Ideas That Never Got off the Ground

As public awareness of the surveillance possibilities of new electronic technology has grown, Congress has at least considered adopting some legislation to protect employee privacy. These proposals, however, have faced uphill sledding since the Republican Party won control of the House of Representatives in 1994. And over the last year, the focus on foreign relations has pushed virtually all domestic legislation onto the back burner.

What's most instructive about these failed pieces of legislation is not so much the specifics of their provisions (although they contained some valuable ideas) as the sheer ferocity with which they were opposed. Shortly after each bill was introduced, a broad coalition of business interests (and to some degree, conservative groups) descended on them like white blood cells on a virus, and consigned each to a slow but certain death by committee.

## The Privacy for Consumers and Workers Act

On February 27, 1991, the late Senator Paul Simon (Illinois) and Representative Pat Williams (Montana) introduced the Privacy for Consumers and Workers Act (PCWA). Under the terms of the bill, employers would have been required to:

- Clearly define their privacy policies.

- Notify prospective employees of electronic monitoring that might affect them.

- Limit surveillance to ensuring job performance.

- Refrain from monitoring personal communications.

- Give employees access to any data about them collected during surveillance.

- Refrain from video monitoring in locker rooms or bathrooms (unless there were specific suspicions of illegal conduct).

- Notify workers when telephone monitoring was taking place (except when the monitoring was being done for quality control).

The bill failed to gain traction during the 102nd Congress and was reintroduced in 1993. Once again, the bill's supporters were unsuccessful in their efforts to get it out of committee.

Opposing the legislation was a wide variety of business organizations ranging from Household Finance Corp. to Associated Builders and Contractors, which worried that the legislation would limit the ability to videotape striking workers. Larry Fineran, an assistant vice president for the National Association of Manufacturers, testified before Congress in 1991 that "random and periodic silent monitoring is a very important management tool." He also stated that the PCWA would interfere "with the ability of modern and future equipment that can assist domestic companies in their fight to remain competitive . . . otherwise the United States may as well let the information age pass it by."

Fineran also came up with the novel "stage fright" objection to providing employees with notice of surveillance. He argued that employees can function better when they don't know that they're being observed, and that it's actually more stressful when they're told that they are being watched.

Insurance organizations, including the American Insurance Society and the Risk and Insurance Management Society, also lobbied heavily against the bill because of their concern that it would limit their ability to conduct surveillance to prevent workman's compensation fraud. Along with assorted finance companies, insurance companies backed up their testimony with $23 million worth of campaign contributions in 1996 to candidates sympathetic to their position on privacy issues.[14]

## The Notice of Electronic Monitoring Act

What would have been, essentially, a narrower and simpler version of the PCWA was introduced on July 20, 2000, by Senator Charles Schumer (New York). Known as the Notice of Electronic Monitoring Act (NEMA), the bill would have subjected employers to civil liability if the employer:

> . . . intentionally, by any electronic means, reads, listens to, or otherwise monitors any wire communication, oral communication, or electronic communication of an employee of the employer, or otherwise monitors the computer usage of an employee of the employer, without first having provided the employee notice . . . .

Under the terms of the law, the employer would be required to tell employees the type of monitoring that would take place, the means of monitoring that would be used, the information that would be gathered (including whether any non-work-related information would be collected), the frequency with which the monitoring would occur, and how the information would be used.

The law contained one exception: An employer could engage in electronic monitoring without notice if the employer had reasonable grounds to believe that the employee was engaged in illegal or dangerous activity, *and* that the electronic surveillance would produce evidence of the undesirable conduct. If an employer violated NEMA, then the affected employee could sue for actual and punitive damages, attorney fees, and litigation costs.

Like its predecessor, NEMA never made it to the floor of the Senate for a vote. The bill was also introduced in the House of Representatives by Representative Charles Canady (Florida), but it met an even less enthusiastic response. It has not been reintroduced.

## The Employment Nondiscrimination Act

Few sectors of the population are more worried about the potential consequences of employer surveillance and invasion of privacy than gays and lesbians. Although large numbers of corporations have adopted nondiscrimination policies, workers who admit that they are gay are reported to earn between 11 percent and 27 percent less than their heterosexual coworkers, which is just one of the reasons that many gay and lesbian employees choose to remain in the closet. Other motivations for silence include the risk of harassment, loss of promotion, and/or termination.

As we saw in Chapter 2, some employers were using lie detector tests in the early 1960s in an effort to determine whether job applicants might be homosexual. The general problem still exists: When Delta Airlines took over Pan American World Airway's European flight routes in 1991, reports surfaced that Delta had hired Equifax to conduct extensive background checks on thousands of Pan Am employees who applied for jobs with Delta. Applicants were required to sign forms consenting to the background checks, including interviews with friends and coworkers. Among the information sought was the sexual orientation of the applicants.[15]

The first efforts to pass nondiscrimination legislation for gays and lesbians was introduced in the 1970s, but received little support. Two decades later, in June 1994, Senator Edward Kennedy (Massachusetts) and Representative Gerry Studds (Massachusetts) introduced the Employment Nondiscrimination Act of 1994 (ENDA). Hearings were held by the Senate Committee on Labor and Human Resources, but the bill never made it to the floor of the Senate. In 1996, supporters tried to attach the Act as an amendment to the Defense of Marriage Act. As a compromise, supporters of the Defense of Marriage Act agreed to allow ENDA to come to the floor of the Senate for a separate vote. It was defeated by a single vote, fifty to forty-nine.

ENDA was reintroduced in the Senate in June 1997 by Senator James Jeffords (Vermont), and again, hearings were held by the Senate Committee on Labor and Human Resources. In his introduction to the bill, Senator Jeffords articulated the need for the legislation:

> By extending to sexual orientation the same Federal employment discrimination protections established for race, religion, gender, national origin, age, and disability, this legislation will further ensure that principals of equality and opportunity apply to all Americans.
> . . . . People who work hard and perform well should not be kept from leading productive and responsible lives because of an irrational, ‘nonwork-related prejudice. Unfortunately, many responsible and productive members of our society face discrimination in their workplaces based on nothing more than their sexual orientation.[16]

ENDA has been reintroduced in each of the last two Congresses—by Senator Jeffords in 1999, and by Senator Kennedy in 2001. Over the course of the last decade, the scope of the law has been narrowed considerably. While it would still prohibit discrimination on the basis of sexual orientation, it also contains a number of explicit statements about what it does *not* do:

- The law would not mandate benefits for domestic partners.

- It would bar the Equal Employment Opportunity Commission from collecting statistics on sexual orientation from covered entities.

- It would prohibit quotas and preferred treatment.

- It would not apply to religious organizations, the military, and laws creating special rights for veterans.

- The law would prohibit the imposition of affirmative action as a remedy for violations.

According to public opinion polls, there is widespread support for legislation that would prohibit employment discrimination based on sexual orientation. Yet Congress has been reluctant to act and is probably less likely to do so given the results of the 2002 midterm election.

## An Employee Bill of Rights

The significance of the laws discussed in the first part of this chapter cannot be underestimated. They amply demonstrate that when sufficiently motivated, Congress can have the willpower to step in and protect the rights of employees. The chief problem is that most of the laws on the books regulate what employers can do with information once they have it, but make no effort to regulate how the employer obtains the information. It seems increasingly evident that the methods used to collect information about employees are as damaging and destructive as the discrimination that often follows.

One can analogize employee privacy in the workplace to the ozone layer. Total employee privacy would be no more workable than an entirely opaque ozone layer; employers are entitled to a certain transparency, for all of the reasons discussed in Chapter 1 and elsewhere in this book. (It's worth noting that most employees are also against workplace violence, theft, sexual harassment, etc.) But employers have been steadily stripping away employee privacy with the same thoughtless avidity that we pumped chlorofluorocarbons (CFCs) into the atmosphere in the 1970s and 1980s. A complete absence of employee privacy is no more tenable and should be no more acceptable than a complete absence of ozone.

Despite the size of the privacy hole that is opening up over employees, it's not too late for Congress to act. We've seen what can happen in the physical world: Thanks to the banning of CFCs, the size of the hole in the ozone layer over the Antarctic has been steadily shrinking. With the adoption of a few well-considered statutory provisions, Congress could begin to restore a healthier balance in the workplace.

The following is a number of general areas in which Congress should take action to better protect employee privacy rights.

## Opt-In Requirements for Collection of Information

At the outset, it is worth restating that employers are entitled to and should collect certain types of information about their employees. It would be wholly impractical and downright silly to argue that employers should be barred, for instance, from verifying the information that prospective employees offer on resumes and job applications.

Nonetheless, the first and most fundamental requirement for improving workplace privacy is that employers be required to obtain specific, informed consent from employees and prospective employees before they acquire personal information about them. There is no incompatibility between informing applicants of the specifics of a background check and protecting the integrity of the workplace.

To a limited degree, the requirement of disclosure already exists: Under the terms of the Fair Credit Reporting Act, an employer (or prospective employer) must obtain your written permission before it can legally obtain a copy of your credit report (apart from the header information, which is essentially available to anyone).

The chief difference between this proposal and current practice is that employers would no longer be able to rely on a broad, generally worded grant of permission by applicants and employees to an essentially unfettered examination of their private life. Instead, an employer would be required to provide all applicants and current employees with the following specific information:

- The nature and scope of the information being sought

- The sources from which the information would be obtained

- The methods by which the information would be obtained

- The specific, work-related purposes for which the information was being sought

Such disclosure would enable employees to make an informed decision about whether or not to apply for a job with a particular employer. In addition, it would bring some much-needed sunlight to the amount of private information that is being routinely obtained by businesses during the job application process.

## Disclosure of Surveillance

The same approach should be taken when it comes to surveillance of employees. The tools and technologies available for conducting surveillance are only going to become smaller, less obtrusive, and hard to detect. Senator Paul Simon had the right approach—an outright ban on hidden surveillance is an appropriate step if we are serious as a society about protecting workplace privacy and the basic dignity of employees.

When Vincent Ruffolo, the head of Security Companies Organized for Legislative Action, testified against Senator Simon's Privacy for Consumers and Workers Act in 1991, he argued that "An employer would be put in the absurd position of having to advise suspected thieves when they are being monitored."[17] However, if informing suspected thieves that they are being monitored brings an end to the unwanted behavior, it would seem that the surveillance has accomplished its ultimate purpose. If the notice of the surveillance does not stop the behavior, presumably the employer would then have the evidence it needed to fire the employee.

The problem with hidden surveillance (and particularly hidden video surveillance) is three-fold: First, it is fundamentally incompatible with the basic values of this country. Secrecy has its place—in national security or trade secrets, for instance—but in general, our society is premised on the free flow of information. We've even gone so far as to pass a Freedom of Information Act at the federal level and in most states to help us learn what information the government might have about us.

Second, the use of hidden surveillance encourages the companies that use it to invade the zone of privacy that each of us is entitled to enjoy, even in the workplace. Admittedly, that zone shrinks when we are on someone else's property and diminishes further when we are supposed to be working for someone else, but even so, it should not vanish altogether. Hidden surveillance is simply not proportional to its objective—in the name of protecting company property or economic interests, it completely obliterates employee privacy.

Third, hidden surveillance panders to a voyeuristic streak that is not our most admirable trait. Even if a company's management or security personnel is not secretly marketing hidden surveillance tapes to sleazy late-night advertisers, there's still a disturbing temptation for camera operators to spend time looking for embarrassing activity. This is hardly an argument to eliminate surveillance cameras so that coworkers can make out in the stairwell, but it is an argument that employees should not have people peering or leering at their unguarded moments.

From the employer's perspective, there is not much practical difference between hidden and obvious surveillance. If anything, a video camera mounted on the wall is capable of watching a wider area than a video camera hidden in an exit sign or desk lamp. The fundamental difference is the level of dignity and choice that each reflects. When surveillance is disclosed and obvious, employees can make an informed decision about whether to work for a particular company, and if so, how to behave in light of the surveillance that is in place.

## Limiting the Casual and Unauthorized Spread of Employee Information

As a practical matter, it is inevitable that an employer will come into possession of private information about its employees. With limited exceptions, there are no legal constraints on what employers can do with the information they collect; employer misuse of employee information has been a problem for decades. Following the passage of the Privacy Act in 1974, which restrained government collection of personal information, Congress established a Privacy Protection Study Commission to evaluate the use of personal information by private industry, appointing University of Illinois professor David Linowes to chair the investigation.

In 1977, the Commission recommended that private employers self-regulate by adopting privacy safeguards for employee information. The Commission's recommendations, however, fell on deaf ears. In a 1979 follow-up study, Professor Linowes found that 85 percent of employers provided information from employee personnel files to creditors. In 1997, Dana Hawkins, a reporter for *U.S. News & World Report*, cited a survey of Fortune 500 companies that found that a majority still routinely shared employee information with creditors, landlords, and even charities.[18]

Just as the collection of employee information should be limited to what is necessary for effective job performance, so too should the distribution of employee information be limited. There is seldom any need for an employer to release employee information to any outside entity in order for an employee to effectively perform his or her job. Establishing clear limits on the redistribution of employee information will go a long way toward buttressing the concept of employee privacy and, at the same time, may make employees and prospective employees far more comfortable with the idea of disclosing personal information that is relevant to their job.

## Restrict the Misuse of Employee Medical Information

From a privacy perspective, employee medical information poses the greatest problem. It is typically the information that you most want to be kept private, yet you are typically forced to reveal extensive amounts of medical information in order to receive adequate care and to have that care covered by your health insurance plan. At the same time, employee medical information is especially valuable to your employer, insofar as knowledge of a potentially expensive medical condition can be an important factor in cutting down on health care costs.

In the 1970s and 1980s, employer misuse of medical records was rampant. In his 1979 study, Professor Linowes found that three out of four employers used employee medical information when making employment decisions. When he conducted a similar investigation in 1989, he found that the percentage of employers misusing medical information was roughly the same.[19]

The level of protection for employee medical records improved slightly in the early 1990s, when Congress passed the Americans with Disabilities Act and the Family and Medical Leave Act (FMLA). Both laws contain provisions that establish confidentiality standards for employee medical records; under the ADA, for instance, employers are required to keep employee medical records in confidential files stored separately from general personnel files.

Largely as a result of those laws, Professor Linowes found in 1996 that the percentage of companies that use medical information in making employment decisions had dropped to about 35 percent.[20] That's certainly an improvement, but it still represents a significant number of employees around the country whose jobs are dependent not so much on how well they work but instead on how expensive their medical care is or is likely to be.

Closely tied to the misuse of medical record information is the collection and misuse of information about how employees spend their personal time, either in their recreational activities or their lifestyle choices. The acquisition of such information should be subject to the same test governing the acquisition of other employee information: Is it reasonably related to your ability to perform your job? If not, then your employer should not be permitted to actively seek that information, and if does acquire it nonetheless, should not be allowed to use it for employment purposes such as hiring or termination.

The problem is that employers have been able to argue that an incredibly wide range of personal information is "relevant" to employment, largely because virtually any human activity can, to one degree or another, have an effect on health insurance costs. But this is simply not an acceptable situation in a nation that prides itself on personal freedom and individual choice.

Obviously, it's a tricky business to eliminate discrimination in a society. We've made some good efforts recently, but thirty-eight years after the passage of the Civil Rights Act, few would argue that we've totally eliminated racism and sexism in this country. And, it is fair to say, we are as a society intrinsically more comfortable trying to eliminate discrimination based on who we are as individuals than the lifestyle choices we make. Hence the passage of the ADA, which attempts to ban discrimination based on personal characteristics we didn't choose, but not the passage of the Employee Nondiscrimination Act, which attempts to ban discrimination against individuals who, rightly or wrongly, are perceived by a significant portion of the population as having made a lifestyle choice.

Businesses will continue to argue that their health insurance premiums should not be subject to the whims of employees who engage in risky behavior, from jet skiing to smoking to gorging on Big Macs. However, it's important to remember that the offering of health insurance is a competitive decision by a business, designed to make its workplace more attractive. Making that offering is itself a risk, which in some cases will simply go bad: An employee might develop a lingering cancer, a child might be born premature and ill, a bad accident may require years of physical therapy.

There is no disagreement that businesses have every right to try and reduce their costs; that is, after all, one of the fundamental principles of a capitalist economy. But if we allow businesses to discriminate against individuals who are capable of performing a particular job but happen to have (or may develop) an expensive medical condition, then we are potentially consigning a large portion of our population to low-paying, non-benefit jobs. An employer should have the burden of showing that the information it seeks about recreational and lifestyle choices is directly related to the work an employee is hired to do, and not to his real or imagined impact on health insurance premiums.

In theory, the ADA was supposed to minimize these types of concerns by limiting the results of a preemployment medical exam to whether a prospective employee is capable of doing the work required, incapable, or capable with reasonable accommodations. No additional information is supposed to be provided to the employer. Yet as we've seen, it's relatively rare that the information provided to an employer is that limited.

The ADA does provide for the filing of a discrimination complaint with the Equal Employment Opportunity Commission and, if necessary, the filing of a lawsuit alleging discrimination. While there is no underestimating the value of private litigation in reining in the worst excesses of corporate behavior, it's at best a scattershot enforcement mechanism. A more comprehensive approach is necessary, consisting of a combination of criminal penalties for the unauthorized disclosure and misuse of employee medical information and statutory penalties to help compensate individuals whose actual damages are limited.

## The Requirement of Reasonable Suspicion for Drug Testing

The most common "lifestyle choice" that employers try to identify is whether its employees are using or have used drugs. With nearly every major U.S. corporation and significant numbers of smaller businesses conducting preemployment tests for drugs, it's not surprising that the detection/antidetection forces are locked in a bit of a contest.

On the surface, it's tempting to applaud businesses for their willingness to bear the expense of random drug testing. The use of most drugs, after all, is against the law, and arguably the prospect of being tested serves as a deterrent to some potential users.

However, there's no statistical evidence to suggest that company drug tests have had any impact at all on drug use in the United States. Moreover, it is legitimate to ask whether a private organization should be attempting to enforce state or federal criminal laws.

Businesses would reply, in part, that they're not actually attempting to enforce criminal laws; they're simply evaluating people's fitness for employment, and if they fail the test, the only consequence is that they don't get the job. No business of which I'm aware refers failed drug test takers to state or federal law enforcement. Moreover, businesses point assiduously to statistics that suggest that drug users are more accident-prone, miss more days of work, and have higher health care costs than nondrug-using employees. Not surprisingly, studies with opposite conclusions exist: in 2001, for instance, the Robert Wood Johnson Foundation concluded that there "was [a] lack of any significant relationships between nonchronic drug use, employment, and labor force participation."[21]

Accurate or not, the statistics regarding drug users and their impact on the workplace give businesses an arguably credible basis for seeking out and acquiring personal information about specific employees for the purposes of extrapolating what is a general outcome. That's an enormously common practice, of course, but we can and should make a decision that in the context of workplace privacy, it is a practice that carries an unnecessarily high social cost.

No one can reasonably disagree that an employer has both the right and—where public safety is concerned—the obligation to make sure that its employees are not actually working under the influence of drugs or alcohol. However, before an employer should be able to require that an employee take a drug test, the employer should be able to state the ways in which the employee's ability to perform is impaired. It is also worth noting that there are a variety of testing methods—those based on coordination, for instance—that can help an employer assess whether an employee's performance capabilities are impaired without acquiring unnecessary information about his medical condition or his personal activities at home.

## Preserving the Boundary Between Work and Home

It would be unreasonable to expect employers to completely ignore the potential problems posed by telecommuting. An employee who works at home with a networked computer is just as capable of causing harm to a business through inappropriate e-mail or stolen trade secrets as someone in the office. Telecommuters also present the potential for greater productivity concerns than employees who can be observed during the course of the day. There is no reasonable basis, then, for arguing that just because you are working at home, you should be free from surveillance software.

That being said, the mere fact that you work at home should not subject you to greater scrutiny or invasion of privacy than is faced by your coworkers in the office.

Of all the potential conflicts between employer and employee, this is the one most easily remedied by employee self-help. If your employer provides you with a computer, for instance, it would be prudent to not use the computer for personal matters unless such use is explicitly authorized. Even then, it is important to keep in mind that the ownership of the computer by your employer could easily expose your private information to unwelcome eyes.

## Enforcement

In order for these protections of employee privacy to be effective, it will be necessary for Congress to create some enforcement provisions. Ideally, these would consist of both civil and criminal remedies. Two pieces of legislation discussed in this chapter, the Electronic Communications Privacy Act and the Health Insurance Portability and Accountability Act, offer compelling models for how such provisions might be structured.

Although the Electronic Communications Privacy Act has not proven so far to be a particularly powerful tool for employees, the basic structure of its enforcement provisions is sound. For instance, the ECPA is primarily a criminal statute: If a person "intentionally intercepts, endeavors to intercept, or procures any other person to intercept or endeavor to intercept, any wire, oral, or electronic communication," and is convicted of doing so, he can be punished by a fine or up to five years in prison.[22]

However, the ECPA takes a dual approach to enforcement by providing civil remedies as well. A person whose communication was "intercepted, disclosed, or intentionally used in violation" of the ECPA may bring a civil action against the violator and request a variety of remedies. Specifically, the ECPA authorizes the awarding of:

■ Preliminary and other equitable or declaratory relief

■ Damages as set out in the statute and punitive damages where appropriate

■ A reasonable attorney's fee and other litigation costs reasonably incurred

The ECPA specifies a certain minimum amount of damages of $100 for each day of violation, up to a maximum of $10,000. However, if a plaintiff's actual damages plus any profits earned by the violator as a result of the interception are greater than the statutory damages, then the plaintiff can try to recover the actual damages instead.[23]

Although it is too early yet to determine just how effective they'll be, particularly given some of the loopholes in the enabling regulations, HIPAA contains some fairly powerful enforcement provisions. For instance, health care plans, providers, and clearinghouses that violate HIPAA's confidentiality provisions are subject to the same type of civil liability as provided for in ECPA, although the upper limit is $25,000 instead of $10,000. In addition, HIPAA makes it a crime to knowingly obtain protected health information:

■ Up to one year in prison and $50,000 in fines for certain violations of HIPAA

■ Up to five years in prison and $100,000 in fines if the crime is committed under "false pretenses" (i.e., pretexting)

■ Up to ten years in prison and $250,000 in fines if the information was obtained "with the intent to sell, transfer or use protected health information for commercial advantage, personal gain or malicious harm"

The remedies laid out in HIPAA and the ECPA offer a useful framework for helping to protect not just communication privacy but workplace privacy in general. By providing for both statutory damages and criminal penalties for unauthorized invasions of privacy, an "employee bill of rights" would effectively place some limits on the hunt for and misuse of private employee information.

## End Notes

1. Jacob Riis, a somewhat older contemporary of Hine, helped spur similar changes in housing conditions in New York with his gripping photographs of tenement houses in the book *How the Other Half Lives* (1890).

2. 477 U.S. 57 (1986).

3. Will Rodger, "Databases Online: What Is Already Known," *Inter@ctive Week* (December 1, 1997).

4. Barbara Kate Repa, Esq., *Your Rights in the Workplace*, 5th ed. (Berkeley, CA: Nolo Press, 2000).

5. Ibid., p. 8/39.

6. ____U.S. ____(2001).

7. 480 U.S. 709, 107 S.Ct. 1492 (1987).

8. 823 F.2d 1328 (Ninth Circuit 1987).

9. Shields v. *Burge*, 874 F.2d 1201 (Seventh Circuit 1989).

10. *In re Colgate-Palmolive*, 323 NLRB 515 (1997).

11. *In re National Steel Corp.*, 335 NLRB No. 60 (2001).

12. *In re E.I. Dupont DeNemours & Co.*, 311 NLRB 893 (1993).

13. "Employee Medical Info Protected: New HIPAA Law Imposes Constraints on Employers," Barney & Barney, LLC (August 23, 2002).

14. Mark Boal, "Spycam City," *The Village Voice* (September 30, 1998).

15. Charles Lewis, "American Workers Beware: Big Brother Is Watching," *USA Today* (May 1999).

16. Senator James Jeffords, *Congressional Record* (June 10, 1997), p. S5457.

17. Charles Lewis, "American Workers Beware: Big Brother Is Watching," *USA Today* (May 1999).

18. Dana Hawkins, "Who's Watching Now?" *U.S. News & World Report* (September 15, 1997).

19. "Employee Monitoring, Investigations, and Privacy Rights," JacksonLewis.com (September 23, 2001).

20. Ibid.

21. "Drug Testing & Employment," DrugWarFacts.com (February 1, 2002). Available online at www.drugwarfacts.org/drugtest.htm.

22. 18 U.S.C. § 2511(1), (4).

23. 18 U.S.C. § 2520(a-c).

# Conclusion

## The State of Workplace Privacy

There's not much to applaud about the current state of workplace privacy in the United States. The technological capability of employers to monitor the activities of their employees surges ahead on a nearly daily basis, and neither Congress nor the nation's labor unions have come up with an effective response. In addition, the events of 9/11 have created an environment in which residents of this country are willing to tolerate—and even welcome—a much higher level of surveillance by both government and businesses.

The chief problem, of course, is that once surveillance cameras, Internet monitoring software, drug tests, GPS, RFIDs, infrared badges, and detailed background checks are in place, they are rarely removed or turned off. As politicians, celebrities, and royalty have known for decades, it's far harder to regain privacy than to defend it in the first place.

There are some signs of grassroots resistance: In the United States, public outcry led to the abandonment of the Terrorism Information and Prevention System (TIPS) program, which sought volunteers to spy on their neighbors, and in Canada, Professor Ronald Deibert of the University of Toronto urged people to participate in "World Sousveillance Day" on December 24, 2002, by using their own cameras to take pictures of surveillance cameras in public spaces.[1]

State snooping and surveillance of daily public activities are attractive targets for citizen outrage; even under the shadow of terrorism, we still retain a deeply ingrained resistance to government agents watching our public activities. If personal privacy is something we truly value, however, we need to bring that resistance to surveillance into the workplace, and find ways to balance the legitimate interests of employers with the equally valid privacy interests of employees.

## Defending Your Privacy at Work

In the popular science fiction series *Star Trek: The Next Generation*, an alien race called the Borg speeds through the universe in massive cubiform structures, absorbing all of the civilizations in their path. As the Borg engage each new foe, they broadcast their intentions and chillingly declare that, "You will be assimilated. Resistance is futile."

It's appropriate to raise the specter of the Borg in the context of workplace privacy: The Borg are portrayed as a semiautonomous collective of cyborg organisms that share a consciousness and an utter lack of personal privacy. The advance of surveillance technology in the workplace has a Borg-like quality to it, a relentless encroachment to which resistance often does in fact feel futile.

Fortunately, science fiction does not necessarily predict the future. Although it is sometimes difficult to do so, there are steps that individuals can take to protect at least some of their privacy at work. More importantly, there are things that we can do together to help better define the proper boundaries between the workplace and personal space.

■ *Assume that you have no privacy at work.* The first and most important step is to be realistic about the current state of workplace privacy. Unless you are told otherwise, your safest assumption is that everything you say and do, particularly on your computer, can be monitored by your employer. With this in mind, you may want to prevent intrusions into your private life by:

■ Limiting the amount of time you spend on personal telephone calls during working hours

■ Limiting or avoiding sending personal e-mails on the company's computer system

■ Avoiding the storage of personal files on the company's computer system

- Removing your badge incorporating infrared technology when you don't want to be located (if your job requires wearing such a badge)

- Being aware that every day you leave "digital footprints" (Credit cards, ETC cards, cell phones, GPS, and other devices used in m-commerce leave a trail of activity in their wake that gives your employer a good idea of how you've been spending your time. Exercise prudence in your use of such devices.)

Even if you are told that your communications are not being monitored, it is very easy for an employer to begin doing so with relatively little expense and no notice to you. The advances in technology make it possible for companies to conduct a wide range of secret surveillance, and in the vast majority of states, companies are under no legal obligation to let you know that they are doing so. It is, however, illegal to record a conversation without the consent of all participants. The following list includes some of the signs that indicate you may be bugged:

- People seem to know your activities when they shouldn't.

- Your AM/FM radio has suddenly developed strange interference.

- Electrical wall plates appear to have been moved slightly or "jarred."

- The smoke detector, clock, lamp, or exit sign in your office or home looks slightly crooked, has a small hole in the surface, or has a quasi-reflective surface.

- Certain types of items have "just appeared" in your office or home, but nobody seems to know how they got there. Examples include clocks, exit signs, sprinkler heads, radios, picture frames, and lamps.

As a practical matter, the only prudent assumption to make is that your employer knows far more about you and how you spend your day than you realize.

*Decide how important workplace privacy is to you.* It may not bother you that your employer is capable of tracking nearly everything that you do in the office. In the type of tough economy that the U.S. has experienced over the last couple of years, workplace privacy can seem like a relatively minor concern. Moreover, despite its Orwellian overtones, there's a seductive appeal to former British Prime Minister John Major's campaign slogan, "If you've got nothing to hide, you've got nothing to fear." Unprompted, many people offer a similar sentiment when asked about the possibility of increased government surveillance to battle terrorism.

But privacy shouldn't be about fear; it should be about choice. When you apply for a job, you routinely take into account the type of work it is, where the job is located, what the work environment is like, how much the job pays, and so forth. An employer's approach to workplace privacy should be on that list as well: the types of background checks done during the application process, the handling of personnel and medical records, visual and electronic surveillance, and monitoring outside of the office. In the specific instance where an employer asks you to take a lie detector test, you should be aware of the following:

- You cannot be legally asked questions about your religious beliefs, sexual preference, racial matters, lawful activities of labor organizations, and political affiliation.

- You have the right to refuse to take a lie detector test.

- An employer cannot require that you take the test as a condition of employment.

- The employer must explain how the test results will be used.

- You have certain rights, which the employer must list, if the test is not properly administered.

- You have the right to stop the test at any time.

- You can request that questions not be asked in a "degrading and needlessly intrusive fashion."

In addition, be certain to educate yourself regarding company drug tests. When a company routinely conducts drug testing of its employees be aware that "false positives" can be affected by what you eat for breakfast (poppy seed rolls are the most notorious for failure to pass a drug test) as well as that caplet you took for your headache.

While virtually all businesses conduct some type of surveillance, the specific types of surveillance conducted varies widely from business to business. You might be comfortable working for a company that monitors phone calls for quality assurance, but less comfortable with a company that keeps track of how long you wash your hands.

If you are in doubt about a company's surveillance methods, ask. The challenge, of course, is getting a straight answer. Companies have no obligation to disclose all of the surveillance tools that they use and may be very reluctant to do so. There's also some risk involved: In some corporate environments, you may be perceived as a troublemaker or security threat if you push too hard for information about the company's surveillance practices. It is worth asking, however, if that's the kind of company for which you do or don't want to work.

- *Be proactive on the issue of privacy.* An important practical step is to educate yourself about the kinds of surveillance that your employer could be conducting. Once you are familiar, for instance, with the various types of software and hardware that can be used to monitor the workplace, you can begin to conduct a realistic assessment of just how closely you are being watched. More importantly, you can ask your employer or potential employer informed questions about the types of surveillance that it conducts.

■ *Pay attention to developments in technology.* If you are concerned about workplace privacy, it's also important to keep abreast of the technological changes that make surveillance easier. This book will help give you an idea of some of the areas to watch: faster and more sensitive biometric tools (Chapter 3), smaller cameras (Chapter 5), more sophisticated Web monitoring software (Chapter 6), and so forth. In order to be proactive on the issue of workplace privacy, you need to know the questions to ask, and paying attention to technological innovations will help provide you with the necessary information.

Also, in the area of computer monitoring, be aware that a company's Web surveillance options usually fall into one of the following four categories:

1.  Log files and cookies—the lists of resources you've visited online. (Both *Internet Explorer* and *Navigator* keep a history of sites visited that can be easily accessed.)

2.  Browser caches—which, in addition to keeping pieces of stored Web pages, track the addresses of downloaded Web pages, the dates they were first accessed, and the dates they were last accessed.

3.  Packet sniffers—programs installed on a gateway server or Internet service provider system that are designed to examine individual packets of electronic data for specific terms.

4.  Filters and monitors—software to filter access to inappropriate material as well as outright monitoring of Web surfing

You should also search your favorite mainstream media website (a few of mine are nytimes.com, globe.com, cnn.com, and salon.com) for the latest developments in surveillance technology. It's also useful to periodically visit somewhat more specialized sites like wired.com or slashdot.com. On all of those sites, searches using some combination of the terms "employee," "workplace," "surveillance," and "privacy" will turn up a variety of relevant articles.

In addition, there are a number of organizations that actively advocate for greater privacy. Although most deal with the issue of privacy in general, virtually all address the issue of workplace privacy as well. Good places to start include the American Civil Liberties Union (aclu.org), the Electronic

Privacy Information Center (epic.org), the National Work Rights Institute (workrights.org), and the Privacy Rights Clearinghouse (privacyrights.org).

■ *Encourage Congress, your state legislature, and your union to strengthen workplace privacy.* Workplace privacy is not something that will be protected effectively by market forces; while competition over workers can have some effect, there are too many competing economic considerations. If workplace privacy is going to be protected in a meaningful way, Congress, the various state legislatures, and labor unions will have to make the establishment of appropriate guidelines a priority. I believe that this issue is large enough and important enough that it should be addressed at the federal level rather than piecemeal by the states. Some of the elements that should be included in such an "Employee Bill of Rights" are:

■ Opt-in requirements for collection of information by employers

■ Disclosure of surveillance by employers

■ Limits on the casual and unauthorized spread of employee information

■ Restrictions on the misuse of employee medical information

■ Requirements for reasonable suspicion for drug testing

■ Preservation of the boundary between work and home

■ Enforcement of these rights that would consist of both civil and criminal remedies

Chapter 10 outlines what legislation Congress has passed, to date, that deals with the issue of employee privacy rights, as well as some good ideas that failed to gain support.

It's understandably tempting to be skeptical about the power of individual voters to influence Congress, but a large enough group of individuals can make a difference. If you think that workplace privacy is important and that Congress should do something about it, let your representative and senator know. Ask them where they stand on the issue of workplace privacy, and ask them to notify you if any relevant bills are filed. If you see reports in the media that privacy-related legislation has been filed, let your representatives know that you are following the issue. It does make a difference.

Thanks to technology, it's never been easier to contact your representatives. Every senator and representative in Congress maintains a website with information regarding their positions on different issues and links for sending them e-mail. In addition, there are a number of websites specifically designed to assist you in contacting your Congressional delegation.

On the local level, not all state senators and representatives have Web pages, but increasing numbers do. At the very least, each state has a website that contains, among other things, information on how to contact your state senators and representatives.

Needless to say, if you're worried about the issue of workplace privacy and possible surveillance by your employer, you probably shouldn't use your office computer or company e-mail account to lobby for more restrictive legislation.

## The Future of Workplace Privacy

Above the door of the federal government's newly established "Information Awareness Office" is the motto *Scientia est potentia*—"Knowledge is power." That's a disturbing attitude on the part of the federal government, but at least there's some safety in numbers: With more than 300 million people in the United States, the odds of any individual coming under random surveillance is relatively small. The odds are considerably higher in most businesses, only a few of which are so large as to number in the tens of thousands.

If knowledge is power, the ability of employers to increase their power over their employees is only going to increase. It does not take a call to phone psychic Miss Cleo to safely predict that surveillance technology will get steadily smaller, cheaper, and more powerful. As the cost of surveillance technology continues to drop, the unavoidable consequence will be that an increasing percentage of Americans will spend significant portions of each day being monitored by their employers. While much of that surveillance will continue to be open, the percentage of secret surveillance will steadily grow, if only because the tools themselves will make it easier to conduct hidden surveillance.

In theory, market forces could limit employer surveillance: If enough employees chose not to work for companies that conduct the more outrageous types of surveillance, eventually those companies either would be unable to function or would change their surveillance practices. Unfortunately, technology often moves faster than the slow tides of market forces. The implementation of most surveillance technologies is so widespread (due in large part to the consistently rapid drops in cost) that it is difficult for individuals to discriminate between different businesses based on their surveillance practices. In addition, market forces are predicated on the theory that individuals have access to all of the necessary information before they make their decision. To the extent that a significant portion of employee surveillance is secret, it's information that's unavailable to the average employee.

The issue of workplace surveillance most directly affects the nation's roughly 140 million employees, but it has important implications for all of us. Either we successfully establish boundaries to protect some privacy in the workplace and pull back the curtain cloaking hidden surveillance, or we run the risks associated with the unmonitored collection and potential misuse of highly personal information. This is precisely the type of broad social issue, like child labor or civil rights, that Congress can and should address.

## End Note

1. Professor Deibert defines "sousveillance" as "to view from below," in contrast to "surveillance," which means "to view from above."

# Index